THE
TENTH MUSE

Lately sprung up in AMERICA.
OR
Severall Poems, compiled

with great variety of VVit
and Learning, full of delight.
Wherein especially is contained a com-
pleat discourse and description of

The Four { Elements,
Constitutions,
Ages of Man,
Seasons of the Year.

Together with an Exact Epitomie of
the Four Monarchies, viz.

The { Assyrian,
Persian,
Grecian,
Roman.

Also a Dialogue between Old *England* and
New, concerning the late troubles.
With divers other pleasant and serious Poems.

By a Gentlewoman in those parts.

Printed at *London* for *Stephen Bowtell* at the signe of the
Bible in Popes Head-Alley. 1650.

EARLY
AMERICAN POETRY

A COMPILATION OF THE TITLES OF VOLUMES
OF VERSE AND BROADSIDES BY WRITERS
BORN OR RESIDING IN NORTH AMERICA
NORTH OF THE MEXICAN BORDER

BY

OSCAR WEGELIN

VOLUME I
1650-1799

"So eine arbeit eigentlich nie fertig wird. . . . Man sie
für fertig erklären muss, wenn man nach zeit und umständen
das möglichste daran gethan hat."—*Goethe.*

SECOND EDITION, REVISED AND ENLARGED

NEW YORK
PETER SMITH
1930

PREFATORY

Twenty-seven years have passed since this work was first issued in a limited edition. It has long been out of print and extremely difficult to obtain. During these years, the compiler has made note of all titles which were unknown to him when the book first appeared. Hundreds of new titles have thus been discovered, and many errors in the early edition detected and corrected.

The growing interest in all forms of early American literature has made a new edition of this bibliography necessary, and the compiler now offers it with the hope, that imperfect as it may be, it will be of value to all those who are interested in a most fascinating phase of American literature.

No serious attempt has been made to indicate the libraries where every title may be found, but those in the possession of The American Antiquarian Society at Worcester, Mass., and Brown University at Providence, R. I., are designated with the letters A and B respectively. A few titles in other libraries are also noted.

In the compilation of this bibliography, I have received much valuable assistance from Messrs. Harry Lyman Koopman, Librarian of Brown University, and Clarence Saunders Brigham, Librarian of The American Antiquarian Society. Thanks are also due to the New York Public Library, The Massachusetts Historical Society, and the Henry E. Huntington Library, at San Gabriel, Calif., for help rendered. I desire also to thank Dr. A. S. W. Rosenbach for permitting me to copy several rare titles in his possession.

OSCAR WEGELIN.

DEDICATION

To Harry Lyman Koopman and Clarence
Saunders Brigham, Librarians, respectively, of
Brown University Library, and The American
Antiquarian Society, without whose assistance
these volumes would be far from complete, I
dedicate this book.

EARLY AMERICAN POETRY
1650-1799

ADAMS, JOHN. Poems | on | Several Occasions, | Original and Translated.| By the late Reverend and Learned | John Adams, M. A.| Hœc placuit semel, hœc decies repetita placebit.| Hor. de Art. Poet. | Boston: | Printed for D. Gookin, in Marlborough-Street, over | against the Old South Meeting House. 1745.| 16mo. pp. [9],-2-176.   A.B. (1).

[ALLEN, JAMES.] The Poem which the Committee of the Town of Boston had voted unanimously to be published with the late [Dr. Warren's] Oration: with Observations, etc. . . and Extracts from an ingenious Composition never yet published. Boston: E. Russell, 1772. 4to. pp. 30.   A. (2).

> Written at the request of Dr. Warren to accompany his oration of March 5, 1772. Owing to doubts of the author's patriotism, the Committee suppressed it. His friends, however, procured a copy from him, and published it, with extracts from another poem [The Retrospect] by the same hand.

ALLEN. A Poem on Occasion of the Horrid Boston Massacre, by British Soldiers on American Citizens. Boston, 1785. 12mo. pp. 6.   (3).

ALLEN, JOHN. A | Morning Thought | upon Viewing the | Dawn of Day; | Being a Poem in Two Parts: | Composed | By John Allen, V.D.M.| A Few Days before His Death.| My Voice shalt thou hear in the Morn- | ing, O Lord: in the Morning will | I direct my prayer unto Thee, and | will lookup. Psalm, 5, 3.| Exeter: | Printed by Lamson and Ranlet, | For John Allen, Stratham, | MDCC, LXXXVIII.| 16mo, pp. [2], I-II, [3], 4-33.   (4).

[ANDRE, JOHN]. Cow-Chase, | in Three Cantos, | Published on Occasion of the | Rebel General Wayne's | Attack of the | Refugees Block-House | On Hudson's River, | On Friday the 21st of July, 1780.| New York.| Printed by James Riving-ton, | MDCCLXXX.| 8vo. pp. 69.   N.Y.P.L. (5).

> The *Cow-Chase* appeared originally in three numbers of *The Royal Gazette*. The last canto appearing on the day of Andre's capture, ends with this prophetic epilogue:—
>
> > "And now I've clos'd my epic strain,
> > I tremble as I show it,
> > Lest this same warrior-drover Wayne
> > Should ever catch the poet."
>
> Besides the *Cow-Chase* the volume is composed of the following: *Yankee Doodle's Expedition to Rhode Island. On the affair between the Rebel Generals Howe and Gaddesden; and The American Times,* a Satire in three parts, by "Camillo Querno," Poet-Laureat to the Congress. [Rev. Jonathan Boucher].

[APLIN, JOHN]. Verses | on | Doctor Mayhew's | Book of Ob-servations | On the Charter and Conduct | of the | Society | for the Propagation of the Gospel in Foreign | Parts: | With Notes, Critical and explanatory.| By a Gentleman of Rhode-Island Colony.| Providence, in New-England: | Printed and sold by William Goddard, at the Sign of | Shakespeare's Head. 1763.| 8vo. pp. [3].-4-19.   A. (6).

ARNOLD, JOSIAS LYNDON. Poems.| By the late | Josias Lyndon Arnold, Esq; | of St. Johnsbury [Vermont] formerly of | Providence, | and a tutor in Rhode Island College.| Printed at Providence, | by Carter and Wilkinson, and sold at their Book- | Store opposite the Market.| M.DCC.XCVII.| 12mo. pp. xii,-13-141.   A.B. (7).

> Edited by James Burrill, Jr., who, as Duyckinck notes, has per-formed his duties carelessly, as he has included *The Dying Indian,* by Freneau, in the above volume.

[BARLOW, JOEL.] An | Elegy | on the Late Honorable | Titus Hosmer, Esq; | One of the Counsellors of the State of Con-necticut, | A Member of Congress, | And a Judge of the | Maritime | Court of Appeals for the | United States of Amer-ica.| Hartford: | Printed by Hudson & Goodwin.| 12mo. pp. [5] 6-15.   A.B. (8).

8

[BARLOW.] A | Poem, | Spoken at the | Public Commencement|
at | Yale College, | in | New: Haven; | September 12, 1781.|
Hartford: | Printed by Hudson & Goodwin.| 12mo. pp. [3],
4-16.   A.B. (9).

BARLOW. The | Vision | of | Columbus; | A Poem in Nine
Books.| By Joel Barlow, Esquire.| Hartford: |Printed by
Hudson and Goodwin, for the Author: | M.DCC.LXXXVII.|
16mo. pp. [7],-viii-xxi, [4], 26-258, [14].   A.B. (10).

    Another edition containing *The Conspiracy of Kings.* Paris,
1793. 8vo. pp. [6],-2-300. Also: London, 1794.

BARLOW. The Prospect of Peace.| A Poetical | Composition, |
Delivered in | Yale-College, | at the | Public Examination, | of
the | Candidates for the Degree of | Bachelor of Arts; | July
23, 1778.| By Joel Barlow, A. B.| New-Haven: | Printed
by Thomas and Samuel Green, | M,dcc,lxxxviii.| 8vo. pp.
[3],-4-12.   A. (11).

BARLOW. A letter to the National Convention of France, on the
defects in the constitution of 1791. . . . To which is added
the Conspiracy of Kings. New York: J. Fellows, [179-?]
8vo. pp. 87.   (12).

[BARLOW.] The | Hasty Pudding: | a Poem, | in Three Cantos.|
Written at Chambery, in Savoy, January, 1793.| [New
Haven: Printed by Tiebout & O'Brien, 1796.] 8vo. pp. 15.
                                                             A.B. (13).

    Other editions as follows:
    [New Haven, 1796:] 16mo. pp. 12.   A.
    New York: 1796. 12mo. pp. v,-6-22.   A.
    New York: Printed for the Purchaser. [C. 1796.]   A.
    Stockbridge: 1797. 8vo. pp. [7],-8-16.   A.
    Catskill: [C. 1797] 16mo. pp. 12.   A.
    [Fairhaven, Vt.] [C. 1797] 24mo. pp. 16.   A.
    Salem: 1799.

    Several editions some with illustrations were also issued after 1800.

BARLOW. The | Conspiracy of Kings; | A Poem: | Addressed | To the Inhabitants of Europe.| From another quarter of the World.| [2 lines from Theognis. 6 lines from Mysterious Mother, Act IV.] | By Joel Barlow, Esq; | Author of "Advice to the Privileged Orders," and of "The Vision of Columbus."| London: | Printed for J. Johnson, St. Paul's Churchyard.| 1792.| 8vo. pp. [5],-6-20. A. (14).
The same: Newburyport, 1794. 8vo. pp. 30.

[BARRELL, JOSEPH.] Tit for Tat; t'other Side; or, | Bounceabout.| Sold at Edes's Printing-Office, in Cornhill. [Boston]. Broadside. A. (15).

BARTLETT, JOSEPH. Physiognomy, | A Poem, | Delivered at the request of the Society of | Φ.B.K, | in the Chapel of Harvard University, | on the Day of their Anniversary, | July 18th, 1799.| By Joseph Bartlett.| [2 lines from Lavater. 1 line from Erasmus.] Boston, Printed by John Russell, | 1799.| 8vo. pp. 16. A.B. (16).

BELKNAP JEREMY. An Eclogue, occasioned by the Death of the Reverend Alexander Cumming, A. M., on the 25th of August, A. D. 1763, Ætat 37. Boston: Printed by D. & F. Kneeland for J. Edwards, 1763. 4to. pp. 8. A. (17).

BEVERIDGE, JOHN. Epistolæ Familiares | et | Alia Quædam Miscellanea.| Familiar Epistles, | and | other miscellaneous Pieces, | Wrote originally in Latin Verse, | by John Beveridge, A. M. | Professor of Languages in the College and Academy | of Philadelphia.| To which are added several Translations into English | Verse, by different Hands, etc.| [One line from Ovid.] | Philadelphia. | Printed for the Author by William Bradford, at the *London Coffee-|House,* at the Corner of *Market* and *Front-Streets.*| M,DCC.LXV.| 8vo. pp. xi,-[1],-2-88. A.B. (18).
The translations are by Thos. Coombe, Jr.; A. Alexander; Stephen Watts; Rev. J. Mayhew, Nath. Evans and others.

BIGELOW, SAMUEL. A | Poem, Suitable | For the Present Day.| In Five Parts: | 1. To the People in General.| II. To Spiritual Mourners.| III. To Sleepy Professors.| IV. To the Openly Profane.| V. To the Christless Soul.| By Samuel Bigelow | Pastor of a Church in New-Salem.| State of Massachusetts-Bay | Worcester: Printed for the Author | MDCC-LXXVI.| 12mo. pp, [2], 3-16. (19).

BIGLOW, WILLIAM. Education; | A Poem:; | Spoken at Cambridge | At the Request of the | Phi Beta Kappa Society; | July 18th, 1799; | By William Biglow.| Salem: | Joshua Cushing.| 1799.| 8vo. pp. [3],-4-17. A.,N.Y.P.L. (20).

BINGHAM, JEREMIAH. Twelve Poems. Norwich: J. Trumbull. [1776]. (21).
>   Advertised in the *Norwich Packet,* July 29, 1776, as just published.

BLEECKER, ANN ELIZA. The | Posthumous Works | of | Ann Eliza Bleecker, | in | Prose and Verse.| To which is added, | A Collection of Essays, | Prose and Poetical, | by | Margaretta V. Faugeres.| New-York: | Printed by T. and J. Swords, No. 27, William-Street.| 1793.| 12mo. pp. [12],-xviii,-19-375. A.B. (22).

BOSWORTH, BENJAMIN. Signs of Apostacy Lamented *with* A Caution to prevent Scandal. n.p. 1693. 8vo. pp. 4.
B., N.Y.P.L. (23).
>   Signed on page 4 by Benjamin Bosworth of New England. In the 81st Year of My age, 1693." The author was a planter of Hingham, Mass., as early as 1635. His son, of the same name, married a daughter of Secretary Nathaniel Morton.

[BOWDOIN, JAMES.] A Paraphrase on part of the Oeconomy of Human Life, inscribed to his Excellency Thomas Pownall, Esq. Governor of the Province of the Massachusetts Bay. Boston, New England: Printed and Sold by Green and Russell, at their Printing Office in Queen St. 1759. 8vo. pp. 88. A. (24).

11

Boyd, William. Woman: | A Poem, | Delivered at | A Public Exhibition, April 19, | at | Harvard University, | in | The College Chapel.| By William Boyd.| Boston: | Printed by John W. Folsom, | 1796.| 12mo. pp. [5],-6-15. A.B. (25).

Boyd. Beauty, a Poem at Commencement, Cambridge, June 20, 1796. n.t.p. 12mo. (26).

[Brackenridge, Hugh Montgomery.] A | Poem | On | Divine Revelation; | Being An | Exercise | Delivered | At the Public Commencement | At | Nassau-Hall, | September 28, 1774.| By the same Person, who on a similar occasion, Sept. 25, 1771. | delivered a small Poem on *the rising Glory of America.*| Philadelphia: | Printed and Sold by R. Aitken, Bookseller, | Opposite the London Coffee-House, | Front-Street.| M.DCC.LXXIV.| 8vo. pp. 22. A. (27).

> In early life Brackenridge called himself "Hugh Montgomery," his later publications however, bear the name Hugh Henry Brackenridge.

[Bradstreet, Anne]. The | Tenth Muse | Lately sprung up in America. | or | Severall Poems, compiled | with great variety of Wit | and Learning, full of delight. | Wherein especially is contained a compleat discourse and description of |

The Four { Elements, Constitutions, Ages of man, Seasons of the Year.

Together with an exact Epitomie of | the Four Monarchies, viz. |

The { Assyrian, Persian, Grecian, Roman.

Also a Dialogue between Old England and | New, concerning the late troubles.| With divers other pleasant and serious Poems.| By a Gentlewoman in those parts.| Printed at London for Stephen Bowtell at the signe of the | Bible in Popes Head-Alley. 1650. 12mo. pp. [14],-1-207. B., N.Y.P.L. (28).

The second edition was issued with the following title:

Several | Poems | Compiled with great variety of Wit and | Learning, full of Delight, | Wherein especially is contained a Compleat | Discourse and Description of |

The Four {
    Elements,
    Constitutions
    Ages of Man,
    Seasons of the Year.
}

Together with an exact Epitome of | the three first Monarchyes

Viz. The {
    Assyrian,
    Persian,
    Grecian.
}

And beginning of the Romane Commonwealth | to the end of their last King: | with diverse other pleasant & serious Poems; | By a Gentlewoman in New-England.| The second Edition, Corrected by the Author, | and enlarged by an Addition of several other | Poems found amongst her papers | after her Death.| Boston, Printed by John Foster, 1678. 24mo. pp. [14],-1-255.
A., N.Y.P.L. (29).

Same. Third Edition. [Boston.] 1758. 16mo. pp. [2],-iii-xiii,- [1],-1-233. A. (30).

BRANCH, AMAZIAH. A Elegiac Poem, on the Death of Mrs. Sarah Branch. Bennington: Printed by Haswell and Russell, 1789. (31).

BRAUN. Ein Lied welches auf die Bestürmung und Einnahme des Forths Mont-Gomery, den 6 ten Octobris anno 1777. Von einen Auspacher Grenadier namens Braun poesirt wurde. [Philadelphia: Gedrucht bey Christoph Saur, jun. und Peter Saur? 1777]. (32).

BREWSTER, MARTHA. Poems | on divers Subjects, Viz.|
*On the four Ages of Man.| On the Day of Judgment.| The 24th Psalm paraphras'd.| A Prayer.| A Letter to some Christian | Friends.| A Dream.| God's Judgments our Monitors.| To the Subjects of the special Grace of God and it's

13

Opposers.| Chronicles IId Book, 6 Chap.|16, 17, 18 ver. para-|
phras'd.| A Poem to the Memory of | Dr. Watts.| Braddock's
Defeat.| The noble Man.| Two wedding Posies.| Two
Letters.| To the Memory of that | worthy man Lieut. Na-|
thaniel Burt of Springfield.| Several Acrosticks.| A Word
of Advice reserv'd | for my two Grand-Sons, | being yet Babes.|
By Martha Brewster, of Lebanon. | New-London Printed:
Boston Re-printed: | And Sold by Edes & Gill, at their Print-
ing-Office next | to the Prison in Queen-Street.| 12mo. pp.
[3],-4-35.   (33).

     Contents in double column.

BROADDUS, ANDREW. An | Elegiac Poem, | on the Late | *Rev.*
Mr. *Lewis Lunsford,* of Northumberland County; | Who Died
October 26, 1793, at Mr. A. | Gregory's, in Essex County, on
his | return Homewards from an Excursion, | which he had
made to an Associa- | tion, and Several other appoint- | ments:
Having been some time | Ill before, He experienced a | relapse
which proved | fatal.| by Andrew Broaddus, V.D.M. | Printed
for the Author in the year 1794.| 12mo. pp. [4],-2-9.   (34).

[BROCKWAY, THOMAS] The | Gospel Tragedy: | An | Epic
Poem.| In four books.| [3 lines from Genesis III. 15.] |
[5 lines from Virgl Ecl. IV.] [Vignette] | Published accord-
ing to Act of Congress.| Printed at Worcester, Massachusetts,
| By James R. Hutchins, | MDCCXCV.| 12mo. pp. [3],-IV,-
[3],-8-119. [Frontispiece view of the Crucifiction engraved
by Doolittle.]   A., N.Y.P.L. (35).

[BUELL, SAMUEL.] The following lines were occasioned by the
Death | of Richard Brown, Samuel Brown, John King and
Peter Brown | who belonged to Oyster-Ponds, on Long-
Island, | and were all Drowned by the over-setting of their
Boat, as they were attempting | a Passage from East-Hampton,
to the Oyster-Ponds March 9th, 1770.| Broadside with Cut
at top representing death, with this motto. "Young & Old
Remember Death." New London, 1770.   (36).

    36 verses with the following at end: East-Hampton, ex meo
Musaoe, March 20th., 1770."

BUELL, SAMUEL. The best New-Year's Gift for Young People: or, The bloom of Youth immortal, by Piety and Glory. A Sermon Preached (summarily) at East Hampton, on the Lord's Day, January 1st, 1775. Wherein the real Glory and Felicity of the Inhabitants of Heaven is described; and in which, they are represented as flourishing in unwithering Beauty and Glory, And as persisting in a perpetual and everlasting Bloom of Youth. To which is added Youth's Triumph, a Poem of Vision. And made publick at the Desire of a number of young people. New-London: Printed and sold by T. Green. [1775]. 8vo. pp. [1],-54-13. (37).

BURLESSON, E. A Lamentation in Memory of the Distressing Sickness in Hartford, from November 5th, 1724, to February 20th, 1724-5. Which took away more than Fifty Persons, hereafter named. [? New London: 1725]. (38).
    Broadside 4to.

BURT, JONATHAN. A Lamentation | Occasion'd by the | Great Sickness & Lamented Deaths of divers Eminent Persons in Springfield.| Composed by Mr. Jonathan Burt, (an Old Disciple,) in his Fourscore and Fifth Year, | (Since Deceased,) Left as a Dying Legacy to his Children, and Surviving Friends. Writ April, 1712. Printed in the Year 1720.| Folio broadside. (39).

BYLES, MATHER. A Poem | on the Death | of His late Majesty | King George, | of glorious Memory.| And the Accession | of our present Sovereign | King George II. | To the British Throne.| By Mr. Byles.| [Quotation: 3 lines from Virgil.] [Boston: 1727.] 12mo. pp. [3],-ii,-v. B. (40).

BYLES. A Poem | Presented | To His Excellency | William Burnet, Esq; | On his Arrival at Boston, | July 19. 1728.| By Mr. Byles.| [Quotation: 3 lines from Ovid.] Published by Order of his Excellency the Governour. [Boston, 1728.] 8vo. pp. [3],-2-6. B. (41).

15

[BYLES.] An Elegy, | Address'd to | His Excellency | Governour
Belcher: | On the Death | of his | Brother-in-Law, | The
Honourable | Daniel Oliver, Esq; | Re ipsa repperi | Facili-
tate nihil esse homini melius, neque clementia.| Clemens,
Placidus; nulli Soedere-arridere omnibus; | Omnes benedicere,
amant. Ter. Adelph.| 8vo. pp. [3],-2-4.   A.B. (42).

> Issued with Sermon on Oliver, by Thomas Prince, Boston: Knee-
> land and Green, 1732.

BYLES. Poems on Several Occasions. By Mr. Byles. Boston:
1736.   (43).

BYLES. To his Excellency Governour Belcher, on the *Death* of
His | Lady.| An Epistle.| By the Reverend Mr. Byles | [line
in Latin, Sen Agamem] | [Boston: 1736], 4to. pp. [3],-II,-
[1],-2-6.   A., N.Y.P.L. (44).

BYLES. On the Death | of the Queen.| A Poem.| Inscribed to
His Excellency | Governour Belcher.| By the Reverend Mr.
Byles.| [Four lines of Latin verse] | Boston in New Eng-
land: | Printed by J. Draper, for D. Henchman in Cornhill.
1738.| 8vo. pp. [5],-2-7.   A. (45).

[BYLES.] The | Comet: | A | Poem.| [Cut of several men gazing
through a telescope] | Boston: Printed and Sold by B. Green
and Comp.| in *Newbury-Street,* and D. Gookin, at the Corner
of | *Water-Street, Cornhil.* [*sic.*] 1744.| 4to. pp. [2],-3-4.
                                          N.Y.P.L. (46).

BYLES. Poems | on | *Several Occasions.*| By Mr. Byles.| [Line
in Latin from Hor. Lib.| Epist. I. V. 10.| [Cut] | Boston:
Printed and Sold by *S. Kneeland* | and | *T. Green, in Queen-
Street,* 1744.| 4to. pp. [4],-1-112,-[4].   J.C.B. (47).

BYLES. Poems.| The Conflagration, | applied to that grand Per-
iod or Catastrophe of | our World, when the Face of Nature is
to | be changed by a Deluge of Fire, as formerly | it was by
that of Water.| The | God of Tempest | and | Earthquake.|
[Printer's ornament] | Boston, Printed; | And Sold by D.
Fowle in Ann-Street, and by Z. Fowle | in Middlestreet.|
[1744] 12mo. pp. [2],-3-8.   A. (48).

16

[BYLES.] An Eclogue Sacred to the Memory of the Rev. Dr. Jonathan Mayhew, who departed this life July 9, anno salutis humanæ. 1766. Ætatis 46. [4 lines of poetry.] Boston: Printed by Thomas and John Fleet. [1766.] pp. 16. A. (49).
Attributed to Mather Byles.

CALEF, JOHN. A | Poem, | on the | much lamented Death | of | Mr. Edmund Titcomb, | Who Died May 26, 1722, in the 41st year of his Age. Broadside. (50).

CAPEN, JOSEPH. A Funeral Elegy | Upon the much to be Lamented Death | and most | Deplorable Expiration of the Pious, Learned, Ingenious, | and Eminently usefull Servant of God | Mr. John Foster | who Expired and Breathed out his Soul quietly into the Arms of His Blessed Redeemer | at Dorchester, Sept. 9th Anno Dorn, 1681.| Ætatis Anno 33.| Broadside. (51).

[CAREY, JAMES.] A Pill for Porcupine: Being a Specific for an obstinate itching. &c., &c. Philadelphia: Printed [by Steuart and Cochran] for the Author, September 1, 1796. 8vo. pp. 83. A. (52).

[CAREY.] He wou'd be | A Poet; | or, | "Nature will be nature still." An | Heroic Poem: | To which is annexed | A Thanksgiving Epistle | on | Electioneering Success.| By Geoffry Touchstone.| Philadelphia: | Printed for the author.| 1796.| 8vo. pp. [5],-6-28. A.B. (53).

CAREY, MATHEW. The | Plagi-Scurriliad: | A Hudibrastic Poem.| Dedicated to Colonel Eleazer Oswald.| By Mathew Carey.| Philadelphia: | Printed and Sold by the Author. | January 16. 1786. 8vo. pp. [3],-iv-vii,-[2],-x-xiv,-[1],-xvi,-17-19,-[1],-21-23,-[2],-26-47,-[1],-49-59. A.B. (54).

CAREY. The | Porcupiniad: | A Hudibrastic Poem.| In Four Cantos.| Addressed to | William Cobbett, | by | Mathew Carey.| Canto I.| [4 quotations from Porcupine's Gazette.] Philadelphia: | Printed for and sold by the Author. | March 2, 1799.| [Copy-right secured according to Act of Congress.] 8vo. pp. [3],-iv-vi,-[1],-viii,-[1],-10-52. A.B. (55).

[CARPENTER, WILLIAM.] A Poem, | On the Execution of William Shaw, | at Springfield, December 13th 1770, for | the Murder of Edward East in Springfield | Goal.| Broadside 4to.   (56).

> There are two issues of this title.

CARPENTER. A Poetical Paraphrase on the Book of Job. Rutland: Printed [By James Kirkaldie] for and sold by the author, [at Chittenden,] M.DCC.XCVI. 8vo. pp. 55.   A. (57).

CARRIGAN, PHILIP.. Agriculture; a Poem, Delivered at the Anniversary Commencement of Dartmouth University, Hanover, August 27, 1794. Hanover. Printed by Dunham and True, 1795.   (58).

[CASE, WHEELER.] Poems, occasioned by Several Circumstances and Occurriencies [sic] in the Present Grand Contest of America for Liberty. New Haven: Printed by Tho. and Samuel Green. 1778. 12mo.   (59).

> This is the second edition.
>
> I have been unable to locate a perfect copy of this book. An imperfect copy is in the Harris collection in the library at Brown University. A reprint from an imperfect copy, with historical appendix, was issued in New York, 1852. An edition [the fifth] was printed by Shepard Kollock, Chatham, N. Y., 1799. 12mo. pp. 24. [Cut of an eagle and crane on page 4.] An edition was also issued in Hartford by B. Wheeler, 1778, and another in Trenton, N. J., by Isaac Collins, 1779.

CATE, JAMES. Remarks on the Death of Mr. George Hancock, jun. By JAMES CATE. [followed by —] [6 lines, woodcut, very crude, and 51 stanzas of 4 lines.] [at end] From your affectionate Friend, JAMES CATE. Mr. George Hancock, Northfield. July 31, 1798. PRINTED BY J. L. FOR THE AUTHOR. Broadside.   (60).

CATE. [Between black rules] Devastation by the "King of Terrours," in the Family of Mr. Jeremiah Sandborn, [&c.] of Sandbornton, in the year 1798, [&c.]. By JAMES CATE. [5 lines, 3 coffins, 43 verses of 4 lines] [at end]. To Mr. Jeremiah Sandborn. From your affectionate friend, JAMES CATE. February 12, 1799. PRINTED BY J. L. FOR THE AUTHOR. Broadside.   (61).

18

[CATE.]   [Between black rules, 4 coffins, &c.]   The following
Lines were composed on the melancholy state of the Family
of Mr. Benjamin Sandborn, of Sandbornton, who departed
this life October 20, 1794, in the 49th year of his age; . . .
[3 lines, and 73 verses of 4 lines, interspersed with 4 coffins.]
Broadside.   (62).

> The above broadsides by James Cate were probably printed in New
> Hampshire. I have not made a personal examination of them, so can-
> not say where.

CHANDLER, WILLIAM.   A Journal of the Survey of Narragansett
Bay.   Broadside.   [Newport: The Widow Franklin] [1741.]
Mass. H.S. (63).

[CHAPLIN, JOHN] A | Journal | Containing some Remarks upon
the | spiritual Operations, Beginning about | the Year *Anno
Domini*, 1740, or 1741.| And also shewing something of the |
Essence of the internal Part of the | Religion of the People
called *New-*| *Lights*, if I mistake not: Also some | Hints at
their inward Conflict, and | a Lamentation for our Backsliding;
| and also for the Withdraw of the | holy Spirit of God.| [12
lines of verse] | Printed, 1757.| 16mo. pp. [I-IV],-5-11.

> Has a half title, A | Journal | Of former and present times, | in |
> New-England.|
> The author's name is given in an acrostic on title, as *John Chap-
> lini*, but I am inclined to believe the last letter was used simply to
> fill out the last line to complete the poem. At end is "Rowley, Nov.
> 18th, 1757."
> The piece consists of five poems mainly on the Whitefield Con-
> troversy.

CHATTERTON, AUGUSTUS.   The | Buds of Beauty; | or, | Par-
nassian Sprig.| Being a collection of | Original Poems, |
upon | Various Subjects.| By Augustus Chatterton, Esq.|

[4 lines from Horace.]| Baltimore: | Printed for the Author,
by John Hayes.| M.DCC.LXXXVII.| 12mo. pp. [5],-vi,-
[1],-viii,-[1],-x,-[3],-12-106.   A.B. (65).

> "Augustus Chatterton' is probably a pseudonym. An edition
> was printed in New York by F. Childs, 1781. 12mo. pp. 106.

19

[CHESTER, STEPHEN?] A | Funeral Elegy | Upon the Death of that Excellent and most worthy Gentleman | John Winthrop Esq. | Late Governor of his Majestyes Colony of Connecticut: | who deceased April 1676. [Boston: John Foster, 1676]. Broadside. (66).

[CHURCH.] The | Choice: | A | Poem, | After the Manner of Mr. *Promfret.* [*sic*].| By a young Gentleman.| Boston: | Printed and Sold by *Edes* and *Gill, in Queen-Street,* 1757. 8vo. pp. [3],-4-15. A. (67).
    Errata at close of poem, "In the Title-Page—for Promfret, read Pomfret."
    Another edition Worcester: 1802. 12mo.

[CHURCH.] Elegy | on the | Death | of the | Reverend | Jonathan Mayhew, D. D. | who departed this life | July 9th, | Anno Domini, 1766.| Aetatis suae 46.| Boston: N. E.| Printed and Sold by Edes and Gill, | in Queen-Street.| 8vo. pp. [3],-4-15. B. (68).

[CHURCH.] An | Address | To | A Provincial Bashaw.| O Shame! where is thy Blush?| By a Son of Liberty. Printed in (the Tyrannic Administration of St. | Francisco) 1769. 8vo. pp. [2],-3-8. B. (69).

[CHURCH.] An Elegy to the memory of that pious and eminent servant of Jesus Christ the Rev. George Whitefield. Boston: Richard Draper, 1770. 4to. pp. 7. A. (70).

[CHURCH]. The | Times.| A | Poem.| By an American.| *Omnes profecto liberi libentius* | Sumus quam servimus.| Plaut. in Captivis.| [Circa 1771.] 8vo. pp. 16. A. (71).
    The title forms a portion of the first page of text.

[CHURCH, EDWARD.] The | Dangerous Vice | A Fragment.| Addressed to all whom it may concern.| By a Gentleman, formerly of Boston.| [Quotation. 4 lines from Pope's Essay on Man.] Columbia printed. | 1789. 8vo. pp. [3],-6-16.
A.B. (72).

CHURCHILL, ——. The following Lines wer Composed | by the | Widow of Mr. George Churchill, | who died at Martha's Vineyard, | September 14, 1796, in the 35th Year of his Age. Broadside. (73).

CLEAVELAND, AARON. [A Poem on Slavery.] Norwich: 1775.
(74).

[CLIFFTON, WILLIAM.] The | Group: | or an | Elegant Representation | illustrated.| Embellished with a beautiful head of | S. Verges, C.S.| Philadelphia: | Printed for Thomas Stephens, | By Lang and Ustich.| M.DCC.XCVI.| 8vo. pp. [7],-8-35. A.B. (75).

CLIFFTON. Tit for Tat. Philadelphia: [1796.] 8vo. pp. 25.
(76).

COBBY, JOHN. Poetic Essays | on | the Glory of Christ, | and on | the Divinity and work | of the | Holy Spirit.| By John Cobby.| Price Eight cents.| New-York: | *Printed by* John Tiebout, No. 358, *Pearl-Street,* | For the author.| 1797.| 8vo. pp. [3],-4-[1],-6-16. (77).

COCKINGS, GEORGE. [half title] War: | An | Heroic Poem.| (Price Three Shillings sew'd.) [Title] War: | An | Heroic Poem. | from the | Taking of Minorca by the French, | To the| Raising of the Siege of Quebec, by | General Murray.| By George Cockings.| [Vignette] | London: | Printed by C. Say, in Newgate-street, for the Author; | And Sold by J. Cook, behind the Chapter House, St. Paul's | Church-yard. M.DCC.LX. | Small 8vo. pp. [5],-vi-xiv, [3],-4-174.
N.Y.P.L. (78).

The only copy of this, the first edition which I have seen, is imperfect, lacking pp. [1-3] and 7-8. These pages were evidently cut out for some purpose known only to the publishers and author, as the copy I have seen was in the finest possible condition and in the original blue wrappers as issued. The pages which are missing evidently contained half titles to the *Argument* and the poem itself, or they may have been blank leaves.

Another edition. Boston, N. E. Printed by S. Adams, for the Author and Sold by T. Leverett, in Cornhill, Edes & Gill, and D. & J. Kneeland, in Queen street. 1762. 8vo, pp. [5],-VI-XVI, [1] 2-190. [1],-2-46, [2]. A.B. (79).

Although the title states this to be the *Second Edition,* this is a mistake, as the London edition of 1762 claims that honor.

The same. Fourth edition. London, 1765. 8vo, pp. XVI, 240.

Another edition. Portsmouth, N. H., 1762. Also, London, J. Wilkie, n. d. 8vo, pp. XVI, 240.

COCKINGS. The American War, A Poem, in six books. In which the names of the Officers who have Distinguished themselves, are Introduced. London: Printed by W. Richardson. MDCC-LXXXI. 8vo. pp. [4], 181. [Plan of Bunker's Hill.]

A. (80).

COCKINGS. Eloquence and Medical Infallibility, a Satire in verse. London: 1771. 8vo. (81).

COCKINGS. Benevolence, | and | Gratitude. | A | Poem.| By George Cockings.| London: | Printed for, and Sold by the Author; and may be | had of all Booksellers in London and Westminster.| MDCCLXXII.| [Price Two Shillings.] 8vo. pp. [3], ii, 9-44. B. (82).

COCKINGS. Arts, | Manufacturers, |and | Commerce: | A | Poem.| By George Cockings, | Author of War; an Heroic Poem: from | the taking of Minorca by the French, to the re-|duction of Manilla by the English.| London: | Printed for the Author; | and Sold by J. Cooke, Bookseller, at Shakespeare's Head, Paternoster-Row. S. Steare, | Bookseller, at No. 93, Fleet-Street; D. Paylett. Book | and Print-seller, in Princes' Street, Leicester Fields; the | Booksellers in London and Westminster; and by the | Author; of whom also may be had, the Fourth Edition | of War, an Heroic Poem. Price 3s. 6d. 8vo. pp. [3], ii.-iv, [1], 2-36. (83).

COLE, J. The American War. An Ode, n.p. [1779.] 12mo. pp. 66. (84).

COLMAN, BENJAMIN. A funeral sermon on the death of . . . the Reverend Mr. Samuel Willard. . . by Ebenezer Pemberton, A. M. To which is annexed, A Poem . . . by the Rev. Mr. Benjamin Colman. Boston: Printed by B. Green, for Benjamin Eliot. 1707. 12mo. pp. [16], 80,-[2],-14.

A.B. (85).

COLMAN. Memoirs | of the | Life and Death | of the Pious and Ingenious | Mrs. Jane Turell, | who expired at Medford, March | 26th, 1735.| Ætat. 27, | Chiefly collected from her own Manuscripts.| Boston, N. E.| Printed in the Year, MDCCXXXV.| Forms pp. 57-129 of Colman's *Reliquiae Turellae*, Boston: 1735. A. (86).

22

[COLLINS, NATHANIEL.] On the much Lamented Death of the Reverend Mr. Noadiah Russel, Late Pastor of the Church of Christ in Middletown, who had his Clayey Tabernacle Dissolved and his Mortality Swallowed up of Life, December 3d, 1713. Ætatis suæ 55. 1 p. folio [New London, 1714] with curious cut at the head. (87).

> The longest poem is signed N. C. Probably the Rev. Nath. Collins, of Enfield. [H. C. 1697].

COOK, EBENEZER. The | Sot-Weed Factor: | or, a Voyage to Maryland.| A | Satyr.| In which is describ'd | The Laws, Government, Courts and | Constitutions of the Country, and also the | Buildings, Feasts, Frolicks, Entertainments | and Drunken Humours of the Inhabitants | of that Part of *America*, | In Burlesque Verse.| By Eben Cook, Esq.| London: | Printed and Sold by *D. Bragg* at the *Raven* in Pater|-Noster Row. 1708. [Price 6d.] 8vo. Title; pp. 1-21.

B., N.Y.P.L. (88).

> Reprinted as No. 11 of Shea's Early Southern Tracts.
>
> Mr. Cook seems to have been "a London 'Gent,' rather decayed by fast living, sent abroad to see the world and be tamed by it, who very soon discovered that Lord Baltimore's Colony was not the Court of her Majesty, Queen Anne, or its taverns frequented by Addison and the wits, and whose disgust became supreme when he was 'finished' on the Eastern Shore by
>
> > 'A pious consientious Rogue,'
>
> who taking advantage of his incapacity for trade, cheated him out of his cargo, and sent him home without a sheaf of the coveted 'Sot-Weed.'" The poem was probably the result of that homeward voyage, and is worth preserving, photographing as it does the manners and customs of the inhabitants of Maryland at that time.

[COOKE.] Sotweed Redivivus; | Or the Planter's | Looking-glass.| In Burlesque Verse.| Calculated for the Meridian of | Maryland.| By E. C., Gent.| Annapolis: | Printed by William Parks, for the Author.| MDCCXXX.| Small 4to. Title, one unnumbered leaf, pp. v-viii; [1]; 2-28.

N.Y.P.L. (89).

> This is probably the earliest poem printed in Maryland. The curious preface begins with this sentence: "May I be canonized for a Saint, if I know what apology to make for this dull Piece of Household stuff."

COOKE. The | Maryland Muse.| Containing | I. The History of Colonel Nathaniel Bacon's Rebellion | in Virginia. Done into *Hudibrastick* Verse, from | an old Ms.| II. The Sotweed Factor, or Voiage to Maryland.| *The Third* Edition, *Corrected and Amended.*| By E. Cooke, Gent.| [2 lines of verse] | [Type Device] | Annapolis: | Printed in the Year M,DCC,XXXI.| Folio, pp. [1-II], 1-25, [26], [1].

B.M. (90).

No trace can be found of copies of the first or second editions. The author promised a second part, but no copy has been located. Other parts were to be issued annually, but were probably never printed.

The first title noted above is probably the first edition, the poem on Bacon's Rebellion having been added to this third edition.

COOMBE, THOS. Edwin: | Or the | Emigrant.| An Eclogue.| To which are added | Three Other Poetical Sketches.| By the Rev. Mr. Coombe.| . . . . | Philadelphia: | Printed by John Dunlap in Market-street.| M,DCC,LXXV.| 4to. pp. 24. (91).

COOMBE. The | Peasant | Of Auburn, | Or; the Emigrant. | A Poem.| By T. Combe, D. D.| . . . | . . . . | [cut.] | Philadelphia: Printed and Sold by Enoch Story, Jun. [1784?] 8vo. pp. 48. (92).

Also, London, 1775. This work was dedicated to Oliver Goldsmith.

COOPER, MYLES. Poems | on | Several Occasions.| By Myles Cooper, | M. A. | Of Queen's College.| [One line from Ovid.] | [View of the Theatre and other edifaces at Oxford.] Oxford, | Printed by W. Jackson.| M.DCC.LXI. 8vo. pp. xxxix; [2]; 3-342. (93).

Myles Cooper was president of King's [now Columbia College] at the outbreak of the Revolution. His writing and leanings toward the Royalist side led to his being mobbed and he fled to England. The above volume was printed prior to his arrival in America.

[COOPER.] THE | PATRIOTS | of | North-America: | a | Sketch with | explanatory notes.| [4 lines in Latin] | New-York: | Printed in the Year M,DCC,LXXV. 8vo. pp. iv, [1], 2-47.

A. (94).

A Tory effusion written at the commencement of the Revolution. The notes occupy pp. 35-47.

[COTTON, JOHN.] Upon the Death of that Aged, Pious, Sincere-hearted Christian, | John Alden, Esq.: | Late Magistrate of New-Plimouth Colony, *who* dyed Sept. 12th, 1687, | being about eighty nine years of age. Broadside, printed *circa* 1714.

(95).

Reprinted, 1806 for T. A. Jun, at Portsmouth, N. H.

COX, JOHN. Rewards | and | Punishments, | or, | Satan's King-dom Aristocratical.| To which is subjoined | A Voyage to London, | and | An Acrostic.| By John Cox, a Native of Philadelphia.| Philadelphia, | Printed for the Author, at No. 41, Chesnut-Street. | May, 1795.| 8vo. pp. [3], 4-20.

B. (96).

[CRAWFORD, CHAS.] The | Christian: | A Poem; | in | Four Books.| To which is prefixed a | Preface in Prose | In De-fence of Christianity; | with an | Address | to the | People of America. | . . . | . . . | . . . . | Philadelphia: | Printed and Sold by Joseph Crukshank, | in Market-Street, between Second and | Third-Streets. MDCCLXXXIII. 12mo. pp. xl, 111.

A. (97).

[CRAWFORD.] Liberty: | A | Pindaric Ode. . . . . | Phila-delphia: | Printed for the Author, by Robert Aitken, at Pope's Head | in Market-Street | M.DCC.LXXXIII. Sq. 8vo. pp. 16.

A. (98).

Another edition entitled *The Progress of Liberty &c.* A new edition. Philadelphia: Ormrod and Conrad, 1796. 12mo. pp. [2],-3-21,-[1].

CRAWFORD. A Poem on the Death of Montgomery. By Charles Crawford. Philadelphia: Robert Aitken [?1783.] (99).

[CRAWFORD.] A | Poetical | Paraphrase | on our | Savior's Sermon | on the | Mount.| . . . | . . . | . . . . | Phila-delphia: | Printed for the Author, by Robert Aitken, at Pope's Head, | in Market-Street. | M.DCC.LXXXIII.| 4to. pp. 24.

(100).

CRAWFORD. Poems on Various Subjects. By Charles Crawford. Philadelphia: Joseph Crukshank. 1784. (101)

DANFORTH, JOHN. Kneeling to | God, | At Parting With Friends: on the | Fraternal | Intercessory Cry | of Faith & Love: | Setting forth and Recommending | the Primitive Mode of taking Leave.| By J. Danforth, Pastor of the Church of Christ in Dorchester.| I Thes. 5.25. Brethren Pray for Us.| Col. 1. 9. We . . do not cease to Pray for you.| I Sam. 12.23. Moreover, as For Me, God Forbid that I should Sin against the Lord, in 'Ceasing to Pray for you, &c.| Boston, Printed by B. Green, and F. Allen.| Sold by S. Phillips, at the Brick Shop 1697.| 12mo. pp. [5], 6-72. A.B. (102).

> On pp. 64-65 is "A Poem to the Memory of Mrs. Jane Eliot," and on pp. 66-72, "A Poem to the Memory of John Eliot."

[DANFORTH, JOHN.] Profit and Loss. An Elegy upon the Decease of Mrs. Mary Gerrish, late virtuous wife of Mr. Samuel Gerrish, and Daughter of the Honorable Judge Sewell, who, on Nov. 17, 1710, the night after public Thanksgiving, entered on the Celebration of Triumphant Hallelujahs to her profit and our loss, aged 19 years and 20 days. Maestise Composiut. J. D. [cut at top.] Folio broadside. (103).

DANFORTH. Honour and Vertue | Elegized: | in an | Poem, | Upon an Honourable, Aged, and Gracious Mother in our Israel, | Madame Elizabeth Hutchinson, | Late Vertuous Consort of our Hon. Judge, Col. Elisha Hutchinson, Esq. in Boston.| She Entered into the Joyes of Paradise, Feb. 2, 1712, 13. Ætatis Suæ 71. Broadside. (104).

DANFORTH. A Poem, Upon the much Honoured and very Exemplarily Gracious | Mrs. Maria Mather, | Late Consort of the very Reverend Increase Mather, Dr. of Divinity | and Teacher of a Church in Boston in New-England.| She exchanged this Life for a better, April 4, Anno Domino 1714. Ætatis suæ 73.| Broadside. (105).

DANFORTH. Memento Mori. Remember Death. [The above motto is seen issuing from between the teeth of a skeleton. Cut of Funeral Procession, Implements of the graveyard, etc.] *Greatness & Goodness* Elegized, | In a Poem, Upon the much Lamented Decease of the Honourable & Vertuous | Madam Hannah Sewell, | Late Consort of the Honourable Judge Sewell, in Boston, in New-England.| She Exchanged *this* Life for a *Better, October* 19th. *Anno Dom.* 1717. Ætatis Suæ. 60.| Broadside, folio. [1717.]   (106).

[DANFORTH.] [cut] The Divine Name Humbly Celebrated, | On Occasion of the Translation to Heaven of the Bright Soul | of the Pious and Vertuous, | Madam Susanna Thatcher | Late Consort of the Reverend Mr. Peter Thacher, Pastor of the Church | of Christ in Milton. September 4. Anno Domini 1724. Ætatis Suæ 59. Broadside.   (107).

DANFORTH. A Poem on the Death of Peter Thacher of Milton and Samuel Danforth of Taunton. 8vo. [Boston, 1727] Broadside.   A. (108).

[DANFORTH, SAMUEL.]   [cut.] A Pindarick Elegy Upon the Renowned, | Mr. Samuel Willard, | Late Reverend Teacher of the South Church in Boston, and | Vice-President of Harvard College in Cambridge; | who Deceased September the 12th. 1707. Ætatis Anno 68.| Broadside.   (109).

DANFORTH. [cut] An Elegy in Memory of the Worshipful | Major Thomas Leonard Esq. | of Taunton in New-England: Who departed this Life on the 24th. Day of November, | Anno Domini 1713. In the 73d. Year of his Age. Broadside.
(110).

DAVID, ENOCH. Offers of Christ | No Gospel Preaching.| To which is added, | A Word of Advice | To | A young Gospel Minister. | written in verse, | By Enoch David.| Philadelphia, | Printed for the Author; | By Henry Miller, in Second-Street, 1770. 16mo. pp. [2],-iii-x, 11-20.   B. (111).

DAVIES, SAMUEL. Elegiac Verses on the lamented | Death of the |
Rev. Mr. Samuel Blair, | who made his triumphant *Excite*
(*sic*) from this Mortal | Stage *July* 5, 1752, (*sic*) with the de-
served Character of a good *Scholar,* a masterly genius, a sin-
cere *Christian,* | and successful *Minister* of the Gospel.| Signed
Sic Cecinit Marensi.

S. DAVIES.

Hanover in *Virginia,*
November 10th, 1751.
Printed on pp. 25-34 of A Sermon preached at Fogs-Mannor
on the Death of Blair, by Samuel Finley: Philadelphi, |
(*sic*) | Printed and Sold by W. Bradford in Second-Stree |
(*sic*) MDCCLII.| 8vo. pp. 34.   (112).

DAVIES. Miscellaneous poems, chiefly on divine subjects. In two
books. Published for the Religious Entertainment of Chris-
tians in General. Williamsburg: Printed and Sold by William
Hunter, at the Printing-Office. 1752.   (113).

DAVIES. An Ode on the Prospect of Peace. Philadelphia: Printed
by Henry Miller. 1761. Folio broadside.   (113B).

DAVIS, JOHN. A | Tribute | to the | United States.| A Poem. |
by John Davis. | [line from Mart.] | New York: | Printed by
Robert M. Hurtin, at the Literary Printing | Office, | No. 29
Gold-Street.| 1798.| 12mo. pp. [3],-4-7.   (114).

[DAWES, THOMAS.] The | Law given at Sinai: | A Poem.| By
a young Gentleman.| Boston: | Printed by Thomas and John
Fleet, in Cornhill, 1777. | 8vo. 6 unnumbered leaves.
A.B. (115).

[DAWKINS, HENRY.] THE PAXTON EXPEDITION. Inscribed to the
Author of the Farce, by H. D. [Philadelphia: 1764.]   (116).
The above is a copperplate representing the Citizens of Philadelphia at the Court House in Arms ot repel the Paxton Boys. Six
doggerel verses follow.

DAYTON, EBENEZER. A Concise, poetical | Body of | Divinity, | Published in Three separate Parts, | Each a Pamphlet: | Being the *Shorter Catechism* First agreed upon | by the Rev'd Assembly of Divines, Sitting at *Westminster;* | wherein each Question is turned into a Divine Hymn, in the Form of a Question and Answer; and fitted to the several | metres, and suitable to be sung in Families and private | Meetings of So-cieties, for the Instruction of Persons of all | Age and Capaci-ties, to Whom they are dedicated, with a | View of promoting Christian Knowledge, Godly Devotion, | and real Piety.| By Ebenezer Dayton, | Of *Brook-Haven,* and late School-Master in *Newport, Rhode-Island.*| [Cut of a Crown.] Part I. | Printed for the Author. 1769. 12mo. pp. iv; 5-27. A. (117).

> The author was a resident of Brookhaven, Long Island, and gained a reputation as a privateersman, operating against the British and Tories on Long Island Sound. An account of him will be found in Sharpe's *History of Seymour, Conn.,* Seymour, 1879. I have been unable to find more than the first part of the above production which is probably all ever printed at Newport. It was probably printed at Newport, as the title is dated from that place. Ebenezer Dayton was the earliest writer in Brookhaven Township.

DAYTON, EBENEZER. A | Serious | Poem | On various Subjects, | Written for the Perusal of Children.| By Ebenezer Dayton, | School-master in *Newport, Rhode Island.*| The Second Edi-tion.| Printed for the Author. 1769.| 16mo. pp. [2],-3, [1], 5-16.   N.E.H. (118).

> The Preface is dated Prison Lane, May 18, 1769.
> The above work was probably printed at Newport, by Solomon Southwick, who had a press there from 1768 to 1787.

[DEVENS, RICHARD.] A | COMMENT | on | Some passages | in the | Book of Job.| Boston: | Printed by Isaiah Thomas, at his Printing-| Office, near the Mill-Bridge. MDCCLXXIII. 8vo. pp. 15.   (119).

[DEVTER, SAMUEL.] The | Progress | of | Science.| A | Poem | Delivered at | Harvard College | Before a Committee of Over-seers, April 21, 1780.| By a Junior Sophister.| Printed in the Year 1780. 4to. pp. [2], 3-10.   A.B. (120).

DICKINSON, JOHN. The Liberty Song. In Freedom we're born [with music] [Boston: Printed and Sold by Mein and Fleeming, September, 1768.] Broadside. (121).

DODGE, PAUL. A Poem: | delivered at the Commencement | of Rhode Island College, | September 6, A. D. 1797. | by Paul Dodge, A.B. O Tempora! O Mores! Cicero | Published by Request.| Providence | 1797.| 8vo. pp. [3],-4-8.
A.B. (122).

[DOVE, DAVID JAMES.] The Lottery.| A Dialogue | Between | Mr. Thomas Trueman and | Mr. Humphrey Dupe.| [Germantown: Christopher Sower. 1758.] 16mo. pp. 16. (123).
Contains also two poems, viz.: "The Academy Garland" and "The Lottery.'

DOW, HENDRICUS. A Poem. In two letters. Argument. A Candidate for the Ministry of the Gospel is highly Censured by a Physician &c., &c., &c. Newfield: [Now Bridgeport, Conn.] Printed by Black and Jones, 1795. 12mo. pp. 11.
See also Evans. 28588. (124).

[DUCHE, JACOB.] PENNSYLVANIA: | A | Poem.| By a Student of the College of Philadelphia.| Philadelphia: | Printed by B. Franklin, and D. Hall.| MDCCLVI.| Folio. pp. 11.
(125).
A poem with the title of "Pennsylvania" was written by Jacob Taylor and published in Philadelphia, 1728. Taylor also wrote some Complimentary verses to Webb's "Bactchelors Hall."

[DUKE, WILLIAM.] Hymns | and | poems, | on | various occasions.| By a Member of the Protestant Episcopal | Church | Baltimore: | Printed by Samuel and John Adams, in | Market-Street.| M,DCC,XC.| 12mo. pp. [3],-iv-vii,-[2],-10-90.
(126).

[DUNLAP, JANE.] Poems, | Upon several Sermons, Preached | by the Rev'd, and Renowned, | George Whitefield, | while in Boston.| [Three quoted lines] | [Cut].| A New-Years Gift, from a Daughter of | Liberty and lover of Truth.| Boston: Printed and Sold, next to the Writing-School | in Queen-Street. 1771. 16mo. pp. [2],-[i]-iii, 4-10,-[1]. A. (127).
[Introduction signed Jane Dunlap and last page signed J. D.]

DWIGHT, TIMOTHY. The | Conquest | of Canâan; | A Poem, in Eleven Books.| By Timothy Dwight.| [2 lines from Pope.] Hartford: | Printed by Elisha Babcock. | M,DCC,LXXXV. 12mo. pp. [8],-304,-[1].   A.B. (128).

[DWIGHT.] The | Triumph | of | Infidelity. | A | Poem.| Printed in the world, | M.DCC,LXXXVIII. 8vo. pp. [3],-iv,-[1],-6-40.   A.B. (129).
    Another edition, London: 1791. 8vo, pp. 27.

DWIGHT. Greenfield Hill: | A | Poem, | in | Seven Parts.| I. The Prospect.| II. The Flourishing Village.| III. The Burning of Fairfield.| IV. The Destruction of the Pequods.| V. The Clergyman's Advice to the Villagers.| VI. The Farmer's Advice to the Villagers.| VII. The Vision, or Prospect of the Future Happiness of America.| By Timothy Dwight, D.D.| New York: Printed by Childs and Swaine.| 1794.| 8vo. pp. [5],-6-183.   A.B. (130).

ELLIOT, JAMES. The | Poetical and Miscellaneous | Works | of | James Elliot, | Citizen of Guilford, Vermont, | and late | A Noncommissioned Officer in the | Legion of the United States.| In Four Books.| [13 lines from Pope.] Greenfield, Massachusetts, | Printed by Thomas Dickman, | For the author.| M,DCC,XCVIII.| 16mo. pp. [3], 10-271, [5]. A.B. (131).
    Only 300 copies were printed.

[EVANS, NATHANIEL.] Ode, | On the late | Glorious Successes | Of his | Majestys Arms, | And present Greatness | Of the English Nation.| Philadelphia: | Printed and Sold by William Dunlap, M.DCC,LXII.| Sq. 8vo. pp. 14.   (132).

EVANS, NATHANIEL. Poems | on | Several Occasions, | with Some other Compositions.| By Nathaniel Evans, A.M. | *Late* Missionary (*appointed by the* Society *for* Pro-|pagating the Gospel) for Gloucester County, | *in* New-Jersey; *and* Chaplain *to the* Lord Vis-|count Kilmorey, *of the* Kingdom *of* Ireland.| Philadelphia: Printed by John Dunlap, in Market-Street.| MDCC,LXXII. 8vo. pp. xxviii, 160, 24; and leaf of errata, which is almost always missing.   A.B. (133).

F. P. A few Verses composed by P. F. on Account of the sudden Death of John | Brown, and Huldy Brown, Son and Daughter, of Elder *Eleazer Brown,* of | *Stonington,* who were killed with Lightning, on *Saturday* the seventh day | of *June* 1788.| The young man was in the 25th Year of his Age, and the young Woman about 18 Years old.—Both in the prime of Life.| (at end) Printed, and Sold at Norwich, 1789.| Folio broadside of XXXVII verses of 4 lines each. Within black border and at top a cut with skull and other insigna of death.   (134).

FAUGERES, MARGARETTA V. An Ode | For the 4th of July, 1798, | *Dedicated to the friends of* | *Liberty* and Independence, | by Margaretta V. Faugeres.| Folio broadside.   (135).

FAUGERES. The | Ghost | of John Young | The Homicide, | Who was Executed the 17th of August last, | For the Murder of Robert Barwick, a Sherif's Officer.| The following Monody is written with a | View of rescuing his Memory from Obloquy, | and showing how inconsistent sanguinary Laws | are, in a Country which boasts of her Freedom | and Happiness.| By Mrs. Faugeres. [Price six pence.] 12mo. pp. [2],-3-6. [1797].   B. (136).

[FESSENDEN, THOS. G.] Jonathan's Courtship.| [4to broadside, 2 columns of verse. Probably printed in New Hampshire about 1795].   A. (137).

FITCH, ELIJAH. The | Beauties | of | Religion.| A Poem.| Addressed to Youth.| In Five Books.| By Elijah Fitch, A M.| Ineunite Aetate Semina Virtutis dissemintur. [Quotation of 3 lines from Young.] Providence. | Printed by John Carter. M,DCC,LXXXIX.| 8vo. pp. [5], 6-129.   A.B. (138).

FITCH. The Choice Providence: Printed by John Carter, 1789. 8vo. pp. 5.   (139).

FOLGER, PETER. A Looking Glass for the Times, etc. to which is added the Report from the Lords of the Committee of Councils, and the King's Order relating to the People called Quakers in New England. By Peter Folger. 1677. A. (140).
    Reprinted in 1763. The author was Benj. Franklin's maternal grandfather.

FORREST, MICHAEL. Travels | Through | America.| A Poem.| By Michael Forrest.| Philadelphia: | Printed by Johnston & Justice, at Frank-|lin's Head, No. 41 Chesnut-street.| 1793.| 12mo. pp. [7],-8-50. A.B. (141).

FRAME, RICHARD. A Short | Description | of | Pennsilvania, | Or, A Relation What things are Known, | enjoyed, and like to be discovered in | in the said Province.| [next line partly obliterated] of England.| By Richard Frame.| Printed and Sold by William Bradford in | Philadelphia, 1692.| 4to. pp. [1],-2-8. (142).
> Reprinted by the Oakwood Press 1867. 118 copies printed.

[FRANKLIN, BENJAMIN.] [The Lighthouse Tragedy.] [Boston: James Franklin, 1719.] Broadside? (143).
> Ford 1. No copy located.

[FRANKLIN, BENJAMIN.] [The Taking of Teach, the Pirate.] [Boston: James Franklin, 1719.] Broadside? (144).
> Ford 2. No capy located.
> See also, *The Yearly Verses of the Printer's Lad* under Anon.

FRENEAU, PHILIP. The | American Village, | a Poem.| To which are added, | Several other original Pieces in Verse.| By Philip Freneau, A.B. [Two lines from Horace.] New-York: Printed by S. Inslee and A. Car, on Moor's Wharf.| M,DCC,LXXII.| 12mo. pp. 27, [1]. L.C., J.C.B. (145).

[FRENEAU.] A | Poem, | on the | Rising Glory | of | America; | being an | Exercise | Delivered at the Public Commencement at | Nassau-Hall, September 25, 1771.| [Six lines from Seneca] | Philadelphia: | Printed by Joseph Crukshank, for R. Aitken, | Bookseller, opposite the London-Coffee-| House, in Front-Street.| M,DCC,LXXII.| 12mo. [3],-27, [1]. (146).
> Written in Collaboration with H. H. Brackenridge.

[FRENEAU.] American Liberty, | A | Poem.| [One line from Virgil] | [Two lines from Pope] | New-York: | Printed by J. Anderson, at Beekman-Slip.| MDCCLXXV.| 12mo. pp. 32. (147).

[FRENEAU.] The | Last Words, Dying Speech, and Confession |
Of J . . . s R . . . . g . . n, P . . . t . . . r, who was
executed at New Brunswick, in | the Province of New Jersey,
on the Thirteenth Day of April, 1775.| Supposed to be written
by himself the Night preceeding the Day of his | Execution.|
(148).

    Small 4to. Broadside, with 48 lines in the style of Freneau's
earlier verse, and probably by him. It was probably printed by
Hugh Gaine, in 1775.

[FRENEAU.] Tom Gage's | Proclamation | versified.| (149).

    Small folio broadside, printed in two columns, in the style of
Freneau's verse, dated "New York, June 30, 1775."

FRENEAU. On the | Conqueror of America | shut up in Boston.|
Published in New York, August 1775. (150).

    The above title is taken from the edition of Freneau's poems, is-
sued in 1786, p. 85. No copy of the original can be found.

FRENEAU. General Gage's Soliloquy. New York: Printed by
Hugh Gaine, 1775. (151).

    A manuscript copy of the above is in the Du Simitiére collection in
The Library Company of Philadelphia. Some one, probably Fre-
neau, has written thereon "Printed in New York August, 1775, By
Gaine." No printed copy can be traced.

[FRENEAU.] A | Voyage | to | Boston.| A | Poem.| [Five
lines from Shakespeare.] | By the Author of *American Liberty,*
a Poem: | General Gage's Soliloquy, &c.| New-York: Printed
by *John Anderson,* | at Beekman's Slip.| [1775.] 12mo. pp.
[iii] and iv; [5]-24. (152).

    Another edition: Philadelphia:| sold by | William Woodhouse | in
Front-Street. | M,DCC,LXXV. | 12mo. pp. [iii] and iv; [5]-24. A.

[FRENEAU.] General Gage's | Confession, | Being the Substance
of | His Excellency's last Conference, | With his Ghostly
Father, Friar Francis.| [One line from Virgil.] By the Au-
thor of the Voyage to Boston.| A Poem, &c.| Printed in the
Year, 1775. [By Hugh Gaine.] 8vo. pp. [3]-8. (153).

FRENEAU. The Expedition of Timothy Taurus, Astrologer, to the Falls of Passaick River, in New Jersey, etc. Formerly printed in New York. (154).

> Reprinted in *Poems*, N. Y., 1809. The original was probably printed in a newspaper, about 1775.

FRENEAU. Mac Swiggin; a Satire. Written 1775. (155).

> The above title is taken from the 1786 edition of the *Poems*. Also printed in the 1809 edition.

[FRENEAU.] The | Travels | of the | Imagination; | a true Journey from | Newcastle to London.| To which are added, | American Independence, | an | everlasting deliverance | from | British Tyranny: | A Poem.| Philadelphia: | Printed, by Robert Bell, in Third-Street.| MDCCLXXVIII. 8vo. pp. [viii] ; 9-126. (156).

> Freneau's poem has its own title page on page 113.
> *American Independence* was also published in a volume entitled *Miscellanies for Sentimentalists,* etc. Phila., R. Bell. M, DCC,- LXXVIII.

[FRENEAU.] Sir Henry Clinton's Invitation to the Refugees. (157).

> Published as a ballad sheet, 1779.

[FRENEAU.] The British Prison-Ship: | A | Poem, | In Four Cantoes. - - -

Viz. Canto {
1. The Capture,
2. The Prison-Ship.
3. The Prison-Ship, Continued
4. The Hospital-Prison-Ship.

To which is added, | A Poem on the Death of Capt. N. Biddle, | who was blown up, in an Engagement with the | Yarmouth, near Barbadoes.| [13 lines from Milton.] Philadelphia: | Printed by F. Bailey, in Market-Street.| M.DCC.LXXXI.| 12mo. pp. [3]-20; 21-23. (158).

[FRENEAU.] Rivington's last will and testament. (159).

> Published in the *Freeman's Journal,* February 27, 1782.

[FRENEAU.] New Year Verses, | Addressed to those Gentlemen who have been | pleased to favour Francis Wrigley, News Car-|rier, with their Custom.| January 1, 1783.| Folio broadside. (160).
Reprinted in 1786 edition of *Poems*.

[FRENEAU.] New Year's Verses, addressed to The Customers of the Pennsylvania Evening Post, by the Printer's Lad who carries it. January 4, 1783. Broadside. (161).

[FRENEAU.] New Year's | Verses | Addressed to the Customers of | The Freeman's Journal, | By the Lad who carries it.| January 8th, 1783.| Folio broadside. (162).

[FRENEAU.] A Newsman's Address. January 1, 1784. Broadside, [Charleston, S. C. ? 1784.] (163).
No copy can be found; it was reprinted in the 1795 edition of Freneau's *Poems*.

[FRENEAU.] New-Year | Verses, | For those who carry the | Pennsylvania Gazette | To the | Customers.| January 1, 1784.| Small folio broadside printed by Hall and Sellers. (164).

[FRENEAU.] New Year's Verses, addressed To the Customers of the Freeman's Journal, by the Lad who carries it. January 1, 1784. Broadside. (165).
See Hildeburn, *Issues of the Press in Pennsylvania,* No. 4524.

[FRENEAU.] New Year's Verses, addressed To the Customers of the Freeman's Journal, by the Lad who Carries it. January 1, 1785. (166).
Broadside; printed in the 1786 edition of his poems.

[FRENEAU.] A Newsman's Address. [1786.] (167).
No copy known; printed in 1795 edition of his poems.

FRENEAU. The | Poems | of | Philip Freneau.| Written Chiefly during the late war.| Philadelphia: | Printed by Francis Bailey, at | Yorick's Head, in Market Street.| MDCCLX-XVI.| 8vo. pp. [v]-vii; [1]; 1-407. A. (168).

[FRENEAU.] A | Journey | from | Philadelphia | to | New-York, | by way of Burlington and South-Amboy.| By | Robert Slender, Stocking Weaver.| Extracted from the Author's Journals.| [Two lines from Horace.] Philadelphia: | Printed by Francis Bailey, at Yorick's Head, in | Market Street.| MDCC-LXXXVII.| 12mo. pp. vi; 7-28.   (169).

[FRENEAU.] New Year's Verses for 1788. [Supposed to be written by the Printer's lad, who supplies the customers with his weekly paper.]   (170).
   Broadside; no copy can be found. Printed in the *Miscellaneous Works*, 1788.

FRENEAU. The | Miscellaneous | Works | of | Mr. Philip Freneau | containing his | Essays, | and | additional Poems.| Philadelphia: | Printed by Francis Bailey, at Yorick's | Head, in Market Street. | MDCCLXXXVIII. 12mo. pp. xii, 429.
                    A. (171).

[FRENEAU.] The | Village Merchant: | A | Poem.| To which is added the | Country Printer.| [Quotation of 4 lines.] Philadelphia: | Printed by Hoff and Derrick, | M,DCC,XCIV.| 12mo. pp. [3]; 4-16.   A. (172).

FRENEAU. Poems | Written between the years 1768 & 1794, | By | Philip Freneau, | of | New Jersey: | A New Edition, Revised and Corrected by the | Author; Including a considerable number of | Pieces never before published.| [2 lines from p. 435.] Monmouth | [N. J.] | Printed | At the Press of the Author, at Mount Pleasant, near | Middletown-Point; M,DCCXCV: | and, of | American Independence.| xix.| 8vo. pp. [ix]-xv; one blank page, [1]-455; [1]. A.B. (173).

[FRENEAU.] Means | for the | Preservation | of | Public Liberty.| An | Oration | delivered in the New Dutch Church, | On the | Fourth of July, 1797. Being the twenty-first | Anniversary of our Independence.| By G. J. Warner.| [Ten lines from Freneau.] New York: | Printed at the Argus Office, | for | Thomas Greenleaf and Naphtali Judah.| 1797. 8vo. pp. 22.   A. (174).
   Contains on pp. 20-21, "Ode | (Composed for the Occasion, by P. Freneau.) | The Musick performed | by the | Uranian Musical Society."

37

[Freneau.] Megara and Altavola. To a female satirist (an English actress) on receiving from her No. 1 of a very satirical and biting attack. (175).

> This is printed in the 1809 edition of his poems—vol. II, pp. 30-34, with a foot-note which states: "Six copies only, of this little Poem were printed and sent to the satirist."

[Freneau.] Letters | on | Various interesting and important Subjects; | many of which have appeared | in the | Aurora.| Corrected and much enlarged.| By Robert Slender, O.S.M.| [Two lines from Pope.] Philadelphia: | Printed for the Author.| From the Press of D. Hogan—| And sold at his Store, No. 222, South Third-street, and at | the Office of the Aurora.| December 30, 1799.| 12mo. pp. viii; 9-142. (176).

> Contains poem entitled "Fourth of July—An Ode." The pagination of page 74 is given as 47.

G., W. A Brief Narrative, or Poem, giving an Account of the Hostile Actions of some Pagan Indians towards Lieutenant Jacob Tilton, and his brother Daniel Tilton, both of Ipswich, . . . Broadside. (177).

> Reissued at Newburyport: J. Thomas and H. W. Tinges, [1774.] See following title.

G., (W.) A Brief Narrative, or poem, giving an account of of the hostile action of some pagan Indians towards Lieut. Jacob Tilton, and his brother Daniel Tilton, both of the Town of Ipswich, as they were on board a small vessel at the eastward: which happened in the summer-time, in the year 1722. With an account of the valiant exploits of the said Tiltons, and their victorious conquest over their insulting enemies. Newburyport—from a reprint of I. Thomas and H. W. Tinges. Printed by W. & J. Gilman, No. 9 State Street, June, 1834. Folio broadside. (178).

> The original, of which no copy is now extant [as far as can be ascertained], was probably printed at the time of the skirmish. The Newburyport edition was issued in 1774.
>
> An edition was also printed in Boston by Robert Weir in 1852, and it was printed under the title "A Tragedy of the Sea" in the N. E. Reg. 2: 271. [1848.]

[GARDINER, JOHN S. J.]   An | Epistle | to | Zenas.| Boston:
Printed by Peter Edes.   [1786.]   8vo.   pp. [2],-ii,-[1],-6-15,
[2].   A. (179).

   The author was assistant and Rector of Trinity Church, Boston.

[GARDINER.]   Remarks on the Jacobinead: revised and corrected
by the author; and embellished with caricatures.   Part First.
[8 lines of Verse] Printed at Boston, by E. W. Weld and W.
Greenough, 1795.   8vo. pp. 54.   [5 Etchings.]   A. (180).

GAY, BUNKER.   To Sing of Mercy and Judgment: | Recommended
and exemplified | in a | Discourse, | delivered on a day of |
Publick Thanksgiving.| by Bunker Gay, A.M.| Minister of the
Church in Hindsdale.| [2 ll. from psalms] | Printed at Green-
field, Massachusetts, | by Thomas Dickman.| MDCCXCIII.|
8vo. pp. [4],-5-19.   A. (181).

      Pp. 10-19 are poetry.
      Half title reads.   Mr. Gay's | Reflections | on the Thanksgiving
   next after | the Death of his wife.|

GODFREY, THOMAS.   The | Court of Fancy; | A | Poem.| By
Thomas Godfrey.| . . . | . . . | . . . | . . . . |
Philadelphia: | Printed and Sold by William Dunlap,
M,DCC,LXII.   Sm. 4to. pp. 24.   (182).

GODFREY.   Juvenile Poems | on | Various Subjects.| With the |
Prince of Parthia, | A Tragedy.| By the Late | Mr. Thomas
Godfrey, Junr. | of Philadelphia.| To which is prefixed, |
Some Account of the Author and his Writings.| Poeta nas-
citur non fit.   Hor. | Philadelphia. | Printed by Henry Miller,
in Second-Street.| 1765.| 8vo. pp. [2] iii-xxvi, [2] 1-223.
                                              B. (183).

GRAHAM, JOHN.   [A Ballad satirizing the Episcopalians.]   [Circa,
1732.]   (183B).

      This item is mentioned in the recently issued Autobiography of
   Rev. Samuel Johnson, first president of Columbia College.   The
   author was the Rev. John Graham of Southbury, Conn., and it is
   possible, if not altogether probable, that this broadside was issued
   from the New London Press, then the only printing establishment
   in Connecticut.

[GRAVE, J.]. A | Song of Sion.| Written by a Citizen thereof, whose outward Habitati- | on is in Virginia ; and being sent over to some of his | Friends in England, the same is found fitting to be | Published, for to warn the Seed of Evil-doers. [10 lines by the Publisher.] With an Additional Post-script from ano-|ther Hand.| Printed in the Year, 1662. 12mo. pp. [2], 3-12.   B. (184).

    A Quaker production. The "Postscript" has been attributed to Martin Mason.

[GREEN, JOSEPH.] Entertainment for a Winter's Evening: Being a full and true Account of a very Strange and Wonder-ful Sight Seen in Boston on the Twenty-seventh of December, 1749, at Noon-Day. The Truth of which can be attested by a Great Number of People who actually saw the Same with their own Eyes. By Me, the Hon. B. B. Esq. Boston: G. Rogers. [1750.] 8vo. pp. 15.   A. (185).

    A satire on a Masonic Procession on St. John's day. A reprint was issued in 1795. 12mo. pp. [2], 3-12.

    Also second edition, Boston: 1750.   A.

[GREEN.] The Grand Arcanum Detected, or a wonderful phe-nomenon explained, which has baffled the scrutiny of many ages. By Me, Phil Arcanos, Gent. Student in Astrology. Printed in the year 1755. 12mo. pp. 14.   (186).

[GREEN.] A | Mournful Lamentation | For the sad and deplor-able death of | Mr. Old Tenor, | A Native of *New-England,* who, after a long Confinement, by a deep and mortal wound | which he received above Twelve Months before, expired on the 31st Day of *March,* 1750. *He lived beloved,* and died lamented.| To the mournful tune of, *Chevy-Chace.*| folio broadside of 12 verses in double column. Surrounded by black lines [mourning] at end.   (187).

    Mr. Old Tenor was born in the year 1702. | Finis. |

[GREEN.] An | Eclog | Sacred to the Memory | of the | Rev. Dr. Jonathan Mayhew, | who departed this life | July 9th, | Anno Salutis Humanæ 1766, | Ætatis 46.| [4 lines of verse] | Bos-ton : | Printed by Thomas and John Fleet.| (1766) 4to. pp. [2],-3-16.   A. (188).

H., I.   Faction, a Sketch; or, A Summary of the Causes of the
Present most unnatural and Indefensible of all Rebellion's.
Written at New-York, February, 1776. By I. H.   New York:
1777.   8vo. pp. 8.   (189).

HAMLIN, AMOS.   The Republic of Reason: Being an Essay on
Nature and Reason.   Albany: Printed for the Author, 1797.
12mo. pp. 12.   (190).

HAMMON, JUPITER.   An | Evening Thought.| Salvation by Christ,
|with Penetential Cries: | Composed by Jupiter Hammon, a
Negro belonging to Mr. Lloyd, of Queen's | Village, on Long-
Island, the 25th of December, 1760.| Broadside of 88 lines,
printed in double column, and word "Finis" at bottom.   Size
10¼x7⅞ inches.   (191).

> The earliest specimen of American Negro Poetry. The only known
> copy is in the Collection of the New York Historical Society.
>
> For an account of Hammon and his writings see Wegelin *Jupiter
> Hammon,* New York: 1915.

HAMMON.   Hartford, August 4, 1778.| An Address to Miss
Phillis Wheatly, [*sic*] Ethiopian Po-|etess, in Boston, who
came from Africa at eight years of age, and | soon became
acquainted with the Gospel of Jesus Christ.| [one line, fol-
lowed by 21 Verses of 4 lines each, printed in double column] |
Composed by Jupiter Hammon, a Negro Man belonging to
Mr. Joseph Lloyd, of Queen's Village, | on Long Island, now
in Hartford.| The above lines are published by the Author,
and a number of his friends, who desire to join with him in
their best | regards to Miss Wheatly. [*sic*] | Broadside. Size
8¾x6 inches [Hartford: 1778].   (192).

> The only known copy is in the Connecticut Historical Society.

HAMMON.   An Essay on the Ten Virgins.   Composed by Jupiter
Hammon, a Negro Man belonging to Mr. Joseph Lloyd of
Queen's Village on Long Island, now in Hartford.   Hartford:
Printed by Hudson and Goodwin, 1779.   (193).

41

HAMMON. A | Winter Piece: | being a | Serious Exhortation, with a call to the | Unconverted: | and a short | Contemplation | on the | Death of Jesus Christ.| Written by Jupiter Hammon, | A Negro Man belonging to Mr. John Lloyd of | Queen's Village, on Long Island, now in Hartford.| Published by the Author with the Assistance | of his Friends.| Hartford: | Printed for the author.| M.DCC.LXXXII: | 8vo. pp. [2]-22,-[1],-24.   (194).

HAMMON, JUPITER. An | Evening's Improvement.| Shewing, | the Necessity of beholding | the Lamb of God.| *To which is added,* | A Dialogue, | Entitled, | The Kind Master and | Dutiful Servant.| Written by Jupiter Hammon, a Negro | Man belonging to Mr. *John Lloyd,* of Queen's | Village, on Long-Island, now in Hartford.| Hartford: | *Printed for the Author, by the Assistance of his Friends.* [Circa, 1790.] 8vo. pp. [2],-3-28.   (195).

HAMMOND, WILLIAM . Advice to Youth: Being the Instructions of a Father to a Son, on several interesting occasions, A Poem. Philadelphia: Printed and Sold by William Evitt, at his Printing-Office, at the Sign of the Bible-in Heart, in Strawberry-Alley. MDCCLXX. 4to. pp. 13,-[1].   (196).

[HARRIS, THADDEUS MASON.] The | Triumphs | of | Superstition: | An | Elegy.| By a Student of Harvard University.| [line from Seneca.] [line from Virgil.] Printed at Boston, | By Isaiah Thomas and Ebenezer T. Andrews.| At Faust's Statue, No. 45, Newbury Street.| 1790.| 12mo. pp. [5]-8-16.
                                                          A.B. (197).

[HAYMAN (ROBERT.).] Quodlibets, | Lately Come Over | From New Britaniola, | Old Newfoundland.| Epigrams and other small parcels, both | *Morall and Diuine.*| The first foure Bookes being the Authors owne: the | rest translated out of that Excellent Epigrammatist, | Mr. *John Owen,* and other rare Authors: | With two Epistles of that excellently wittie Doctor, | *Francis Rablais:* Translated out of his French at large.| *All* of *them* | Composed and done at Harbor-Grace in | Britan-

42

iola, anciently called *Newfound-Land.* | By R. H. | Sometimes Gouernour of the Plantation there.| London, | Printed by *Elizabeth All-de,* for *Roger* | *Michell,* dwelling in *Pauls* Church-yard, | at the signe of the Bulls-Head.| 1628.| Sm. 4to. Title, 3 unnumbered leaves, pp. 1-64.   (198).

[HAYMAN.] Certaine | Epigrams Ovt. | of The First Foure | Bookes of the Ex-|cellent Epigrammatist, Master John Owen : | Translated Into English | At Harbor-Grace In | Bristols Hope in Britaniola, anciently | called *New-found-land* : | By R. H. | [Device] | At London | Imprinted for *Roger Michell* and are to be sold at | the signe of the Buls head in Pauls Church-|yard. 1628.| Small 4to. Title, 2 nunumbered leaves, pp. 1-58.   (199).

HAZARD, JOSEPH. Juvenile | Poems | on a | Diversity of Sub-jects | By Joseph Hazard | Litchfield, (Connecticut) | Printed by Thomas Collier, for the Author | MDCCLXXXIX. 12mo. pp. 43.   (200).

HENDERSON, HUGH. The Confession and Dying Warning of | Hugh Henderson . . . [Also] A Poem | Occasioned by the untimely Death of Hugh Henderson . . . [cut] Boston : Printed and Sold at the Printing House in Queen Street over against the Prison. Broadside.   A. (201).

[HONEYWOOD, ST. JOHN.] A | Poem | on reading the | Presi-dent's Address ; | with a sketch of the Character | of a | Candidate | for the | Presidency.| Philadelphia : | Printed by Ormrod & Conrad, | No. 41 Chesnut-Street, | 1796.| 8vo. pp. [3],-4-7.   (202).
   Another edition with the Author's initials [S. J. H. Esquire] on title. Albany, Printed by Charles R. and George Webster. [1796] 8vo, pp.8.

[HOPKINS, JOSEPH.] A Line to the | Modern Ladies, | Found among the Writings of | Joseph Hopkins, | Late of Farming-ton, deceased.| [17 Verses in 2 columns] [4to Broadside.] Printed in the Year 1769.   A. (203).

[HOPKINS, LEMUEL.] Echo ; | or a Satirical Poem on the Virtu-ous Ten and other Celebrated Characters : | Hartford : 1795. 12mo. pp. 22.   A. (204).

43

[HOPKINS.] The | Guillotina, | or a | Democratic Dirge, | A | Poem.| By the Author of the "Democratiad."| [Quotation of 12 lines.] Philadelphia: | Sold at | The Political Book-Store, | South Front-Street, | No. 8.| 8vo. pp. [3]-4-14, [2]. A.B. (205).

[HOPKINS.] The | Democratiad, | A | Poem, | in | Retaliation, | for the | "Philadelphia Jockey Club."| Lo! the dire Hedge-Hog from another sty, | At tilted Folly lets his arrows fly.| By a Gentleman of Connecticut.| Philadelphia: | Published by Thomas Bradford, Printer, | Book-Seller & Stationer, | No. 8, South Front Street.| 1795.| 8vo. pp. [3]-iv-22, [1]. (206).
Second edition, Philadelphia, 1795. 8vo. pp. (3), IV-22,[1]. A.B.
Third edition, Philadelphia, 1796. A.

[HOPKINSON, FRANCIS.] An | Exercise, | Containing | A Dialogue and Ode | On the Accession of His present gracious Majesty, | George III. | Preformed at the public commencement in the College of | Philadelphia, May 18th, 1762.| Philadelphia: | Printed by W. Dunlap, in Market-Street, M,DCC,-LXII, | 4to. pp. 8. (207).

HOPKINSON. Science.| A | Poem.| By Francis Hopkinson, Esq; | . . . | . . . . | Philadelphia: | Printed by William Dunlap, in Market-Street, | MDCCLXII.| 4to. pp. 19. (208).
A pirated edition was issued in the same year as the above by Andrew Steuart, in Philadelphia, Sm. 8vo. pp. 8.
An edition was also issued in New York by Hugh Gaine in 1762, which contains a quaintly worded card of excuse for printing the work without the author's permission.

[HOPKINSON.] An | Exercise, | Containing | A Dialogue and Ode | Sacred to the Memory of His late gracious Majesty, | George II. | Performed at the public Commencement in the College of | Philadelphia, May 23d, 1761.| The Ode written and set to Music.| By Francis Hopkinson, Esq; M.A. in said College.| Philadelphia: | Printed by W. Dunlap, in Market-Street, MDCCLXI. 4to. pp. 8. (209).

[HOPKINSON.] A Tory Medley.| [Philadelphia: 1777.] Folio, 1 leaf. (210).
By F. Hopkinson (?) It consists of four songs and a "Medley."

44

Hopkinson. Poems | on | Several Subjects.| [Philadelphia, M,DCC.XCII.] 8vo. pp. [3], 4-204. A.B. (211).
   Vol. 3 of *Miscellaneous Essays.*

Hopkinson, Joseph. Song | adapted to the| President's March, | Sung at the Theatre | by Mr. Fox, | at his Benefit.| Composed by Joseph Hopkinson, Esq.| Printed by J. Ormrod, 41, Chestnut-Street. | [1798]. 12mo. pp. 6. A. (212).

[Hopkinson, Thos.] An | Exercise, | containing | a | Dialogue and two Odes | Performed at the Public Commencement in the College of | Philadelphia, May 20th, 1766.| Philadelphia: | Printed by W. Dunlap, in Market-Street, M,DCC,LXVI.| Sm. 4to. pp. 8. (213).

[Hopkinson.] Liberty, | A | Poem, | lately found in a bundle of papers. | Said to be written by | A Hermit in New Jersey.| "Whoever would give up *essential liberty,* to purchase a | "little *temporary safety,* Deserves neither liberty nor safety.". Message from the *Pennsylvania* Assembly to their Governor.| Philadelphia: | Printed by William Goddard, in Market-Street.| MDCCLXIX. 8vo. pp. 12. (214).

Howe, Solomon. Columbia | Triumphant | A Poem, | on the | Independence, | of the United States-| designed to perpetuate the | Memory of that Glorious | Event.| By Solomon Howe, A.M.| [4 lines of poetry.] | Copyright Secured, | Greenwich: | [Mass.] Printed and Sold, Price 6 cents.| 12mo. pp. 16. [Two curious woodcuts on reverse of title.]
                                        N.Y.H.S. (215).

[Hubbard, John.] a monumental gratitude | attempted, | In a Poetical | Relation | of the | Danger and Deliverance | of | Several of the Members | of | Yale-College, | in | Passing the Sound, | from | South-hold to New-Haven, | Aug. 20th. 1726.| New-London: | Printed & sold by L. Green.| 1727.| 12mo. pp. [2]-1-10. A.B. (216).

[Hubbard.] The | Benefactors | of | Yale-College.| A Poetical Attempt.| [2 lines from Hor.] | [6 lines from Mr. Pope's Essay on Criticism] | Boston: | Printed by S. Kneeland and T. Green.| M,DCC,XXXIII.| 8vo. pp. [2],-1-13. (217).

[HUBBARD.] A | Poem | Occasioned by the Death | Of the Honourable | Jonathan Law Esq; | Late | Governor | of | Connecticut.| [4 lines from Pope's "Essay on Criticism."] Printed in the Year, 1751.| 12mo. pp. [5]-2-8. A.B. (218).
Generally attributed to Benj. Church.

HUGHES, G. Religious Reflections, | Particularly on the late dreadful Fire of the Governor's House in Fort George.| [Printed for the Author, G. Hughes.] [by John Holt, June 1774, in Ms. on Copy in N. Y. H. Soc.] Folio broadside.
(219).

[HUMPHREYS, DAVID.] A | Poem, | Addressed to the Armies | of the | United States of America.| By a Gentleman of the Army. [4 lines from Horace] [one line from Virgil.] New Haven: | Printed by T. and S. Green, | 1780.| 12mo. pp. [4] 5-6, [1] 8-16. B. (220).
The same: New Haven, T. & S. Green, 1784, 4to.
Also issued in London and Paris in 1785.

HUMPHREYS. A | Poem | on the | Happiness of America; | addressed to the | Citizens | of the | United States.| By D. Humphreys.| London Printed 1780.| Hartford: Reprinted by Hudson and Goodwin. 8vo. pp. [3], 4-51. B. (221).
Also: New Haven, 1780. 8vo. pp. 66. The same: Albany, C. R. & G. Webster. n. d. 16mo. pp. 41. Also Hartford: 1786; Portsmouth: 1790. A.

[HUMPHREYS.] The | Glory | of | America; | or, | Peace triumphant over War: | A | Poem.| Philadelphia: | Printed for the Author, by E. Oswald and D. Humphreys, | at the Coffee-House.| M.DCC.LXXXIII.| Sq. 8vo. pp. 16. A. (222).

HUMPHREYS. Poems. Philadelphia: Mathew Carey. 1789. 8vo. pp. 90, [1]. A. (223).

HUMPHREYS. The | Miscellaneous | Works | of | Colonel Humphreys.| New York: | Printed by Hodge, Allen, and Campbell; | and Sold at their respective Book-Stores.| M.DCC.XC.| [With Copy-right according to Law.] | 8vo. pp. [3], 4-13, [2], 16-348. A.B. (224).

46

HUMPHREYS. A | Poem | on | Industry.| Addressed | to the Citizens of | the | United States of America.| By Colonel David Humphreys, Minister Resident | At the Court of Lisbon.| Philadelphia: | Printed for Mathew Carey, | No. 118, Market-Street. | October 14, 1794. 8vo. pp. [3], iv, [3], 8-22, [2].   A.B. (225).

JACOB, STEPHEN. A | Poetical Essay, | delivered at | Bennington, | on the | Anniversary | of the | 16th of August, 1777, | by Stephen Jacob, | 1778.| Hartford: | Printed by Watson & Goodwin.| MDCCLXXIX.| 12mo. pp. 8.   (226).
> Reprinted in Vol. 1 of the Coll. of the Vermont Historical Society. Montpelier, 1870. The above collation is from the reprint and may vary from the original.

JOHNSON, JOHN. The | Rape of Bethesda; | or | The Georgia Orphan House | Destroyed.| A Poem.| By John Johnson.| *Where now are all my hopes! Oh never more | shall they revive! Nor death her rapes restore!*| Sandys.| Charleston: | Printed by Markland & M'Iver, No. 47, Bay.| MDCCXCII.| 16mo. pp. 16.   A. (227).

[JOY, GEORGE.] Innocency's Complaint. [Cambridge, Samuel Green.] 1677.   (228).
> Broadside. Two columns of poetry, signed at end of second column: "George Joy, Mariner, 1677."

[KEIMER, SAMUEL.] An Elegy on the much Lamented Death of the Ingenious and Well-Beloved Aquila Rose, Clerk to the Honourable Assembly at Philadelphia, who died the 24th of the 4th Month, 1723. Aged 28. Philadelphia: Printed and Sold by Samuel Kiemer, in High Street. 1723. Folio. 1 leaf.
(229).
> Reprinted in *Hazard Register,* November, 1828, p. 262.
> Franklin says, "He could not be said to write them, for his manner was to compose them in the types directly out of his head."
> The above is the first issue of Keimer's press, and was worked off by Franklin.
> Keimer was also the author of *Caribbeana.* 2 vols., London, 1741.

KENNA, J. JR. Anna's Tomb. A Poem. Written by J. Kenna, Jun. Fredericksburg: Printed by Timothy Green, 1790.

(230).

[KNAPP, FRANCIS.] Gloria Britannorum: or The British Worthies. A Poem. To which is added "An Ode on his Majesty's Coronation, and an Elegy on the Death of the late Glorious Duke of Marlborough." By a Lover of the present happy Constitution. Boston: Printed by J. Franklin for N. Buttolph, and Sold at his Shop in Cornhill, 1723. 12mo. pp. 30.

A. (231).

Attributed to Francis Knapp, of Watertown, Mass.

KUNZE, JOHANN CHRISTOPH. Einige | Gedichte und Lieder | von | Johann Christoph Kunze, | Ev. Luth. Pred. zu Philadelphia, in Nordame | rika.| Philadelphia: | Gedrukt und zu finden bei Christoph und Peter Saur.| 1778.| 12mo. pp. [42]-[1,]-2-132,-[1].

(232).

[LADD, JOSEPH BROWN.] The | Poems | of | Arouet.| [4 lines from Lucan.] [6 lines from Rowe.] | Charleston, South-Carolina: | Printed by Bowen and Markland, No. 53 Church-Street, | and No. 11, Elliot-Street. 1786.| 12mo. pp. [7], viii-xvi, [5], vi, [1], 8-128.

B. (233).

[LEE, RICHARD.] [cut] Lines | Composed on the last and Dying Words of the Rev. Oliver Williams, Pastor or the | Baptist Church in Grafton, who died August 29th, 1790, aged 39 years.| Warren [R. I.] Printed [by Nathaniel Phillips] for Richard Lee. [1792] 4to. broadside.

A. (234).

Has an "Acrostick" on Richard Lee.

[LEE.] The | Melancholy End | of | Ungrateful Children.| Exemplified in the dreadful fate of the Son | and Daughter of a wealthy Farmer, who, | after receiving and dividing the wealth of | their Parents, refused them, in their old | age, the shelter of their roof, or a morsel | of bread. With an account of the won-| derful scenes the Daughter beheld in her | trance.| Printed for the benefit of the rising Generation, at | the particular request of all who were eye-witnesses | to the scene.| [4 lines of verse] |-Rutland :-| Printed for Richard Lee.| M,DCC,-XCV.| 12mo. pp. [2],-3-8.

A. (235).

LELAND, JOHN. The Virginia Chronicle: With Judicious and Critical Remarks under XXIV heads. [3 lines of quot.] Norfolk: Printed by Prentiss and Baxter, M.DCC.XC. 16mo. pp. 45,-[3]. A. (236).

> Another edition. Fredericksburg. Printed by Timothy Green, 1790. 8vo, pp. 46,-[2]. J.C.B. (237).

[LE MERCIER, ANDRE.] THE | CHRISTIAN RAPTURE.| A | Poem.| Boston: | Printed by Rogers and Towle, for D. Goodkin, in *Malborough-|Street,* near the Old South Meeting House.| MDCCXVII.| 4to. pp. 11. A. (238).

LEWIS, ELI. St. Clair's | Defeat.| A Poem.| By Eli Lewis.| A Tale, which strongly Claims the pitying tear, | And ev'ry feeling heart, must bleed to hear.| Harrisburgh: Printed MDCCXCII.| 16mo. pp. [3],-2-14. (239).

LEWIS, RICHARD. Carmen Seculare, | for the Year | M,DCC,-XXXII.| [Two lines, Hor. Ode VI. Lib. IV., Four lines from Bacon, Advance. of Learn.; Baltimore arms] To the Right Honourable Charles, | Absolute Lord and Proprietary of the | Provinces of Maryland, and Avalon, | Lord Baron of Baltimore, &c.| [Annapolis: Printed by William Parks. 1732.] Folio 2 leaves; pages [1-4]. Md., H.S. (240).

> Reprinted in *American Museum* for 1789, 6: 413, under title of "A Description of Maryland."

[LEWIS, RICHARD.]? March 1, 1731-2 | A | Rhapsody.| [Four lines quoted, "Tacitus, velut aliis placet Quintil, in Dialogo de Oratoribus."] Annapolis: Printed by William Parks. 1732.] Folio 1 leaf, printed both sides. Md., H.S. (241).

[LINN, JOHN BLAIR.] Miscellaneous Works, | Prose and Poetical.| By A | Young Gentleman | of New-York.| [1 line from Horace.] | New-York | Printed by Thomas Greenleaf.| 1795.| 16mo. pp. 353, [1]. A.B. (242).

LINN. The | Poetical Wanderer: | Containing, | Dissertations | On the early poetry of Greece, | On Tragic Poetry, and on the Power | of Noble actions on the Mind.| To which are added, | Several Poems.| *By the Author of Miscellaneous Works.*| [10 lines from Akenside] | New-York: | *Printed for the* author, by G. Forman, | *opposite the Post-Office.* 1796.| 16mo. pp. [7],-8-112,-[6].   A.B. (243).

[LIVINGSTON, HENRY BROCKHOLST.] Democracy: | An | Epic Poem, | By Aqualine Nimble-Chops, Democrat.| Canto First.| New-York: | Printed for the Author | [1794] 8vo. pp. [1], 6-20.   A.B. (244).

[LIVINGSTON, WILLIAM.] Philosophic Solitude: or, The Choice of a Rural Life. A Poem. By a Gentleman educated at Yale College. New York, James Parker, 1747. 4to. pp. 44. (245).
> The first edition.
> Same: Boston, B. Mecom, 1762, 8vo.   A.
> Also: N. Y., J. Holt, n. d. [1769]. And Trenton: Isaac Collins, 1782.

[LIVINGSTON.] America: or, a Poem on the Settlement of the British Colonies; Addressed to the Friends of Freedom, and their Country. By a Gentleman educated in Yale College. New Haven: T. & S. Green. [after 1767] 4to. pp. 12.
(246).
> Evans, 16766, gives the author's name erroneously as Timothy Dwight.

[LOVELL, JOHN.] The | Seasons.| An | Interlocutory Exercise | at the | South Grammar School, | June 26. 1765.| Being the Day of the annual Visitation of the Schools | in Boston.| [4 lines from Horace.] Boston: | Printed by T. & J. Fleet, at the Heart and Crown, | 1765.| 8vo. pp. [2] 3-8. A.B. (247).

[LOW, SAMUEL.] Winter Displayed, | a | poem.| Describing the Season. | in all its | Stages and Viccissitudes; | and Occasionally interspersed with | a variety of | Moral and sentimental remarks.| [4 lines from Pope.] By An American.| New-York: Printed by Samuel Loudon, | MDCC,-LXXXIV.| 8vo. pp. 40.   A (248).
> Attributed to Samuel Low, a well known poet and playwright of the day.

Low. Ode | To Charity: | *Composed by Brother* Low; of *Hol-land-Lodge;* | *And Sung in* St. Paul's Chapel, *on the* 24th *day* | *of June,* 1789, *being the* Anniversary of the Festival *of* St. John *the* Bap-|tist.| 4to. broadside.   (249).

Low. Ode, | *For* St. John's Day, | June 24, 5790, Performed at the Consecration of the New Building for the use of | Holland Lodge, | and the Washington Chapter of Royal-Arch Masons.| [Composed by Brother Low, of Holland Lodge. Printed by Harrison & Purdy.] Folio broadside.   (250.)

Low. Anthem | to be sung in | Trinity Church, on St. John's Day, *June* 24, 5793, | *By the* Episcopal Charity Children.| Composed by Brother Low.| 10 verses in double column. Under verses is. To be Sung | by Mrs. Pownall before Service.| Recitative | Song | etc. T. & J. Swords, impress.| [1793] Sm. folio broadside.   (251).

[Lowell, Percival.]   A Funeral Elegie On the Death of the Memorable and truly Honourable John Winthrope, Esq. [Cambridge, Samuel Green, 1665.]   (252).
    4to. broadside, 2 columns in Verse, Signed "Perciful Lowle."

M., S. A Country Treat | Upon the Second Paragraph in His Excellency's | Speech, *Decem.* 17, 1730.| Folio broadside, printed in double column [Boston: 1730].

                            Photostat copy in N.Y.P.L. (253).

Mackay, J. Quebec Hill; | or, | Canadian Scenery.| A Poem.| In two parts.| by J. Mackay.| [2 lines in Latin from Hor.] | [cut] | London: | Printed by W. Blackader, Tooke's Court, Chancery Lane, | For the Author; | and sold by Elliot & Kay, Strand, and W. Richardson, | Royal-Exchange.| 1797.| [Price Two Shillings and six pence.] 4to. pp. [3],-II,-[1],-4- 34.   (254).
    "By far the greatest part of the Poem was written in Canada, where the writer has spent a considerable portion of his time."

MARKOE, PETER. Miscellaneous | Poems, | by | Peter Markoe.|
[Two lines from Horace.] Imitated.| Some read with Rap-
ture, others judge with Phlegm; | Thus all may not reject
what you condemn.| Philadelphia: | Printed by W. Prichard
and P. Hall, in Market Street, | Between Front and Second
Streets.| 1787.| 8vo. pp. [4], 1-30.   A.B. (255).

[MARKOE.] THE | STORM, | A Poem.| Descriptive of the late |
Tempest, | Which raged with such destructive Fury through-
out the | Southern Parts of North-America, in July, 1788.|
By a Citizen of Philadelphia.| [6 lines from Young.] Phila-
delphia: | Printed and sold by Prichard & Hall, in | Market
Street, near Front Street.| M.DCC.LXXXVIII.| A.B. (256).
Forms pp. 107-123 of "The Shipwreck." by Thomas Falconer.

[MARKOE.] The | Times; | A | Poem.| [Line from Juvenal.]
Imitated.| To whom, you cry are these harsh lines ad-
dressed? | Let ev'ry feeling reader ask his breast.| Phila-
delphia. | Printed by William Spotswood.| 1788.| 8vo. pp.
[5], 2-22.   A.B. (257).
Another issue: Phila., Prichard and Hall, 1788. 8vo. pp. 35.

MARSHALL (HUMPHREY). The | Aliens: | A Patriotic Poem, | by |
H. Marshall, | A Senator | of | The United States.| Occas-
ioned by the Alien Bill, now | Before the Senate, | May 15th,
1798.| Copy-right Secured.| Philadelphia: | Printed for the
Author.| 1798.| 8vo. pp. [3], iv-v, [1], 7-24.   B. (258).

MARTIN, ALEXANDER. America.| A | Poem.| By Alexander
Martin, Esq; | . . . | . . . | . . . | . . . | . . . . |
To which is added, | Liberty. | A Poem.| By Rusticus.|
. . . . | The Second Edition. longe. emendatior priore: |
Likewise from Mr. Addison, in Praise of Li-|berty with
Something suitable to the Times.| [Philadelphia: Andrew
Steuart, ?1769.] 12mo. pp. 28.   (259).

[MATHER, COTTON.] A Poem | Dedicated to the Memory | of |
The Reverend and Excellent Mr. Urian Oakes, | the late
Pastor to Christ's Flock, | and Præsident of Harvard Col-
ledge, | in Cambridge, | Who was gathered to his People on

25d 5mo. 1681. | In the fifty'th Year of his Age.| I Sam. 25. 1. And Samuel dyed, and all the Israelites were gathered together, and Lamented | him.| Scidentur Vestes Gemmæ frangentur, et Aurum; | Carmina quam tribuunt Fama perennis erit. Ovid. | Magna dabit qui magna potest; mihi parva potenti | Parvaq; poscenti, parva dedisse sat est.| Boston in New England, | Printed for John Ratcliff. 1682. 16mo. pp. [4], 1-16.   B. (260).

The first published work of Cotton Mather, written when but nineteen years of age. The only copy which I can trace is in the Brown University collection. It was purchased by C. F. Harris at the Brinley Sale.

[MATHER.] An | Elegy | On The Much-to-be-deplored Death | Of That Never-to-be-forgotten Person, | The Reverend | Mr. Nathanael Collins; | Who After he had been many years a faithful | Pastor to the Church at Middletown of | Connecticut in New-England, | about the Forty-third year of his Age Expired; | On 28th. 10. moneth 1684.| Testor, Christianum hic de christiano vera proferre.| Hier. Epist. Paulae.| Sic oculos, sic ille manus, sic ora ferebat.| Dignum laude virum musa vetat mori. Horat | Boston in New-England | Printed by Richard Pierce for Obadiah Gill.| Anno Christi 1685.| 24mo. pp. [4], 1-20.   B. (261).

Copy of this scarce book is in the Brown University Library. It is the Brinley copy and was purchased at the sale of that collection by C. Fiske Harris for $205.

MATHER. Johannes in Eremo.| Memoirs, Relating to the | Lives, | of the | Ever Memorable, | Mr. John Cotton, | Who Dyed, 23d 10. m. 1652.| Mr. John Norton, |who Dyed, 5.d. 2.m. 1663.| Mr. John Wilson, | Who Dyed 7.d. 6.m. 1667.| Mr. John Davenport, | Who Dyed, 15.d. 1.m. 1670. | Reverend and Renowned Ministers of the | Gospel, All, in the more Imediate Service | of One Church, in Boston; | And | Mr. Thomas Hooker, | Who Dyed, 7.d. 5.m. 1647. | Pastor of the Church at Hartford; New England.| Written, by Cotton Mather.| [3 lines] Printed for and Sold by Michael Perry, at his Shop, |under the West End of the Town-House. 1695.| 12mo. Title, and pp. [6].   A. (262).

[MATHER.] A LACRYMATORY, designed for the tears let fall at the funeral of Mrs. Sarah Leveret, who died 2d. 11mo. 1704, 5. Boston: Samuel Phillips, 1705. 18mo. pp. 4.   263).
Second title of *Monica Americana,* 1705.

[MATHER.] Vigilantius. | or, | A Servant of the Lord | Found Ready for the | Coming of the Lord.| A Discourse | Occasioned by the Early Death | of Seven Young | Ministers, | Within a Little while one of another: | With some Essay, upon their | very Commendable and Inimitable | Character.| And an Elegy upon them.| [4 lines from Aug. ad. Dioscor.] Boston: Printed and sold by B. Green. | At the South End of the Town. 1706.| 12mo. title followed by pp. 7. (264).

[MATHER.] Corderius Americanus.| An Essay | upon | The Good Education of Children.| And what may Hopefully be Attempted for the *Hope of the* Flock.| In a | Funeral Sermon | upon Mr. Ezekiel Cheever.| The *Ancient* and *Honourable* Master of the | Free-school in Boston.| Vho [*sic*] left off, but when Mortality took him off, in | *August,* 1708. the Ninety Fourth Year of his Age.| With an Elegy and an Epitaph upon him.| [one line] Boston, Printed by *John Allen,* for *Nicholas Boone,* | at the Sign of the *Bible* in *Cornhill,* near the | Corner of *School-Street.* 1708.| 12mo. title and 5 leaves.   A.B. (265).

MATHER. Hades Look'd into. | The Power of Our Great | Saviour | Over the | Invisible World, | and the | Gates of Death | which lead into that world.| Considered, In | A Sermon | Preached at the Funeral | of the Honourable, | Wait Winthrop Esq; Who Expired, 7d. ix m. 1717.| In the LXXVI year of his Age.| By C. Mather, D.D. & F. R. S.| [3 lines from Claud. *de Christ Servatore.*] Boston: Printed by T. Crump, 1717.| 12mo. title and 2 leaves.   A. (266).

[MATHER, SAMUEL.] The | Sacred Minister: | A New | Poem, | In Five Parts; | Representing his Qualifications for the | Ministry, | And his Life and Death in it.| By | Aurelius

54

Prudentius, *Americanus.*| Apostoli, et rectores reliqui, *Dona, quae* Christus *dedit* | *Ecclesiae: Nullibi autem dicitur e converso, dedisse* Ecclesiam | Apostolis, *nedum rectoribus reliquis.*| Pet. Cabeljavii *Defensio Potestat. Ecclesiae in exercenda* | *Disciplina.* p. 272 and 273.| Ecce indocti *surgunt, et coelum rapiunt; Et nos, cum nostris Disputationibus,* in Carne and Sanguine *volutamur.*| Augustini *Querela* in Confessionibus *suis* | *Ego quidem sic judico, tum demum fore beatus* Ecclesias, *si* | veri Philosophi *dent Orpeum* Theologiæ, aut Philosophantur | pié | Jacobi Seegkii *Philosophi, Verba.*| Boston: | Printed by John Boyles in Malborough-Street.| MDCCLXXIII.| 4to. pp. [3], 4-22, [1]. A. (267).

MATTHEWS, MORDECAI. The Christian's Daily Exercise. By Mordecai Matthews. Newport: Printed by the Widow Franklin, 1738. 12mo. pp. 12. (268).

MAYLEM, JOHN. Gallic | Perfidy: | A Poem.| *By* John Maylem. *Philo-Bellum.*| [cut of an Indian] | Boston: New-England: | Printed and Sold by *Benjamin Mecom,* at The New | Printing-Office, July 13, 1758. . . . Where may | be had that *noted* little Book, called *Father.* Abra-| Ham's Speech.| 12mo. pp. [4],-7-16. A., N.Y.P.L. (269).

[MAYLEM.] The Conquest of Louisbourg | 12mo. pp. [1]-16. [Caption title. No title page.] A. (270).

[MECOM, BENJAMIN.] A Poem addressed to a Young Lady. St. Johns: 1757. (271).

> A copy of this item was sold in London several years ago. It was described as "the first book printed in Antigua." This is an error. See under Wm. Shervington in this volume. See also No. 714 in this list.

MEIGS, RETURN JONATHAN. A | Poem | Spoken | in the Chapel | of Yale-College, | at the Quarterly Exhibitions, | March 9th, 1784.| By R. J. Meigs.| New-Haven: Printed by | Meigs, Bowen nad Dana, in Chapel-Street.| 12mo. pp. [3], 4-16. B. (272).

[MORRELL, (WILLIAM).] [Small cut representing a leaf, etc.]
New-England. | or | A Briefe | Enarration | of the Ayre, |
Earth, Water, Fish and | Fowles of that Country.| With |
A Description | of the Natures, Orders, Habits, | and Re-
ligion of the Natiues; | in | Latine and English Verse.| Sat
brevé si sat bené.| London, | Imprinted by I. D. | 1625.|
8vo. Collation: Title. To the "Understanding Reader." 1 p.
Dedication 2 pp; Lectori. 1 p.; pp. 1-24; Postscript 2 pp.
(273).

> The Rev. William Morrell came to Massachusetts in 1623 and
> lived at Plymouth for about one year. The results of his visit are
> found in the above poem which was printed after his return to
> England. The poem is one of the earliest which relates to this
> part of the world. A copy is in the British Museum. Reprinted
> by The Club of Odd Volumes, Boston, 1895.

MORTON, MRS. PEREZ. Reanimation.| A Hymn for the Humane
Society. [1791] Broadside. (274).

[MORTON, SARAH WENTWORTH.] Ouâbi: | or the | Virtues of
Nature | An Indian Tale. | in Four Cantos.| By Philenia, a
Lady of Boston.| [1 line from Spenser.] Printed at Bos-
ton, | By I. Thomas and E. T. Andwers, | At Faust's Statue,
No. 45 Newbury Street. | 1790.| 8vo. pp. [7], vi-viii, [1],
10-51, [1]. A.B. (275).

[MORTON.] Beacon Hill.| A Local Poem, | Historic and De-
scriptive.| Book I.| Published according to Act of Con-
gress.| Boston. | Printed by Manning & Loring for the
Author. | 1797.| 4to. pp. [7], viii-ix, [2], 12-56. [Frontis-
piece engraved by S. Hill.] A.B. (276).

[MORTON.] The Virtues of Society.| A Tale, | Founded on
Fact.| *By the Author of The Virtues of Nature.*| [2 lines
from Cartwright] | Published according to Act of Congress.|
Boston.| Printed by Manning & Loring, for the Author |
1799.| 4to. pp. [5],-6-46. A. (277).

MUNFORD, ROBERT. A | Collection | of | Plays and Poems, |
By the Late | Col. Robert Munford, | of Mecklenburg County,
in the State of | Virginia.| Now first published together.|
Petersburg: | Printed by William Prentis. | 1798.| 8vo.
pp. [5], 6-206.   .   B. (278).

MUNFORD, WILLIAM. Poems, | and | Compositions | In Prose |
on several occasions.| By William Munford, | of the County
of Mecklenburg, and State of Virginia.| [Line from Pope's
Essay on Criticism.] Richmond: | Printed by Samuel Pleas-
ants, Jun. | 1798.| 8vo. title, pp. [5], 6-189, [1].

A.B. (279).

NESBET or NISBETT, RICHARD. Numbers of Poetry—Serious and
Comic.| By Richard Nesbet, Barrister at Law.| No. 1.| The
simple, soft Leylock.| Once more I tune the vocal shell—Gar-
rick.| No general title. 8vo. pp. 4. [n.p. 1799. Printed for
the author.]

NESBET. Numbers of Poetry—Serious and Comic. By Richard
Nisbet. No. 11.| The Fruits of Sermon-Hunting: | or, The
Expounder Refuted.| A tale, founded on Real Incident: |
Being the Third Canto of the Author's Catawessiad.| Decet
esse Pium, Religosum Nefas.| Printed for the Author. 8vo.
pp. 16.   N.Y.H.S. (280).

Richard Nesbet or Nisbett was a native of the Island of Nevis.
He resided for some time near Catawessy on the Susquehanna, from
whence he removed, in consequence of mental derangement, to
Philadelphia, where he was for a time employed as clerk in a
scrivener's office. The malady under which he labored compelled
him after a time to enter the Pennsylvania Hospital, where he
wrote a monody on the death of Washington, published in the
Aurora newspaper. Its classic language and noble sentiments
attracted considerable attention.

The above numbers are fragments and are, as far as known, all
that were issued. No. 1 contains the poem "The Simple, Soft
Leylock," extolling the virtues of Washington and John Adams.
No. II contains "The Fruits of Sermon Hunting, etc." and ends
rather abruptly. See also No. 285.

NEVILL, VALENTINE. The | Reduction | of | Louisbourg.| A | Poem, | Wrote on board His Majesty's Ship Orford, | in *Louisbourg* Harbour. | By Valentine Nevill. Esquire, | of *Greenwich* in *Kent,* Secretary to the Honour- | able Admiral Townsend.| Portsmouth: | Printed for J. Wilkinson; and sold by T. Osborne | in *Gray's Inn;* and W. Owen, near *Temple-* | *Bar, London.* M.DCC.LVIII. 4to. pp. [5],-6-16.
(281).

NEWLAND, JEREMIAH. Verses | Occasioned by the Earthquakes in the Month of November, 1755.| By Jeremiah Newland. Broadside. (282).

NILES, NATHANIEL. The American Hero; a Sapphick Ode by Nathaniel Niles, A. M. Norwich, Conn., October, 1775. Broadside of 15 verses. Small folio. B. (283).

NILES, SAMUEL. A Brief and Plain Essay on God's Wonder-Working Providence for New-England, in the Reduction of Louisburg, and Fortresses thereto belonging on Cape-Breton. New London: Printed and Sold by T. Green, 1747. 12mo.
(284).

NISBET, RICHARD. The Source of Virtue: A Poem. Baltimore: Sold by Rice and Co., 1792. (285).

NOYES, NICHOLAS. May 28, 1706. To my worthy Friend, Mr. James Bayley, living (if living) in Roxbury. A Poem by Nicholas Noyes. Folio broadside. (286).

NOYES. Upon the Much Lamented Death, | of that Pious and Hopeful Young Gentlewoman, | Wife of Mr. Samuel Gerrish, the Daughter of the Honourable | Samuel Sewall Esqr. Who Departed this Life November 17th, 1710.| Being the Night after Publick Thanksgiving.| Broadside. (287).

NOYES. Funeral Poem on the Death of Rev. Joseph Green. Boston: B. Green, 1716. 12mo. (288).
Printed with Sermon on the Death of Green, by Thomas Blowers.

[NURSE, JOHN.] [cut] John Nurse, Carrier of the Essex Gazette | humbly presents the following lines to the Gentlemen and Ladies to whom he Carries the News, on the Beginning of the | Year 1774. Broadside. (289).

[OAKES, URIAN.] An Elegie | upon | The Death of the Reverend | Mr. Thomas Shepard, | Late Teacher of the Church at | Charlestown in New-England: | By a great Admirer of his Worth, and true Mourner for his Death.| [3 lines from Isaiah; 4 from Zech; 3 from Heb.] Cambridge.| Printed by Samuel Green. 1667.| 12mo. pp. [2],-3-16. B. (290).

    This is one of the earliest poems printed and published in this country.

OCCUM, SAMSON. Mr. Occom's Address to his Indian Brethren, on the Day that *Moses Paul,* an Indian, was executed at *New Haven,* on the 2d of *September,* 1772, for the murder of *Moses Cook.* Put in Metre. Sold at the *Heart* and *Crown* in *Boston;* and by *Bulkeley Emerson* at *Newbury-Port.* Broadside of 18 verses of 4 lines each. Folio. 1 p. (291).

[ODELL, JOHN.] The American Times. A Satire. London: 1780. 4to. (292).

    The author was a Loyalist preacher in New Jersey during the Revolution.

ODIORNE, THOMAS. The Progress of Refinement, | a Poem, | in Three Books.| to which are added, | a Poem on Fame, | and | Miscellanies.| By Thomas Odiorne.| Boston: | Printed by Young and Etheridge, | Opposite the Entrance of the Branch-Bank, | State-Street.| MDCCXCII. 12mo. pp. x, [2], 13-176. [Plate engraved by Seymour.] A.B. (293).

OKELY, FRANCIS. The | Disjointed Watch, | or | Truth | rent asunder and divided: | a similitude, | attemted (*sic*) in Metre, | by Francis Okely, | Formerly of St. John's College, Cambridge. | [5 lines from Col. 11, 8-10.] | Baltimore: | Printed by Samuel Sower, | 1795.| 12mo. 4 unnumbered leaves. (294).

[OLIVER, PETER.] A | Poem | Sacred to the Memory of the | Honorable | Josiah Willard, Esq; | Late Secretary of the Province of the | Massachusetts-Bay, | in | New-England; | Who Deceased December 6th, 1756.| Aetatis 76.| Boston: | Printed by Green and Russell, in Queen-street.| M.DCC.-LVII.| 12mo. pp. [5],-6-16. A.B. (295).

OTTO, JOHANN HEINRICH. Ein Geistlich Lied auf Paul Springs Selbstmord Mit einer Pistole, so sich im Jahr 1772 im monat September in Lancaster County. Cocallico Taunschip, Zut-rug. [Philadelphia: Gedruckt bey Heinrich Miller? 1772.] Folio broadside. (296).

P., J. [cut.] A Funeral Elegy | Upon the much Lamented Death of | Daniel Rogers Esq; | who travelling from Hampton to Ipswich on Saturday, Decemb.-|. 1722 | ('tis thought) mistook the Road, and going down to Salisbury-Beach was there benighted, and lost his Life; his Body was found the 14th of January | following, in a deep Cove, and was decently Interr'd at Ipswich the 16th, in the | 56 Year of his Age.| Signed, "J. P." and dated December 10th, 1722. Broadside. (297).

PACKOM, REUBEN. The Ardent Desire and Sincere Cry of a true Believer. Boston: James Franklin, 1729. Broadside. (298).

PAIN, PHILIP. Daily | Meditations: | Or, | *Quotidian Preparations for,* | And | Considerations of | Death | And | Eternity.| Begun *July* 19, 1666.| By *Philip Pain*: Who lately suffering | Shipwrack, was drowned.| [2 lines from Job 30.23.] | [2 lines from Eccles. 12.1.] | Cambridge· | Printed by *Marmaduke Johnson.* 1668.| 12mo. Title, verso blank. 1 p. "The Porch," verso blank. pp. 16; one leaf (recto, with caption-title: A Postscript To the Reader; verso signed J. T.) H.E.H. (299).

This work is the earliest known specimen of original American verse printed in the English Colonies. Until the finding of a copy of the first edition at the dispersal of the Christie-Miller Collection in London several years ago by Dr. A. S. W. Rosenbach, this item was known as one of the "lost books" issued from the Cambridge Press. The following is the title of the second edition. A copy is in the Massachusetts Historical Society.

PAIN. Daily | Meditations: | or, | Quotidian Preparations for | and | Considerations of | Death | and | Eternity.| Began July 19. 1666.| By *Philip Pain:* Who lately suffering | Shipwrack, [*sic*] was drowned.| [2 lines from Job 30.23.] | [2 lines from Eccles. 12.1.] | Cambridge: | Printed by S. G. and

M. J. 1670.| 12mo. Title page, verso blank; 1 p. "The Porch," verso blank, pp. 1-16. (300).

[PAINE, ROBERT, TREAT, JR.] The Invention of Letters: A Poem written at the Request of the President of Harvard University, and deilvered on the day of Annual Commencement, July 15, 1795. Boston: Printed for the Subscribers, July 27, 1795. 4to. pp. 15. A. (301).

> Same: Second edition, Boston, August, 1795.
> Written by Thomas Paine, who changed his name to Robert Treat Paine, Jr., as he did not care to have his name mixed with that of the author of *Common Sense*.

[PAINE.] The | Ruling Passion: An Occasional Poem.| Written by the Appointment of the | Society of the | ΦBK, | and spoken, on their Anniversary, | in the | Chapel of the University, *Cambridge*, | July 20, 1797.| By Thomas Paine, A.M.| Published according to Act of Congress.| Boston: | Printed by Manning & Loring, for the Author.| 1797. 8vo. pp. 32. A.B. (302).

[PARKE, JOHN.] The | Lyric Works | of | Horace, | Translated into | English Verse: | to which are added, | a number of | Original Poems.| By a Native of America.| Two lines in Latin] Philadelphia: | Printed by Eleazer Oswald, at the Coffee-House. MDCCLXXXVI. 8vo, pp. xli, [1] 334, 18 pages of Subscribers Names, [6] [front engraved by Jas. Peller Malcolm.] A.B. (303).

> The earliest American translation of Horace. At the end is a play entitled *Virginia*, etc., which is the earliest known attempt to celebrate Washington's Birthday.

PECK, JOHN. A | Description | of the | Last Judgment; | With | Some Reflections thereon.| The Happiness of being ready.| And the Misery of being unready for | such a Day.| Also, | A Poem on Death, | and | One on the Resurrection | (The Second Edition.) | By | John Peck, | Of Rehoboth.| [2 lines from Acts xvii. 31] | [2 lines from Matt. xxx. 46.] | Boston; N. E.| Printed and sold by E. Russell, adjoining the Cornfield, | in Union-street, near the Market. M,dcc,lxxiii.| 8vo. pp. [3],-4-31, [1]. A. (304).

> Two cuts, one on verso of title, the other on the last page.

PEPPER, HENRY. Juvenile Essays; | or, a | Collection of Poems: | Inscribed to my valued friend, | Henry Mac-Neale Kennedy.| By Henry Pepper.| [Line from Moliere] Philadelphia: | Printed by Richard Folwell, | No. 33, Carter's-Alley.| [1798.] 8vo. pp. 75 [1].   B. (305).

[PETERS, RICHARD.] Dialogue, etc. | For the Commencement in the College of | Philadelphia, May 30th, 1765.| [Philadelphia: W. Dunlap. 1765.] 8vo. pp. 4.   (306).

[PHILLY, JOHN.] A Paraphrastical Exposition | on a | Letter | From a Gentleman in | Philadelphia | To his Friend in | Boston | Concerning a certain Person who com-| pared himself to *Mordecai.*| *Printed in the Year* 1693.| 4to. pp. 8.
                                                        (307).

The author's name is also spelled Phillips. The only known copy is in the possession of Dr. A. S. W. Rosenbach. Mr. Wilberforce Eames lists this item in "The first year of Printing in New York," but states that the evidence of its having been printed in New York was not conclusive, and that it may have been printed in Philadelphia just prior to Bradford's removal to New York.

[PITCHER, NATHANIEL.] A Sorrowful Poem upon that Desirable Youth | Isaac Stetson of Scituate, who was | cast-away in a Sloop near the Mouth of the | North-River in Scituate, the 7th day of No- | vember, 1718. Anno Ætatis Suæ 22.| Signed By a Friend. Broadside.   (308).

Printed on same sheet as "Words of Consolation" &c. By Nathaniel Pitcher. The Poem is without doubt by another hand.

PLUMMER, JONATHAN, JR. Elegy | on the death of the Rev. Mr. John Murray, late | Pastor of the Presbyterian Church in Newburyport, who died the 13th March, Anno Domini 1793; | together with a sketch of his Character, by Jonathan Plummer, jun. Broadside.   (309).

PLUMMER. The awful Malignant Fever at Newburyport, in the Year 1796. [cuts of 44 coffins.] An Elegiac Epistle to the Mourners, on the Death of forty-four Persons, who died of a Malignant Fever in | Newburyport and the adjacent towns, in the Summer and Autumn of the Year 1796—Together with a short account of that | alarming disorder—By Jonathan

Plummer, jun. Printed for and sold by the Author—Price
4½d. Broadside. (310).
For other titles by this author see volume 2 of this bibliography.

PORTER, SARAH. The Royal Penitent, in three parts, to which
is added David's Lamentation over Saul and Jonathan. By
Mrs. Sarah Porter of Plymouth in New Hampshire. Concord: George Hough, 1791. 12mo. pp. 19. A. (311).
Also Newburyport: 1793. 12mo. pp. 21-[1]. A

POTTER, JAMES. A Poem on the Death of Deacon Wm. Barns,
of New-Fairfield. Hartford: Green & Watson, 1769. (312).

PRENTISS, CHARLES. A | Collection | of | Fugitive Essays, | in |
Prose and Verse.| Written by | Charles Prentiss.| [1 line
from Johnson.] | *Published according to* Act *of* Congress.|
Leominster, (Massachusetts) | Printed by and for the Au-
thor.| 1797.| 12mo. pp. [5],-6-204. Leaf of errata pasted
on verso of p. [3]. A. (313).
Contains the following play on pp. [171]-204:
Haven, | or, | the Merited Gallows. | in three acts. |

[PRIME, BENJAMIN YOUNG.] The | Patriot Muse, | or | Poems |
on some of the | Principal Events | of | the Late War; | to-
gether with | A Poem on the peace.| *Vincit amor patriae.*| By
an American Gentleman.| London, | Printed for John Bird, in
Ave-Maria-Lane.| MDCCLXIV.| [Price One Shilling and
Six-pence.] 8vo. pp. vi; [8]-94. (314).
A copy is in the Smithtown, L. I., N. Y., Library.

[PRIME.] An Excellent | New Song, | For the Sons of Liberty in
America.| By a Gentleman of the City of New York.| Printed
by John Holt, at the Exchange.| Broadside containing 13
verses of 4 or 5 lines each. (315).
This song was written at the time of the passage of the "Stamp
Act" and was very popular with the Whigs. It has been reprinted
in several collections of Revolutionary ballads. The original broadside is now very scarce; in fact I know of but one copy, the one in
the Smithtown, L. I., N. Y., Library. It was formerly in the collection of the Late Richard H. Handley.

63

PRIME. Columbia's Glory, | or | British Pride Humbled; | A Poem | on the | American Revolution: | some part of it being | A Parody on an Ode, | entitled | Britain's Glory | or | Gallic Pride Humbled; | Composed on the Capture of Quebec, A. D. 1759.| By Benjamin Young Prime, M.D.| [2 lines from Horace. 9 lines from Horace.] New York: Printed by Thomas Greenleaf, For the Author, M,DCC,XCI. 8vo. pp. [2], iii-vi, [1], 2-42. B. (316).

PURDON, JOHN. A Leisure Hour; or, a series of Poetical Letters, mostly written during the prevalence of the Yellow Fever. By a Citizen of Philadelphia. Philadelphia: 1794. (317).

[RALLING, JOHN.] Miscellanies, | Viz. | I. The Time-Piece; or, An honest Servant's | Advice to his Master.| II. Verses on the Month of May.| III. An affectionate Father's dying Advice.| Frugibus maturis, Frumentandum | Ferro candente, elaborandum, | Quippe tempus elabitur.| Philadelphia: | Printed for the Author, by John McCulloch.| M.DCC.XC.| 12mo. pp. [2], 3-24. A.B. (318).

RALLING. Miscellanies, | Moral and Instructive, | In | Prose and Verse; | Collected from | Various Authors, | for the | Use of Schools, | and Improvement of | Young Persons of both Sexes: | A New Edition, with Additions | [2 lines from Pope] | Philadelphia Printed: | London | Reprinted by James Phillips, Georgeyard, Lombard Street.| MDCCXC.| 12mo. pp. [2],-11-13, [1],-23-45, 166, 47-60. (319).

RALLING. Miscellaneous Sketches, | in Prose and Verse: | Written | For the Spiritual Improvement and Instruction | of Mankind.| By John Ralling.| [2 lines from Herbert. 2 lines from Prov. iii. 35. 11 lines, no author.] Newbury-Port: | Printed by William Barrett, Market square.| 1796.| 12mo. pp. [3], 4-24. B. (320).

REMINGTON, E. [cut, showing Death, Gabriel and a vault containing three Coffins] | A Short Account | of Three men that were Kill'd by | Lightning, at Suffield, May 20, | 1766, Viz.| Samuel Remington, | James Bagg, | Jonathan Bagg.| [Hartford, Thomas Green,?1766.| Broadside, 4to. (321).

RICH, ELISHA. A | Poem | On the Bloody engagement that was Fought on | Bunker's Hill | In Charlestown | New-England, | On the 17th of June, 1775: Together with some Remarks of the Cruelty and Barbarity of the | British Troops, by Destroying the above Mention'd Town by Fire, by which a Number of | Distres'd Inhabitants were forced to Flee from the Flames, to seek Relief and Shelter among their | Sympathizing Brethren in the neighbouring Towns.| By Elisha Rich, Minister of the Gospel.| [Chelmsford: Printed and Sold by Nathaniel Coverly, 1775.] Broadside with twenty-six four line stanzas. Folio, with curious cut of the Battle above the poem. (322).

[RICH.] Poetical | Remarks upon the Fight at the Boston | Light-House | Which happen'd between a Party of Troops belonging to the United Colonies, commanded by Major Tupper, and a Number of Regulars.| [Signed E. R.] Chelmsford Printed and Sold by Nathaniel Coverly [rest of the imprint destroyed] [1775.] With cut of the Battle above the verses.] Folio broadside. (323).

RICH. Poetical | Dialogues, | Calculated for the help of | Timorous and Tempted | Christians.| Also Suited to the case of Disponding | [sic] Sinners, | And the Nature of *Truth* and *Error* | Distinguished, &c. &c.| By *Elisha Rich,* | Preacher of the Gospel, and *Pastor* of a | *Baptist-Church* of Christ | in Chelmsford.| Boston: | Printed, by *Nathaniel Coverly,* for the Author.| M,DCCLXXV.| 12mo. pp. [3],-5-36. A. (324).

RICH. The | Number of the | Beast | Found out by Spiritual | Arithmetic.| . . . By | E. Rich.| . . . . | Chelmsford, N. E.| Printed by Nathaniel Coverly.| M,DCCLXXV.| 12mo. pp. 29,-[1]. A. (325).

RICH. [Cut] A | Poem | on the late distress of the | Town of | Boston.| With some Remarks on the sudden Flight of the Ministerial Troops, after plundering and Destroying the Property of the | Worthy Inhabitants, they left the town in the greatest Confusion imaginable, not allowing themselves time to take with them great | part of their Warlike Stores,

In short, they fled like Murderers' pursued by the Hand of Justice. Chelmsford: Printed and Sold at H. Coverly's Printing-Office: Where may be had, Verses by the Groze | or Dozen. M.DCCLXXVI. [Broadside.] (326).

RICH, R. NEVVUS from Virginia. The Lost flock triumphant. With the happy arriual of that famous and worthy Knight Sr. Thomas Gates: and the well reputed and valiant captaine Mr. Christopher Newporte, and others, into England. With the maner of their distresse in the Iland of Deuils (otherwise called Bemoothawes) where they remayned 42 weeks, and builded two pynaces, in which they returned into Virginia. By R. Rich, gent., one of the voyage. London Printed by Edw: Allde, and are to be solde by John Wright, at Christ-Church dore. 1610. 4to. (327).

    The first published metrical effusion relating to America, by one who had resided there.

    Only one copy of the original edition seems to be extant. Reprinted in an edition of 25 copies. London, 1874. 4to. pp. 19.

[RICHARDS, GEORGE.] THE POLITICAL PASSING BELL | an | Elegy.| Written in a Country Meeting House, *April,* 1789.| Parodized from Gray; | and | Accompanied with a Correct Copy of the sublime | Original.| For the Entertainment of those, who Laugh at | All Parties.| [3 lines from Horace] | [4 lines imitated] | [Device] | Printed at Boston, | by Isaiah Thomas and Company.| MDCCLXXXIX.| 8vo. pp. [5],-6-15. A. (328).

    Gray's "Elegy" printed on one side while the parody is printed on the opposite pages. The "Redbreast" stanza is not in this work, however.

[RICHARDS, GEORGE.] The | Declaration | of Independence; | A | Poem: | accompanied by Odes, Songs, &c.| Adapted to the Day.| A firm, unshaken, uncorrupted soul, | A steady spirit, regularly free.—Thomson.| By a Citizen of Boston.| Printed at Boston, | Faust's Statue, No. 45, Newbury Street.| MDCC-XCIII.| 8vo. pp. [5], 6-24. A.B. (329)

RICKMAN, THOMAS C. The Fallen Cottage; a Poem. By T. C. Rickman. [line from Cowper] Philadelphia: Printed for the Proprietors, 1793. 12mo. pp. 24. L.C. (330).

POEMS

On several Occasions,

B Y

𝕬𝖖𝖚𝖎𝖑𝖆 𝕽𝖔𝖘𝖊:

To which are prefixed,

Some other Pieces writ to him, and to his Memory after his Deceaſe.

Collected and publiſhed by his Son *Joſeph Roſe,* of *Philadelphia.*

PHILADELPHIA:
Printed at the *New Printing-Office,* near the
Market. 1740.

ROBINSON, NATHANIEL. Verses | upon Fourteen | Different Oc-
casions: | Composed in Albany Goal, in | the year 1768. | by
Nathaniel Robinson, | The Third Edition. | Boston: | Printed
and Sold by William McAlpine, | in Marlborough Street, |
1773.| 16mo. pp. [2],-3-24. (331).

> Contains poem *On the taking* of Fort William Henry."

ROBINSON. Verses | Composed by | Nathaniel Robinson, |
when he was in | Albany Goal, | in the Year | 1758.| The
Third Edition.| Norwich: | Printed and Sold by Green &
Spooner | 1774.| 16mo. pp. [3],-4-30. (332).

> The copy seen had 30 pp. but was not complete.

ROSE, AQUILA. Poems | On Several Occasions, | by | Aquila
Rose: | To which are prefixed, | Some other Pieces writ to
him, | and to his Memory after | his Decease.| Collected and
Published by his Son Joseph Rose, | of Philadelphia.| Phila-
delphia: | Printed at the New Printing-Office, near the |
Market. 1740. 8vo, pp. 56. (333).

> On page 45 is the following title: A | Poem | to the | Memory
> | of | Aquila Rose: | Who died at Philadelphia, August the | 22d,
> 1723. Ætat 28. by Elias Bockett.| London: Printed.| Philadelphia:
> Reprinted at the New— | Printing Office. [By Benjamin Franklin.]

ROWSON, SUSANNAH. The Standard of Liberty; A Poetical
Address. Baltimore: 1795. 12mo. (334).

[RUGELY ROWLAND.] The | Story | of Æneas and Dido | Bur-
lesqued: | from the fourth book of the Æneid of Virgil.| Vive
la Bagatelle. | Charleston: | Printed and Sold by Robert Wells.|
MDCCLXXIV. 12mo. pp. xvi, 94. N.Y.P.L. (335).

> A curious and rather facetious work. The copy which I have
> seen and collated contained the author's name written in pencil on
> the title-page by a former owner. The preface, which is dated
> "South Carolina, 1774," shows by its contents that the work is un-
> doubtedly an American production.

RUSSELL, JOHN MILLER. A | Poem, | on | The fourth of July,
1798, | being the | Anniversary of the Independence | of the
United States of America.| By John Miller Russell, A.M.|
Boston: | Printed by Manning & Loring.| 1798.| 8vo. pp.
[3], 4-16. B. (336).

RUSSELL. The Pastoral Songs of P. Virgil Maro, to which are added poems sentimental and descriptive. by John Miller Russell. Boston: Manning & Loring, 1799. 12mo. pp. 92.

(337).

S., M. The following lines were Composed and sent to the Rev. E. L. soon after | his recovery from a long confinement by sickness, and during a season | of very distressing affliction, accompanied with the following note from | a female member of his Church. Broadside. (338).

ST. JOHN, PETER. Poetical Relation of the Capture of the Congregation at Middlesex [now Darien], Conn., (who were assembled for Divine Worship, July 22nd, 1781) by a Party of the Enemy from Long Island; With an Account of their Sufferings while in Captivity. Printed for the Author. [1781]. 12mo. (339).

Evans lists an edition printed by Douglas & Ely, Danbury: 1791.

ST. JOHN. Death of Abel. An Historical or rather Conjectural Poem. Danbury, Nathan Douglas, 1793. 12mo. pp. 186, [2].

(340)

[ST. JOHN, SAMUEL.] Taxation of America. [1778.] Broadside. (341).

Ford 2121. Duychinck gives the author's name as above, but it has also been attributed to Peter St. John. Other issues listed by Mr. Ford are as follows:

American Taxation: Nathaniel Coverly, Printer Milk-Street. American Taxation. | A Song of Seventy-Nine. Printed by Nathaniel Coverly, Jun. | Milk-Street, Corner of Theatre-alley, Boston, 1811. (342).

American Taxation. | Or the Spirit of Seventy-six exemplified in a song written in the golden days which tried Men's Souls. This popular piece was probably first issued at or about the period of the Stamp Act, [1765] and reissued in 1776 and 1779. (343).

SAUR, CHRISTOPHER. Ein Einfältiges Reim-Gedichte, welches Christoph | Saur gemacht hat auf seinen Namen und Ge- | burts-Tag, als er sechtig Jahr alt war den 26sten | September, 1781.| [n.p. 1781.] 8vo. pp. 4. (344).

[SCHNEEBERGER, ANDREW.] Wurde abgesungen den 31sten August, 1793 bey B. A. S. auf dem jährlichen Fest an der Antitum. Ephrata. Folio broadside. (345).

[SCULL, NICHOLAS.] Kawanio Che Keeteru: | A true | Relation | of a | Bloody Battle Fought | between | George and Lewis, | in the Year | 1755.| [Philadelphia:] Printed [by William Bradford] in the Year M,DCC,LVI. 8vo. pp. 16. (346).

> Second Edition, Philadelphia: James Chattin, 1756.
>
> Said to be by Nicholas Scull, "A poetical attack on the Quakers for preventing proper measures being taken to defend the province against the French and Indians."

SEARSON, JOHN. Poems | on | Various Subjects and Different Occasions, | chiefly adapted to | Rural Entertainment | in the | United States of America.| By John Searson, | Formerly of Philadelphia, Merchant.| [6 lines from Thomson's "Seasons."| Philadelphia: | Printed by Snowden & McCorkle, No. 47, North Fourth-street.| 1797.| 8vo. pp. [3), iv, [1], vi, 7-94, [9]. A.B. (347)

SEARSON. Mount Vernon, A Poem: | Being The Seat of his Excellency George Washington, in the | State of Virginia; | Lieutenant-General and Commander in Chief of the land forces of the | United States of America | ☞ This rural, romantic and descriptive poem of the seat of so | great a Character, it is hoped may please, with a Copperplate like | ness of the General. It was taken from an actual view on the spot | by the Author, 15th May, 1799. Also a cursory view of George | town, City of Washington, and the Capitol.| By John Searson, *formerly of Philadelphia, Merchant* | [3 lines from Thomson's Seasons.] | Philadelphia: | Printed for the author by Folwell.| [1799.] 8vo. pp. vi. [3], 10-83, 4. [Portrait of Washington.]
A. (348).

> Added to the work are "Elegiac Verses on the decease of General George Washington." pp. 4.

69

SEARSON. *Art* | of | Contentment; | with several | Entertaining Pieces | of | Poetry, | Descriptive of the Present Times, | in the | U. States *of* America.| [line] | By John Searson, | *Formerly a Merchant of Philadelphia.*| [4 lines from Dryden] | [line] | [2 lines from Phil. 4th & 11th] | Baltimore: | *Printed for the* Author *by W. Pechin.*| 12mo. pp. [3],-iv.-[1],-vi,-[1],-8-225, [1]. B. (349).

Dedicated to Washington. The poetry is on pp. (210)-225.

SECCOMBE, JOHN and JOHN HUBBARD. [Cut.] Father Abbey's Will.| To which is added, A Letter of Courtship to his virtuous and amiable widow.| Cambridge, December, 1731 . . . New-Haven, January 1731-2. Our Sweeper having lately buried his Spouse, and accidently hearing of the Death and Will of his deceas'd Cambridge Brother, has conceiv'd a violent Passion for the Relict.·. . . Broadside. A. (350).

A number of editions of this famous poem were printed, some without Hubbard's Poem.

SEVER, THOMAS, JR. An Ode, | On the sudden death of Mr. Daniel Holt, late of *Town-|send,* who was instantly killed by the unexpected fall of a Tree, | August 31st, 1798.| *Addressed to the Public in general, nad his Friends in particular.*| By Thomas Sever, Jun.| Folio broadside of XXX verses of four lines each. Probably printed at Hartford, 1798. B. (351).

SEWALL, JONATHAN MITCHELL. Gen. Washington, | A New Favorite Song, at the American Camp.| To the Tune of the British Grenadiers. [1776] Broadside. (352).

Also issued with variations of title.

[SEWALL.] Verses | occasioned by reading the | Answer | of the | President | of the | United States, | to the | House of Representatives, | requesting certain papers | relative to the | Treaty | with | Great Britain.| Boston: Printed in the Year 1797. 16mo. pp. 1, [7]. B. (353).

[SEWALL.] Versification | of | President Washington's | excellent | Farewell-Address.| To the | Citizens of the | United States.| By a Gentleman of Portsmouth, N. H.| Published According to Act of Congress.| Portsmouth, New Hampshire: | Printed and Sold by Charles Peirce, at the | Columbian Bookstore, No. 5, Daniel-Street, | 1798. 8vo. pp. [5] 6-54.

A. (354).

[SEWALL, SAMUEL.] Upon Mr. Samuel Willard, his first | coming into the Assembly, and Praying, | after a long and dangerous Fit of | Sickness; November 21, 1700. at | 3 in the Afternoon, being a Day of | Publick Thanksgiving.| [Boston: B. Green and J. Allen, 1700.] Broadside. (355).

Reissued in 1720.

[SEWALL.] Wednesday, January 1, 1701, a little before Break-a-Day, at Boston | of the Massachusetts.| A. (356).

Issued at end of *Proposals touching the Accomplishment of Prophesies, Humbly Offered,* by Samuel Sewall. Boston: B. Green, 1713. Some copies may also have been issued separately as a broadside.

Dr. Rosenbach in his admirable *An American Jewish Bibliography,* claims that Samuel Willard was its author, but Dr. Samuel Abbott Green, a student and authority on early New England Literature, claims that Sewall was the author. I am much inclined to believe the latter authority to be correct. This poem was reissued in *Phænomena quadam Apocalyptica,* by Sewall. Boston, 1727.

SEWALL. Upon the drying up of that Ancient River, | the River Merrymak. Dated January 15, 1719-20, and signed S. S. [And] Connecticut's Flood, | on Merrymak's Ebb. Dated March 10, 1720-21, and signed Anthropos. Broadside. (357).

Two poems on same sheet.

[SEWALL.] In Remembrance of Mr. Samuel Hirst, the Eldest and only Surviving Son of Grove Hirst, Esq., . . . and died very suddenly when he was in his way upon the Long Wharff, at two in the Afternoon, January 14, 1726, 7. [Boston: 1727.] Broadside. 12mo. (358).

71

[Sewall, Stephen.] Nocte Cogitata, | Auctore, Anglice Scripta, | Young, D.D.| Quæ | Lingua Latii Donavit | America.| Sunt lachrymæ rerum, et mentem mortalia tangunt.| Virg.| Caroloppidi: | Typis Allen & Cushing, Massachusettensium, | M, DCC,LXXXVI.| 12mo. pp. [5], 6-21.

A.B. (359).

[Shervington, William.] Occasional | Poems.| [2 ll. in Latin from Horace.] Antigua: | Printed by T. Smith, for the Author.| MDCCXLIX.| 4to. pp. [3],-iv,-9-92.   (360)

> Printed from the type of Benj. Franklin. The copy noted lacks pp. 5-8 and pp. 83-84, slightly mutilated. It contains on pp. 30-39 *The Antigonian Beauties,* which with a change in title were reissued at Boston by D. Fowle, about 1750. This is probably the first book printed at Antigua.

[Shervington.] The | *Antigonian* and *Bostonian* Beauties; | A | Poem.| Occasion'd by seeing the Assembly, at St.| *John's Antigua,* on Thursday the 7th | of *July,* and afterwards at *Boston,* in | King-street.| [Three lines from Milton.] | By W. S. A. B.| Boston: | *Printed and Sold* by D. Fowle *in Queen-street.*| [Circa 1750]. 12mo.   A. (361).

[Smith, William.] Indian Songs | of | Peace: | with | A Proposal, in a prefatory Epistle, | for erecting | Indian Schools.| and | A Postscript by the Editor, introducing | Yariza, an Indian Maid's Letter, | to the principal Ladies of the Province and | City of New-York.| By the Author of the American Fables.| [2 lines in Latin from Virgil.] | [2 lines translated from above.] | New-York: | Printed by J. Parker, and W. Wayman, (*sic*) at the | *New Printing Office* in *Beaver-Street,* MDCCLII.| Small 8vo. Collation. pp. [3],-4-27.

H.E.H. (362).

> The *Indian Songs* occupy pp. [13]-22.
>
> This scarce volume is presumed to be by William Smith, Provost of the College of Philadelphia.
>
> Republished in a pamphlet entitled *Some Account of the North American Indians, &c.* London: [1754].
>
> The *Songs* are on pp. 49-64.

[SMITH.] Ode | on the | New-Year, | 1753.| *Labuntur Anni*————— | New-York: | Printed by *J. Parker,* at the New-Printing-Office, | in *Beaver-Street.*| 12mo. pp. [ii]-iv, [5]-16. H.E.H. (363).

By Rev. William Smith, first Provost of the College and Academy of Philadelphia. A copy is in the Collection of E. Dwight Church of Brooklyn, N. Y.

[SMITH.] A | Copy of Verses | written on | A Passage to Queen's Village | on | Long Island. By W. S.| [1761] Broadside, small folio of 38 lines. N.Y.H.S. (364).

[SMITH.] A | Poem | On visiting the | Academy | of | Philadelphia, June 1753.| [3 lines of quotes] Philadelphia: | Printed [by Franklin and Hall] in the Year MDCC-LIII.| 4to. pp. [2],-iii-iv-5-16. (365).

[SMITH.] Poems, | on | Several Occasions, | Written in | Pennsylvania.| "Nec Lusisse Pudet."| Philadelphia. | Printed and Sold by Enoch Story, in Se-|cond, between Chesnut and Walnut-streets. | M,DCCLXXXVI.| 16mo. pp. [5],-6-141.
B. (366).

SMITH. The | Flowret.| A Collection of | Poems, | written by | William Smith, Esq.| Attorney at Law, Philadelphia.| "Nec Lusisse Pudet."| The Third Edition | [cut] | First American Edition Printed by E. S. in | Philadelphia . . . Re-printed in London and now | Baltimore, | Printed and Sold by E. Story.| 1799.| 12mo. pp. [5],-6-141, [blank page], [2]. [plate.] (367).

First published in *Poems on Several Occasions.*

SMITH. Consolation | from | Homar, | An Hermit of the East.| [ornament] | To which is added | A | Soliloquy, | By the Rev. William Smith, A.M.| Rector of St. Paul's Church, Narragansett, | Rhode-Island State.| Newport: | Printed by Henry Barber.| M,DCC,LXXXIX.| 12mo. A. (368).

73

[SNOWDEN, R.] The Columbiad: or, a Poem on the American War. In Thirteen Cantos. Philadelphia: 1795. 12mo. pp. 46. A.B. 369).

Preface signed "A New Jersey Farmer."

STEARNS, CHARLES. The Ladies' | Philosophy of Love.| A Poem, | In Four Cantos.| Written in 1774.| By Charles Stearns, A.B. | Since Pastor of the Church, and Preceptor of the | Liberal School in Lincoln.| Now first published— According to Act of Congress.| Leominster, Mass.| Printed by John Prentiss & Co. For the author. | 1797.| 8vo. pp. iv, 5-76. A.B. (370).

STEEDAM, JACOB JACOBSZ. Den | Distelvink.| Erste Deel, Minne-sang: | behelsende | Eerlijke Minne-Sinne-Beel-den, Vaarsen, en Liede-kens: op verscheyden Oude | en Nuwe Sang-koustige | Stemmen.| Door | J. J. Steendam.| t'Amsterdam, | Voor Gerrit van Goedesberg, Boek-verkooper, | op het Water over de Nieuwe-brugh, in de | Delssche Bybel. 1649.| 8vo. pp. [2],-2-101,-[21],-1-207,-[9],-1-78,-76-80,-199,-[1]. 3 vols. in one. B. (371).

Volume I, Minnesang; Volume II, Zegensang; Volume III, Hemelsang.

[STEENDAM.] Klacht van Nieuw-Amsterdam, in Nieuw-Neder-landt, tot haar Moeder; van haar begin, wasdom en tegen-woordigen stand. T'Amsterdam, by Pieter Dirksz, 1659. folio broadside. [Complaint of New Amsterdam, in New Nether-land.] (372).

A translation by Henry C. Murphy was printed at The Hague, in 1861.

STEEDAM. Zeedes-angen voor de Batavische jonkheyt. Behel-sende verscheyden bedenkelijke en stichtelijke stoffen, op bekende en vermakelijke sangtoonen gepast. Batavia, 1671. 8vo. (373).

Only one copy of this work seems to be known. It contains poems upon events in private life in New Netherland. For a fur-ther account of the author and his work see *Memoir of the first poet in New Netherland*. By H. C. Murphy, The Hague, 1861.

STEERE, RICHARD. A | Monumental | Memorial | of | Marine |
Mercy | being | An acknowledgment of an High Hand of |
Divine Deliverance on the *Deep* | in the Time of distress, |
in | a late voyage from *Boston* in *New England* | To London,
Anno 1683.| In a Poem. *By Richard Steere.*| To which
is added *Another* Occasioned by Several | *Remarkable Passages*
happening at the *Birth* | of a *Male Child* on Board the Same
Ship | in her voyage *Returning* 1684.| By the same *Author*
then a *Passenger.*| Printed at Boston in *New-England* by
Richard Pierce for *James Cowse,* Stationer | Anno 1684.|
12mo. pp. [4],-1-12.   (374).

[STEERE.] The Daniel Catcher.| The | Life | of the Prophet |
Daniel: | In a | Poem.| To which is added, | *Earth's Felicities,*
Heaven's Allowances, | A blank Poem. | With Several other
Poems. | by R. S. | Printed in the year 1713.| 12mo. pp. [2],-
1-90.   A. (375).
>   For a splendid account of Steere see Littlefield. *Early Massa-*
> *chusetts Press.* Club of Odd Volumes, Boston, 1907.

STEINER, J. CONRAD. Wächter-Stimm aus dem verwüsteten Sion
in Pennsylvanien an dessen Lehrer und Wächter, insbesonder
an das gesamte Volck insgemein. Germantown: Christopher
Saur. 1752. 4to. pp. 16.   (376).
>   The author of the above "Watchman's Call," was pastor of the
> Reformed Congregation at Germantown.

[STEWART, JOHN.] The | Revelation of Nature, | with the |
Prophesy of Reason. | [2 lines of Verse] | New-York: |
Printed by Mott & Lyon, for the Author.| *In the fifth year*
of intellectual existence, or the | publication of the Apocalyse
of Nature, 3000 years from the Grecian Olympiads, and
4800 from recorded | Knowledge in the Chinese tables of
eclipses beyond | which Chronology is lost in fable.| 12mo. pp.
[3],-iv-xxxix, [1], 2-104. [1796].   N.Y.P.L. (377).

[STORY, ISAAC, JR.] An | Epistle from Yarico to Inkle, | together |
With their Characters, as related in the | Spectator.| Quod
genus hoc hominum? quaeve hunc tam | barbara morem |
Permittit patria?' Marblehead: | Printed for the sons and
daughters of Columbia.| M.DCC.XCII.| 12mo. pp. [5],
6-31.   A.B. (378).

[STORY.]   Liberty, | a | Poem, | delivered on the Fourth of July.|
[6 lines from Gustavus Vasa.] | The Stranger.| Newbury-
port: | Printed by William Barrett, | Market-Square.—
M,DCC,XCV.| 8vo. pp. [5],-6-10.   (379).

[STORY.] All the World's a Stage.| A | Poem, | in | Three Parts.|
[5 lines from Pope's *Essay on Man.*] | The Stranger.| New-
buryport: | Printed by William Barrett.| 1796.| 8vo. pp.
[3],-4-15.   (380).

SULLIVAN, J. An Ode, | Sung at the Lecture of the Congrega-|
tional Charitable Society, in Boston, | on the 12th of Febru-
ary, 1795.| By Mr. Rea. Broadside.   (381).

SUMNER, CHARLES P. The | Compass | a | Poetical Perform-
ance | at the | Literary Exhibition | in September, 1795, | at |
Harvard University. | by | Charles P. Sumner.| Boston:
Printed by William Spotswood | for the subscribers.| 12mo.
pp. [3] 4-12.   A.B. (382).

SWANWICK, JOHN. Poems | on | Several Occasions. | by | John
Swanwick, Esq. | One of the Representatives in the Congress
of the | United States, from the State of Pennsylvania.| Phila-
delphia: | Printed by F. and R. Bailey, at Yor-|ick's Head,
No. 116, High-Street. | 1797.| 24mo. pp. [5], 2-174.
                                               A.B. (383).

T., J. A | *Moral Reflection,* | on the | Sudden Death | of the
Two | Miss Visschers, | Daughters of | Col. John Visscher, |
of Green-Bush, | who were unfortunately drowned in the
River | Hudson, March 15, 1790.| Very respectfully presented
to the | Disconsolate Mourners, | By their sympathic young
Friend, | J. T.| Printed and Sold at Webster's Printing-|office,
State-street, Albany.| [1790]. 12mo. pp. 8.   A. (384).

T., M. Some Consolatory Reflections and Lamentations, | Occas-
ioned by the premature Deaths of three of the Children of |
Capt. Joseph and Mrs. Mary Hinckley, of Barnstahle: (1732-
1733.) Broadside.   (385).

[TEALL, BENJAMIN.] The following Composed on the lamented Death of | *Michael Griswold,* Junior, | of Killingworth, who was killed at a Raising, in | the Year 1771. (*Written by* B. T.). Broadside, folio, 26 Verses of 4ll. each; on same sheet. The following written to the Young People.| By the same Hand.| [at end Benjamin Teall.]   (386).

THARP, PETER. An | Elegy | On the Death of Capt. Annanias Valentine, Thomas Pinkney, Isaac Elliot, Jacamiah Cropsey and | Leonard Merrit, all respectable Citizens of the Town of Marlborough who were unfortunately drowned on | the Flatts, in front of the town, in attempting to go on shore, on Friday morning, the 12th of December, | 1800, in a violent storm of Wind and Rain.—By Peter Tharp.| [cut of 5 coffins, 19 Verses in 2 Columns] Kingston, (Ulster County.) Printed by Samuel S. Freer | Folio broadside.   A. (387).

THOME, ANASTASIA. Ein Lob-Lied dem in Gott Geehrten Vatter Friedsam Zum Andencken abgesungen &c., &c. Ephrata: Der Brüderschaft, 1768.   (388).

THOMPSON, ABRAHAM. Poems on the most solemn subjects. [New Haven] [1790].   (389).

THOMPSON, OTIS. A Poem delivered in the Chapel of Rhode Island College, at the Public Exhibition of the Senior Class, Dec. 27, 1797. [Providence] B. Wheeler. [1798.] 8vo. pp. 8.   A. (390).

TILDEN, STEPHEN. Tilden's | Miscellaneous | Poems, | on | Divers Occasions; | Chiefly to Animate & Rouse | the | Soldiers.| *Printed* 1756.| 16mo. pp. 30.   (391).

TILDEN. Tilden's | Miscellaneous | Poems, | on | Divers Occasions; | Chiefly to animate and rouse the | Soldiers.| The Third Edition, with sundry Additions.| New-London, T. Green.| n.d. 16mo. pp. 58,-[1].   (392).

TILESTON, THOMAS. Funeral Elegy | Dedicated to the Memory of His Worthy Friend | The Learned & Religious | Mr. John Foster who Deceased in Dorchester the 9 of Sepbr. 1681.| Broadside.   (393).

[TOMPSON, BENJAMIN.] *New Englands Crisis.|* Or a Brief |
Narrative, | Of New-Englands Lamentable | Estate at present,
Compar'd with the for-|mer (but few) years of | Prosperity.|
Occasioned by many unheard of *Cruel* | *tyes* practised upon
the *Persons* and *Estates* | of its united *Colonyes,* without re-
spect of | *Sex, Age* or *Quality* of Persons, by the | Barbarous
Heathen thereof.| *Poetically Described.|* By a Well wisher
to his | *Countrey.|* Boston, | Printed and sold by *John Foster,*
over against | the Sign of the *Dove.* 1676.| 4to. pp. [4]-5-31.
(394).

The above, with variations, was issued also under the following
title. Each of these titles contains matter not in the other.

New Englands Tears | for her | Present Miseries : | or, | A
Late and True Relation of | the Calamities of | New-England |
Since April last past.| With an Account of the Battel between
the | *English* and *Indians* upon *Seaconk Plain* : | And of the
Indians Burning and Destroying of *Marlbury, Rehoboth,
Chelmsford, Sudbury,* | and Providence.| With the Death of
Antononies the Grand *Indian* Sachem ; | And a Relation of a
Fortification begun by | Women upon *Boston Neck.* Together
with an Elegy on the Death of *John Winthrop,* Esq ; late Gov-
ernour of Con- | necticott, and Fellow of the *Royal Society.|
Written by an Inhabitant of* Boston *in* New England | *to his
Friend in* London. With Allowance.| London : Printed for
N. S. 1676. 8vo. pp. 14.   (395).

[TOMPSON.] A | Funeral Tribute | *To the Honourable Dust of
that most Charitable* | Christian, *Unbiassed* Politician, | *And
unimitable* Pyrotechnist | John Winthrope esq : | *A Member
of the* Royal Society, *&* Governour *of* | Conecticut Colony
in | New-England.| Who expired in his Countreys Service,
April 6th, | 1676.| Broadside.   (396).

TOMPSON. Memento Mori.| A Neighbor's Tears | Sprinkled
on the Dust of the Amiable Virgin, | Mrs. Rebekah Sewall, |
Who was born December 30, 1704, and dyed | suddenly August
3, 1710. Ætatis 6. 4to. 1p.   (397).

In early times it was customary to address ladies of high position
as Mistress or Mrs., but this seems to be the only instance where
a child of 6 years was so styled.

78

TOMPSON. The Grammarians Funeral. | or, | An Elegy composed upon the Death of Mr. *John Woodmancy,* | formerly a School-Master in *Boston*: But now Published upon | the Death of the Venerable | Mr. Ezekiel Chevers, | the late and famous School-Master of *Boston* in *New-England;* Who Departed this Life the | *Twenty-first* of *August* 1708. Early in the Morning. In the Ninety-fourth Year of his Age.| 4to. Broadside. (398).

TOMPSON, EDWARD. An | Elegiack Tribute to the Sacred Dust of the Reverend and Worthy | Mr. Seaborn Cotton | Pastour of the Church of Christ at Hampton in New-England: who was discharged | from his Work and Office, to be admitted into Heaven, April 20th, 1686.| [Boston: Printed by Samuel Green.] Broadside. (399).

TOWNSEND, WALTER. Elegy, | On the Death of Mr. Daniel Parish, who departed | this life August 21, 1795—aged 24 years.| by Walter Townsend.| Broadside of 12 verses of 4 lines each. Small folio. (400).

[TRUMBULL, JOHN.] An | Elegy, | On the Death of Mr. Buckingham St. John, | Tutor of Yale College, who was drowned in his Passage from *New-|Haven* to *Norwalk, May* the 5th, 1771.| Broadside. Small folio. N.Y.H.S. (401).

> Trumbull's first separate publication. Only two copies can be located, one of which is in the Collection of the New York Historical Society. Another copy was sold in the Sturges Sale, 1922.
>
> Reprinted, with preface by Oscar Wegelin, Heartman's Historical Series, No. 12. New York: 1915.

[TRUMBULL.] The Progress of Dulness.

Part I. The Rare Adventures of Tom Brainless. Printed in the year 1772. 12mo. pp. 26.

Part II. The Life and Character of Dick Hairbrain, of finical memory. Printed in the year 1773. 12mo. pp. 27.

Part III. The Adventures of Miss Harriet Simper, of the Colony of Connecticut. New Haven: Thos. & Samuel Green, 1773. 12mo. pp. 28. (402).

> Same: Three parts complete. Exeter H. Ranley, 1794. 16mo. A. Several other editions.

TRUMBULL. [Royal Arms.] A New Proclamation! By Thomas Gage, Whom British frenzy, stil'd Honourable and Excellency o'er Massachusett's . . . [Hartford: Printed by Ebenezer Watson, 1775.] 8vo. pp. [8]. (403).

[TRUMBULL.] An | Elegy | on the | Times: | First Printed at Boston, | September 20th, A. D. 1774.| New-Haven: | Re-printed by Thomas and Samuel Green. 1775.| 12mo. pp. [5],-6-15. A.B. (404).

[TRUMBULL.] McFingal: | A Modern | Epic Poem.| Canto First, | or | The Town-Meeting.| Philadelphia: | Printed and Sold by William and Thomas Brad-|ford, at the London Coffee-House, 1775.| Small 8vo. Title; 1 leaf; pp. 40. (405).

> This is the first publication of this popular poem, Part One being all that was issued at the time.

> The Same: London, 1776. 8o. pp. [3], 4-44. A.

> The first complete edition was published in Hartford: Hudson and Goodwin, 1782. A.

> Hartford: Nathaniel Patten, 1782.

> Other editions before 1800 are as follows:

> Boston: Peter Edes, 1785. 16mo. pp. [5], 6-110. A.

> Philadelphia: 1787. A.

> Philadelphia: M. Carey, 1791. 12mo. pp. 95 and leaf of Advertisements. This is the first edition bearing the author's name. A.

> London, 1792. 8vo. pp. [2], 2-142, with explanatory notes. A.

> London, 1793. Same as the London, 1792, edition. A.

> New York: John Buel, 1795. With portrait and eight copper-plates engraved by E. Tisdale. This is the first illustrated edition. A.

> Boston: Manning & Loring, 1799. 12mo. pp. [1], iv-v, [2], 8-141 and three leaves of advertisements. A.

[TUCKER, NATHANIEL.] The | Bermudian.| A | Poem.| *Ille terrarum mihi, praeter omnes,* | *Angulus ridet.*| Hor.| Williamsburg: | Printed by Alexander Purdie & John Dixon.| M,DCC,LXXIV.| 4to. pp. 15. A. (406).

> Another edition, London: Printed for the author, etc., MDCCLXXIV. 4to. pp. [3],-2-16. This has author's name printed on title.

[TUCKER, ST. GEORGE.] The | Probationary Odes | of | Jonathan Pindar; Esq. | A | Cousin of Peter's, | and | Candidate for the Post of Poet Laureat | To the C. U. S.| In two parts.| [2 lines from Horace.] Philadelphia: | Printed for Benj. Franklin Bache, | M.DCC.XCVI.| [Copyright secured.] 12mo. Part 1. pp. viii, 9-46. Part 2. [7] 53-103. (407).

TUCKER. The Knight and Friars. An Historical Tale; after the Manner of John Gilpin. [Line in Latin from Horace]. New-York: Printed and sold by Eleazer Oswald, No. 25, Water-Street. 1786. (408).

TYLER, ROYALL. The Origin of Evil. An Elegy. [12ll. of quot.]. Printed in the Year MDCCXCIII. 4to. pp. 8. A. (409).

TYTLER, J. The | Rising of the Sun | In the | West: | Or the | Origin and Progress | Of | Liberty.| By J. Tytler | One of the Compilers of the Encyclopœdia Britannica in | Scotland.— Exiled from that Country, on Account of his writings | in the Cause of Liberty, Jan. 7th 1793, and lately arrived in A|merica from Belfast in Ireland.| *Composed during the Voyage.*| Salem: | Printed By William Carlton. | 1795.| 8vo. pp. 24. A. (410).

VAIL, JOSEPH. Noah's Flood: | A | Poem.| In two Parts.| Part I. | Contains an Historical account of the De | luge, Taken from the Bible; interspersed | with conjectural observations.| Part II. | Is designed as a Moral Improvement of | the Subject.| To which are added, | The Following pieces in | Poetry, viz. | Youth Cautioned Against Vice.| On Happiness.| A New-Year's Hymn.| [2 lines from Psalmist.] | *By Joseph Vail, A.M.* | Pastor of the Third Church in East Haddam.| *New-London*: Printed by Samuel Green.| 1796.| 8vo. pp. [2],-5-28. A. (411).

[VAUGHAN, WILLIAM.] The | Golden | Fleece | Diuided into three Parts, | Under which are discovered the Errours | of Religion, the Vices and Decayes of the King-|dome, and lastly the wayes to get wealth, and to | restore Trading so much Com-|playned of.| Transported From | Cambrioll Colchos, out of

81

the Southermost | Part of the Island, commonly called the | Newfoundland, | By Orpheus Junior, | For the generall and perpetuall Good of | Great Britaine.| London, | Printed for Francis Williams, and are to bee sold | at his Shop at the signe of the Globe, over | against the Royall Exchange, | 1626.| Sm. 4to. Collation. Part 1. Title, 13 unnumbered leaves ; pp. 1-149. Part 2, pp. 1-105. Part 3. pp. 1-96. [Map of Newfoundland at beginning of Part One.] · (412).

A large part of this work is prose, but enough poetry remains to entitle it to a place in this list.

W., J. *Meditations* | on the | Incomprehensibility of God, | in his | Works of Creation, Providence, | and Redemption ; | As also, | On the General Judgment.| By Jxxxxx Wxxxxx.| Boston: Printed and Sold by Fowle and Draper . . . .| M.DCC.LXII.| 12mo. pp. 8. A. (413).

WALTER, NEHEMIAH. An Elegiack verse, on the Death of the Pious and Profound Grammarian and Rhetorician, Mr. Elijah Corlet, Schoolmaster of Cambridge, who Deceased Anno Aetatis 77, Feb. 24, 1687. [Cambridge] [1687.] Folio Broadside. 1 p., 2 columns within mourning borders. (414).

The only known copy is in the Library of Harvard University.

WAREING, ELIJAH. On the Death of | John Wagstaffe.| An elegiac Poem.| Philadelphia: Printed (at the Desire of many Friends) by Andrew Steuart, in Second-street. 1760.| Folio, broadside. (415).

WARREN, JOHN. A monody | On the Death of the Hon. Thomas Russell, Esq.| Sung after the Eulogy delivered by Doctor John Warren, in the church in Brattle-Street on Wednesday, May 14, 1796. Broadside. (416).

WARREN, MERCY Poems, | Dramatic and Miscellaneous.| By Mrs. M. Warren.| 'Tis a stranger sues, | A virgin tragedy, an orphan muse.—Pope.| Printed at Boston, | By I. Thomas and E. T. Andrews | At Faust's Statue, No. 45, Newbury Street.| MDCCXC.| 12mo. pp. [3],-iv, vi,-[1],-viii,-[1],-10-12-[3], 1-6-252. A.B. (417).

WEBB, GEORGE. Batchelors-Hall; | A | Poem.| By George Webb. | . . . | . . . | . . . | . . . | . . . | . . , | Philadelphia: | Printed and Sold [by B. Franklin and H. Meredith] at the New Printing-Office, | MDCCXXXI.| Price One Shilling.| Folio. pp. 12. (418).

WELD, EDMUND. A | Funeral Elegy | By Way of a | Dialogue; | Between *Death, Soul, Body* and *Jesus Christ.* Composed by *Edmund Weld,* formerly of *Harvard* College, who moving hence into *Ireland,* became a Preacher of the Gospel at *Innis-kean, there;* who upon the Meditation and | Apprehension of his own Death [which was soon after, the Second Day of *March* 1785] | made this following Poem, which was sent hither in a letter from his Widow, there | living, for the benefit of the People of *Massachusetts* in America.| [Springfield, | Mas-sachusetts.] | Printed at the Chronicle Printing-| Office.] [For the Purchasers.] Folio broadside, (419).

> An earlier edition with the wording slightly different was "Re-printed and Sold by S. Kneeland, in *Queen Street."* 1 p. folio.
>
> I cannot trace the first edition, but the date must be considerably earlier than 1785, the date given in the above, as S. Kneeland was not printing for some time prior to that date.
>
> See Ford, Mass. broadsides for the title of the earliest issues of this poem.

[WHARTON, CHARLES HENRY.] A Poetical Epistle | to his Ex-cellency | George Washington, Esq. | Commander in Chief of the Armies of the | United States of America, | from | an Inhabitant of the State of Maryland.| To which is Annexed, | A short sketch | of | General Washington's Life and Character.| [6 lines from Leonidas. 2 lines from Virgil.] | Annapolis Printed 1779: | London Printed by C. Dilly, in the Poultry; J. Almor, Picadilly; | W. Tesseyman, York; T. & J. Merrill, Cambridge; | R. Crutwell Bath; and T. Becket, Bristol.| MDCCLXXX | [Price Half a Crown.] 8vo. pp. iv, 5-24. (420).

> The first edition was printed at Annapolis, Md., in 1779. 4to. pp. 24.

[WHARTON.] A | Poetical Epistle | To His Excellency | George Washington Esq. | Commander in Chief of the | Armies of the United States | of America, | from | An Inhabitant of the State of Maryland.| London Printed: | Philadelphia Re-printed and sold | By George Kline, | In Third-Street, near Arch-Street. 1781.| 12mo. pp. [3], 4-10.   B. (421).

    Same: Providence, 1781.   A
    Also: Springfield, 1782. 4to. pp. 11.   A

[WHARTON.] An | Elegy | to the memory of | Mrs. Mary Wharton, | *Who died at Philadelphia, on the second day of June, 1798.*| By Her Husband.| [Philadelphia: Printed by John Ormrod, 41, Chestnut-Street, 1798.] 12mo. pp. [3] 4-7.
A. (422).

WHEATLEY, PHILLIS. An Elegiac Poem, on the Death of . . . the Reverend and learned George Whitefield . . By Phillis, a Servant Girl, of 17 Years of age. Boston: Ezekiel Russell & J. Boyles. 1770. 4to. pp. 8.   (423).

WHEATLEY, PHILLIS An | elegiac | Poem, | On the Death of that celebrated Divine, and eminent | Servant of Jesus Christ, the Reverend and | learned | George Whitefield, |Chaplain to the Right Honourable the Countess of | Huntingdon, &c.| Who made his Exit from this transitory State, | to dwell in the celestial Realms of bliss, on Lord's Day, | 30th of September, 1770, &c. . . . . By Phillis, A Servant Girl, of 17 Years of Age, belonging to Mr. | J. Wheatley, of Boston. . . . Boston: | Printed and Sold by Ezekiel Russell, in Queen-Street, | And John Boyles, in Marlboro-Street.| [1770.] 12mo. pp. 8.   (424).

    Other issues as follows:
    [Boston:] Sold by Ezekiel Russell, in Queen-Street, and John Boyles, in Marlboro-Street. [1770]. Folio Broadside.
    New York: Printed and sold by Samuel Inslee and Anthony Car, 1770.

Phillis's Poem | on the | Death of Mr. Whitefield [cut at top] [Also on same sheet, Bedlam Garland, [and] The Spinning Wheel.] [Boston: 1770]. Folio broadside. A. (425).

WHEATLEY. An Elegiac Poem, on the Death of that celebrated Divine and eminent servant of Jesus Christ the Rev. Geo. Whitefield. By Philis Wheatley. Philadelphia: William Goddard, 1770. (426).

WHEATLEY. An Ode of Verses | on the much-lamented Death of the | Rev. Mr. George Whitefield, | Late Chaplain to the Countess of *Huntingdon*, ... Printed and sold for the benefit of a poor family burnt out a few weeks since near *Shore-ditch Church,* that lost all they possessed, | having nothing insur'd.| *Price a Penny a piece or 5s a Hundred to those that sell them again.|* Broadside. Small folio. [London? 1771]. (427).

> This issue differs from the usual version, for after the line "'Till Life Divine reanimate his dust," there follow eight lines in double column, and "The Conclusion," six lines. The whole is printed in double column.
>
> An Elegiac Poem, on the Death of that celebrated Divine, *George Whitefield.* By Phillis, a servant Girl belonging to Mr. J. Wheatley of Boston. [Boston, 1770.] Broadside. Also printed on pp. 29-31, in Ebenezar Pemberton's Sermon on the Death of Whitefield, London: 1771. The Boston edition does not contain the Poem.

WHEATLEY. *To Mrs.* Leonard, *on the Death of her* | Husband.| [Boston: 1771]. Folio broadside. (428).

WHEATLEY. To the Rev. Mr. *Pitkin,* on the Death of his Lady.| Broadside, dated Boston, June 16th, 1772. (429).

WHEATLEY. To the Hon'ble Thomas Hubbard, Esq; | *On the Death of* | *Mrs.* Thankfull Leonard.| Broadside, dated *Boston, January 2,* 1773. (430).

WHEATLEY. Heaven the Residence of the Saints.| A | Sermon | Occasioned by the sudden and much lamented Death of the | Rev. George Whitefield, A.M.| Chaplain to the Right Honourable the | Countess of Huntington.| Delivered at the | Thursday Lecture at Boston, in *America,* | *October* 11, 1770. | By Ebenezer Pemberton, D.D. | Pastor of a Church in *Boston.|* To which is added, | An Elegiac Poem on his Death, | By Phillis, A Negro Girl, of Seventeen Years of Age, | Belonging to Mr. *J. Wheatley* of *Boston.|* Boston, Printed: London, Reprinted, | For E. and C. Dilly in the Poultry; | And sold at the

Chapel in Tottenham-Court Road, | And at the Tabernacle near Moorfields.| M.DCC.LXXI.| [Price Sixpence.] 8vo. pp. 31, [1]. A. (431).
The poem occupies pp. 29-31.

WHEATLEY. Poems | on | Various subjects, | Religious and Moral.| By | Phillis Wheatley, | Negro Servant to Mr. John Wheatley, | of Boston, in New England.| London: | Printed for A. Bell, Bookseller, Aldgate; and sold by | Messrs. Cox and Berry, King-Street, Boston.| MDCCLXXIII.| 12mo. pp. [5],-v,-[4],-10-124,-[3]. [Portrait.] A.B. (432).

WHEATLEY. Poems | on | Various Subjects, | Religious and Moral.| By Phillis Wheatley, | Negro servant to Mr. John Wheatley, | of Boston, in New-England.| London: Printed.| Philadelphia: Re-Printed, | and sold by Joseph Crukshank, in Market-Street, Between Second and Third Streets. | MDCC-LXXXVI.| 12mo. pp. [2] 9-66, [2]. (433).
Another edition, Philadelphia: 1787. 16mo. pp. 55. A.

WHEATLEY. Poems on Various Subjects, Religious and Moral. By Phillis Wheatley, Negro Servant to Mr. John Wheatley, of Boston, in New England. London: Printed for A. Bell, Book-seller, Aldgate; and sold by Messrs Cox and Berry, King-Street, Boston. MDCCLXXIII. [Portrait.] 12mo. pp. 124,-[3], and one page adv. (434).
Other editions as follows:
Poems on Comic, Serious, and Moral Subjects. The Second edition, corrected. London: [1773] 12mo. pp. 124,-[3], and one page adv. [Portrait.] Philadelphia: W. and T. Bradford, 1774.
Philadelphia: Re-printed and sold by Joseph Crukshank in Market-Street, Between Second and Third Streets. M,DCC,LXXVI. 12mo. pp. [2],-9-66,-[2].
Albany: Re-printed from the London edition, by Barber and Southwick, for Thomas Spencer, Book-seller, Market-Street, 1793. 16mo. pp. [7],-8-89,-[3]. Walpole, N. H. Printed for Thomas & Thomas, by David Newhall. 1802. 12mo. pp. 86.
Hartford: Printed by Oliver Steele, 1804. 12mo. pp. 92,-[2]. London Printed, Re-printed, in New England, 1816. 16mo. pp. 120. Also printed in *The Negro Equalled by few Europeans.* Translated from l'Abbe La Vallee. Philadelphia: Printed by and for William W. Woodward, No. 17, Chestnut Street, 1801. 2 volumes, 12mo. pp. 259; 248, [238]. Also in Narrative of Olandah Equiano. Halifax: 1813.

WHEATLEY. An Elegy, Sacred to the Memory of that great Divine, the Reverend and Learned *Dr. Samuel Cooper,* Who departed this Life December 29, 1783. Ætatis 59. By Phillis Peters. Boston: Printed and Sold by E. Russell, in Essex-Street near Liberty-Pole. M,DCC,LXXXIV. 4to. pp. 8. [Included are *Words for a Funeral Anthem, performed at the funeral of Dr. Cooper.*   A. (435).

WHEATLEY. Liberty and Peace, | A | Poem.| By Phillis Peters.| Boston: | Printed by Warden and Russell, | At their Office in Marlborough-Street.| M,DCC,LXXXIV.| 4to. pp. 4.

A. (436).

[WHEATLEY.] A | Beautiful | Poem | on | Providence; | written by a young female slave.| To which is subjoined | A short Account of this extraordinary Writer.| Halifax, | [N. S.] Printed by E. Gay.| 1805.| 12mo. pp. [3],-4-8.   (437).
> For further information regarding the writings of Miss Wheatley, see *Phillis Wheatley (Phillis Peters).* By Charles F. Heartman, New York: 1915.   (438).

WHEATON, HANNAH. A | New Year's Wish. January, 1795. Broadside.   (439).

WHEATON. An Elegiac Ode | on the Death of | Mr. Ephraim May. Signed H. W. [1798]. Broadside.   (440).

WHEATON. On taking an affectionate | Farewell to my kind Bene-|factors in Boston. Broadside. [1799].   (441).

WHEATON. The Author wishing it may be improved and | enlarged, by some abler pen, now casts in her | mite, to the Memory of that worthy Person, | whose Loss we severely feel [Washington] [1799]. Broadside.   (442).

[WHEELOCK, JOHN.] Cohos. The Wilderness shall blossom as the Rose. To His Excellency John Wentworth, Captain-General Governor . . . of New Hampshire on his Grant of a very generous Charter of Incorporation of Dartmouth College. [By] A member of Dartmouth College.—A New Song. Upon the flourishing state of the Settlement at Cohos. To the tune of "Indulgent Parents, Dear." Printed and Sold in New London. [1774?] Folio broadside of two columns. (443).

> The longer poem was probably written by John Wheelock, son of Eleazer Wheelock, and his successor in the presidency of the College.

WHITCOMB, CHAPMAN. Miscellaneous | Poems.| By Chapman Whitcomb, A.B.| Printed at Worcester, Massachusetts.| MDCCXCV.| 8vo. pp. 12. A. (444).

[WHITCOMB.] A | concise View | of | Antient and Modern | Religion; | with a | Letter, | from a | deformed gentleman | to a | Young Lady, | who | slighted him, &c.| Printed for Chapman Whitcomb.| [Circa 1796]. 12mo. pp. 12.

A. (445).

> This poem, although differently titled, is the same as the "Comparative View of Religion" in Chapman Whitcomb's "Miscellaneous Poems," Worcester, 1795.

[WHITCOMB.] A | Poem, | on | Religious Ignorance, | Pride and Avarice: | or, the | Modern Priest.| Boston: | Printed in the Year of our Lord, | M,DCC,XCV.| 12mo. pp. 4. A. (446).

> This poem, by Chapman Whitcomb, consists of part of his poem "Concise View of Ancient and Modern Religions," although with slight changes in wording.

[WHITCOMB.] A Poem, on Religious Ignorance, Pride and | Avarice; or the Modern Priest.| Broadside, 2 columns of poetry. [Printed at Leominster, Mass., about 1800.] See note to 1795 edition. A. (447).

[WHITCOMB.] Geography | Epitomized.| A short but comprehensive | Description | of the | Terraqueous Globe, | in Verse, | to assist the memory.| Printed for Chapman Whitcomb.| With privilege of Copy Right.| 12mo. pp. 60. [Leominster, about 1796.] A. (448).

WHITEFIELD, GEORGE. Two Funeral Hymns Composed by George Whitefield. [Boston: 1770.] Folio broadside. [cut.] (449).

WHITEFIELD. Hymn, | composed by the late Reverend Mr. | George Whitefield, | With a Design to be sung at his own Funeral.| Now Re-published at the Request of a Number of Friends to that | truly worthy and pious Gentleman. [Also] New-England | Hymn, | By the late Reverend | Dr. Byles.| [Adapted to America Tune.] Printed by E. Russell, next Liberty-Stump. 1790. Broadside. A. (450).

WIGGLESWORTH, MICHAEL. The Day of Doom, &c. London. Printed by J. G. for P. C. 1666. (451).

> This is without doubt the third edition of this famous poem. A copy is in the British Museum. No copy of either the first of second editions are extant although a fragment in the N. E. Historic Genealogical Society may be a part of a copy of the premier issue. A fragment of one of the earliest issues is also in the Mass. Historical Society, and also in the Antiquarian Society.

[WIGGLESWORTH.] The Day of Doom: | or, a | Description | Of the Great and Last Judgment | With | a Short Discourse about | Eternity| — |Eccless. 12, 14.| For God shall bring . . . it be evil.| — |London | Printed by W. G. for *John Sims,* at the *Kings-|Head* at *Sweetings Alley* in *Cornhill* | Next House to the *Royal-Exchange,* 1673. 12mo. title, pp. [2]-1-92.
N.Y.P.L., B.M. (452).

WIGGLESWORTH. The Day of | Doom: | or, A Poetical Description | Of | The Great and Last | Judgment.| With | A *Short* Discourse about | Eternity.| By Michael Wigglesworth, Teacher of the | Church at Maldon in N. E.| The Fifth Edition, enlarged with | *Scripture* and *Marginal Notes.* [3 lines from Acts 17.31. 4 lines from Mat. 24.30.] Boston: Printed by B. Green, and J. Allen, | for *Benjamin Eliot,* at his Shop under the | West End of the Town-House, 1701. Sm. 12mo. title, 1 leaf.

To the Reader. 3 leaves, on the following Work and Its Author. By J. Mitchel. 1 leaf, A Prayer. 1 leaf, pp. 1-80. the lower half of page 80 is taken up with an advertisement of B: Eliot, advertising "Meat out of the Eater." (453).

> This is the earliest complete copy of an American edition known to exist. The New York Public Library possesses a copy and there

are copies at Harvard, The Boston Public Library and in several private collections. Also American Antiquarian Society. The following are probably, as nearly as can be ascertained the dates of the various editions, printed prior to 1800:

(1) Cambridge: Printed by Samuel Green and Marmaduke Johnson, 1662 or 1663. (2) Cambridge, probably 1666. (3) London: 1666. (4) London: 1673. (5) Boston: 1701. (6) New-Castle-upon-Tyne: 1711. (7) Boston: 1715, The title calls it the sixth edition. (8) Boston: 1751. The title calls is the seventh edition. (9) Abridged edition Norwich, Conn., 1774. (10) Abridged edition, Norwich, Conn., 1777.

For a good bibliographical account of the several editions of *The Day of Doom* and *Meat out of the Eater,* see Bibliography of these books by Matt. B. Jones, *Amer Ant. Soc. Proc., April, 1929.*

WIGGLESWORTH, MICHAEL. Meat out of the Eater, or Meditations Concerning the Necessity, End, and Usefullness of Affliction unto God's Children. Cambridge: Green & Johnson, 1670. (454).

No copy of this work earlier than the fourth edition, issued in 1689, is known at the present day. An edition was issued in 1706.

WIGGLESWORTH. Meat | out of the | Eater | or Meditations | Concerning | The Necessity, End and Usefullness of | Afflictions | unto God's Children.| All tending to Prepare them *For,* | and Comfort them *under* the Cross. By Michael Wigglesworth.| The Fourth Edition.| Boston.| Printed by R. P. for *John Usher,* 1689.| Sm. 12mo. title (1 leaf) pp. 3-208. A., N.Y.P.L. (455).

WIGGLESWORTH. Meat | Out of the | Eater: | or, | Meditations | Concerning the Necessity, End, | and Usefulness of | Afflictions | unto | God's Children | All tending to Prepare them For, and | Comfort them Under the | Cross.| By Michael Wigglesworth.| Corrected and Amended by the Author, | in the Year 1703.| The Fifth Edition.| Boston. Printed by J. Allen, for Nicholas Buttolph, | at his Shop in Cornhill. 1717.| 24mo. pp. [2] 3-143. A. (456).

There are at least five issues of this edition each bearing the name of a different bookseller.

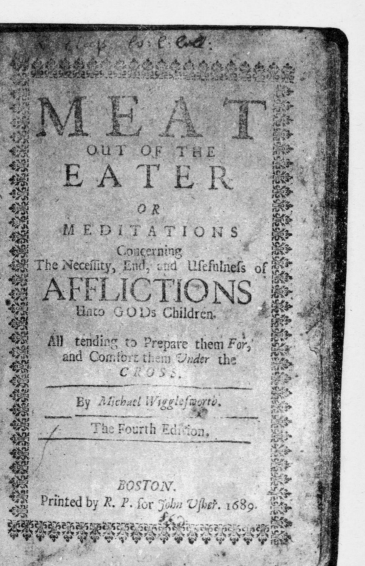

MEAT
OUT OF THE
EATER
OR
MEDITATIONS
Concerning
The Necessity, End, and Usefulness of
AFFLICTIONS
Unto GODs Children.

All tending to Prepare them *For*,
and Comfort them *Under* the
CROSS.

By *Michael Wigglesworth*.

The Fourth Edition.

BOSTON.
Printed by R. P. for *John Usher*. 1689.

WIGGLESWORTH. Meat | out of the | Eater: | or, | Meditations | concerning the Necessity, End,* and | Usefulness of | Afflictions, | unto God's Children, | etc. . . The Sixth Edition, | New London, T. Green for Seth White, 1770. 12mo. pp. [2],-3-240.   Boston Public (457).

WIGGLESWORTH. The Church Moves.| A | Curiosity of Literature and Theology.| Extracts from a Poem of nearly 2,000 lines, | entitled | The Day of Doom, | by | Michael Wigglesworth, A.M., | Teacher of the Church at Malden, in New England.| From the sixth London Edition, 1715.| Boston: | Published by R. Thayer, | Sold by Usher & Quinby, | 37 Cornhill.| 12mo. pp. [3]-4-15, [1].   B. (458).

    For an account of the Life and Writings of Wigglesworth see the Memoir by John Ward Dean. Albany: Munsell, 1871.

[WILLIAMSON, HUGH.] What is Sauce for a Goose is also sauce for a | Gander.| Being | A Small Touch in the Lapidary Way.| Or | Tit for Tat, in your own Way.| An Epitaph | On a certain great Man.| Written by a departed Spirit and now | most humbly inscrib'd to all dutiful Sons and | Children Who may hereafter chose to dis-|tinguish him by the name of | A Patriot.| Dear Children, | [4 lines of verse] | *Thou hast taught us to speak evil of Dignities.*| *Philadelphia,* | Printed in *Arch-Street* [by Anthony Armbruster] 1764. 8vo. pp. [1],-2-8,-[1],-2-4.   (459).

    The last four pages, [Nancey Dawson] do not seem to be in all copies.

WILSON, JOHN. A Song of | Deliverance | For The | Lasting Remembrance | Of God's Wonderful Works | never to be Forgotten.| Containing in it the Wonderful defeat of the Spanish | Armado, *Anno,* 1588. the woful Plague, *Anno,* 1603.| soon upon the entrance of King James of famous memo-|ry, unto the Crown of England.| With the discovery of the Powder Plot, *Anno,* 1605, | and down Fall of Black Fryers, when an hellish Crew of Papists met to hear *Drury* a Popish Priest, *An* 1623.| Also the grievous Plague, *Anno,* 1625. with Poems both Latin | and English, and the Verses of that Learned *Theodore Beza.*| By that Reverend, and eminent man of God, Mr. *John Wilson,* formerly Christs faithful Shepherd in *Sudbury,* in *Suffolk* in | great Brittain, where these heavenly Poems, and spiritual | Songs were Compiled, and at *London* printed, *Anno,* | 1626. since Pastor to the first Church of Christ in | *Boston* in *New-England.*| For the sake of several who have much desired to see and | read this work, it is reprinted.| [3 lines from Ps. 107. 8.] Boston, Printed in the Year; 1680.| 12mo. (460).

> The New York Public Library, possesses an imperfect copy of this work, which contains pp. [8], 36. It will be seen by consulting the above title, that the work was first printed in London, 1626.

WILSON. A Copy of Verses | *Made by that Reverend Man of God Mr.* John Wilson, *Pastor to the* | first Church in *Boston;* On the sudden Death of | Mr. Joseph Brisco, | Who was translated from Earth to Heaven *Jan.* 1. 1657.| 4to. Broadside. (461).

WINCHESTER, ELHANAN. A | New Book | Of | Poems, | On | Several Occasions.| By Elhanan Winchester, jun.| Preacher of the Gospel, and | Author of the Collection of Psalms, Hymns and Poems, designed for | the Use and Edification of Christians.| Boston: | Printed by Isaiah Thomas, for the Author.| M,DCC,LXXIII.| 8vo. pp. 72. A. (462)

WINCHESTER. An Elegy on the Death of the Rev. Mr. John Wesley, who departed this Life March 2d 1791, in the 88th year of his age. London, 1793. 12mo. pp. 6. (463).

[WINTHROP, WAIT.] Some Meditations | concerning our Honourable | Gentlemen and Fellow-Souldiers, | In Pursuit of those | Barbarous Natives in the Narragansit-Country; | and their Service there.| Committed with Plain Verse for the Benefit of those that Read it. By an Unfeigned Friend.| Reprined at N. London, April 4, 1721. Broadside. (464).

> Dated December 28, 1675. No copy of the original has been found.

POETICAL

Meditations,

BEING THE

IMPROVEMENT

OF SOME

Vacant Hours,

By ROGER WOLCOTT, Esq;

WITH A

PREFACE

By the REVEREND

Mr. Bulkley of Colchester.

NEW-LONDON:

Printed and Sold by T. Green,

1725.

WOLCOTT, ROGER. Poetical | Meditations, | Being the | Improvement | of some | Vacant Hours.| By Roger Wolcott, Esq; | With a | Preface | By the Reverend | Mr. Bulkley of Colchester. | New London: | Printed and Sold by T. Green | 1725.| 16mo. pp. lvi, ii, 78.   A.B., N.Y.P.L. (465).

The first volume of verse published in Connecticut. The preface, which gives an account of the agency of John Winthrop in the court of Charles the Second in 1662, when he obtained the charter for the Colony of Connecticut, is of great value and interest. In fact, many of the succeeding writers on the early history of Connecticut have used this volume as a basis for their work. The poems themselves are of vast interest and value, giving full accounts of the obtaining of the charter. The Wars with the Pequots, Narragansetts, etc. The work ends with an advertisement of Joseph Dewey, cloth merchant, of Dorchester, which is missing in most copies. The book was reprinted by The Club of Odd Volumes.

[WOLCOTT, WILLIAM.] Grateful Reflections | On the Divine Goodness vouchsaf'd to the | American Arms in their remark-| able successes in the Northern De | partment, after the giving up of our | Fortresses at *Ticonderoga,* on the 6th of | July, A. D. 1777.| With some Account of the Battles fought, | and the Transactions of that memorable | Campaign.| Occasioned | By the Surrendry of the King's Forces by | Lieutenant-General Burgoyne | to Major-General Gates, on the | 23rd Day of October, in said Year.| In Four Parts.| *He doth according to his Will in the Army of | Heaven, and among the Inhabitants of the | Earth, and none can stay his hand.|* Nebuchadnezzar.| Hartford: | Printed and Sold by Hudson & Goodwin.| [1779] 12mo. pp. 60.   A. (466).

WOLCOTT. A | Devout Wish for the Revival | of | Religion, | or | Orthodoxy and Union, | by William Wolcott Esq. | Hartford: Printed by Bavil Webster.] Folio broadside.   (467).

WORCESTER, THOMAS. A Sacred | Ode, | On the Sudden Death of Lieut. | Emerson, | Late of Hollis, who was in-|stantly killed by the untimely | Discharge of a Field-Piece in | Time of Military Exercise, Octo-|ber, 1790.| Composed and set to

Musick, by | the Rev. Thomas Worcester, | of Hollis, Tune-Littleton.| (at end) Printed next Liberty Pole, | 1791.| (Crude woodcut of an officer at upper left hand corner.) Broadside, small folio. (468).

YOUNG, ROBERT. The Dying Criminal: | A | Poem. | by Robert Young, on his own execution, which was on Thursday last, November 11th, 1779, for a | Rape Committed on the body of Jane Green, a Child eleven years of age, at Brookfield, in the County of | Worcester, on the 3d day of September last. Corrected from .his own manuscript.| [Sold at the Printing-Office, New-London.] Curious cut at top. (469).

   Broadside poem on one side; on other, "Last Words and Dying Speech of Robert Young, executed at Worcester 1779." [Cut at top.] Folio. 1 p. A.

YOUNG, ROBERT. The Dying Criminal: Poem by Robert Young, on his own execution, which is to be on this day Nov. 11, 1779, for Rape Committed on the body of Jane Green, a child eleven years of age, at Brookfield, in the County of Worcester, on the third day of September last. Broadside, with curious woodcut of the execution at the top. Small folio. (470).

   Another issue [Worcester, Isaiah Thomas, 1779.] A

[YOUNG, THOMAS.] A | Poem | Sacred to the | Memory of | James Wolfe, Esq; | Major-General, and Commander in Chief of | His Majesty's Forces, destined for the | Reduction of Quebec.| Who was slain upon the Plains of Abraham, near | that Capital, gloriously disputing the Cause of | Liberty, and his Country; | September 13, 1759. [2 lines in Latin] | New-Haven; | Printed by James Parker, and Company, | At the Post-Office.| 12mo. pp. [3],-4-19. (471).
   Adv. in Conn. Gazette, 1761.

ADDENDA

[DELANO, STEPHEN.] Elegiac | Poems; | also, | A Small Collection | of| Hymns.| By a Country Farmer, in | *Woodstock*, (Vermont.)| Printed at Windsor, | By Alden Spooner.| M,DCC,XCIV.| 12mo. pp. (3),-4-47. A. (471B).

ANNONYMOUS TITLES

An Account of a Famous | Sea-Fight, | Between | Capt. Ward a noted Pirate, | And His Majesty's Ship, | called the Rainbow.| Sold in New-London, | [Two cuts of ships.] Folio broadside.   (472).

An | Account | of the Pirates, | with divers of their | Speeches, Letters, etc. | And a | Poem | made by One of them: | *Who were Executed* at Newport, *on* Rhode-Island, | *July* 19th, 1723.| Reprinted in the Year 1769.| 12mo. 8 unnumbered leaves.   (473).

> The "Poem" which is entitled "One versified some of his Lamentations after this Manner," beginning as follows:
> To mortal men that daily live,
> In Wickedness and Sin.
> Will be found on the 6th and 7th leaves.

Address | of | Robbin | The Carrier of the Daily Advertiser.| To his Kind Customers.| n.p. Folio broadside.   (474).

An Address to a Deist. A Poem. New London: Printed by James Springer, for the Author. 1796. 12mo. pp. 12.
                                                            (475).

An Address to the Freemen of the State of Connecticut; a Poem. By Horatio Juvenal, Esquire. Hartford: Printed and Sold by Hudson and Goodwin? 1790.   (476).

> Also Second Address. Litchfield: Printed and Sold by Thomas Collier? 1790.

Addressed by the Boy who carries the *American Mercury,* to the Subscribers.| Hartford, January 1, 1793.| Folio broadside.   (477).

An Address to the inhabitants of Boston, occasioned by the execution of Levi Ames, tried and condemned for burglary, Sept. 7th, [Boston: 1773.] 2 columns with mourning borders. Folio broadside.   B. (477b).

ADVICE FROM the Dead to the Living, or a Solemn warning to the World. Occasioned by the untimely death of poor Julian, &c. Boston: Printed and Sold at the Heart and Crown in Cornhill. 30 Stanzas. [Woodcut at top.] Folio broadside. (478).

THE ADVANTAGES of Repentance. A Moral tale, attempted in Blank Verse and founded on the Anecdotes of a private family in ——shire. [quot. from Hamlet] [Newport:] Peter Edes. August 16, 1787. (479).
Title from Hammett's Bibliography of Newport, R. I.

THE AGE OF ERROR; | or, A | Poetical Essay | on the | Course | of | Human Action.| By a Philadelphian.| O curas hominum! O quantum est in rebus inane! | Per. Sat. I.I.| Philadelphia: Printed for the Author. | 1797.| 8vo. pp. [5],-vi,-[1],-8-16. A.B. (480).

[CUT.] THE AGONIES of a Soul departing out of Time | into Eternity.| A few Lines Occasioned by the untimely End of John Harrington, | Who is to be Executed at Cambridge this Day, being the 17th of March, 1757, for the | Murder of Paul Learnard, the 1st of September last. Broadside. (481).

THE | ALBANIAD, | an | epic poem, | in three Cantos, | by Pilgarlic, | Printed for the Author, | 1791.| 12mo. pp. [2],-3-24. (482).

THE | ALGERINE SLAVES.| A | Poem.| By a citizen of Newburyport.| "O give me Liberty! | "For were e'en Paradise itself my prison, | "Still I should long to leap the chrystal Walls." | Newburyport: | Printed by Angier March, Middle-Street. | 1798.| 12mo. pp. [3],-178-189. A.B. (483).
Published with the above is A Journal of John Foss: (prose) pp. 1-174.

ALL YOU THAT COME this curious Art to see, &c. [1761.] Broadside. Ford 1226. (484).

AMERICA INVINCIBLE, an Heroic Poem in two books, etc. By an officer of rank in the Continental Army. Danvers, near Boston, E. Russell, 1779. 8vo. pp. 40. (485).

96

America in Tears: A Pastoral Elegy, on the Death of His Most Sacred Majesty King George the Second. Philadelphia: Andrew Steuart, 1761. (486).

The American Hero: | Made on the battle of Bunker-Hill, and the burning of Charlestown.| [1775]. Broadside, 4to.
(487).

The | American in Algiers, | or The | Patriot of Seventy-Six | in | Captivity.| A Poem, | in Two Cantos.| When God from Chaos gave this world to be, | Man then he form'd and form'd him to be free.| Freneau.| New-York: | Printed and Sold by J. Buel, No. 153, Water-|Street, corner of Fly-Market.| 1797.| 12mo. pp. [5] 6-36. B. (488).

American Poems, original and selected. Vol. 1. Litchfield: Collier and Buel. [1793.] 8vo. pp. 304, [7]. A.B. (489).
This, the first collection of American Poetry, was compiled by Elihu Hubbard Smith. Volume I is all that was issued.

The American Union, and the Birth of Gen. Washington. Broadside [circa 1797]. A. (490).

[Cut.] *Americans* | to | Arms.| Sung to the Tune of, Britons to Arms. [1774] Broadside. (491).

An | Answer | To | A Piece, Entitled | A Line Drawn Between | Christ, | and | Anti-Christ.| Printed For The Author, | A. D. 1765.| 12mo. pp. 12. A. (492).
Signed H. W.

Anthem | *To be sung by the* Charity Scholars, *on* Sunday, *the* | 22d of November, *at* St. Paul's Church, *After the Charity Sermon for the Benefit of the School.* [New York, 1788.] Folio broadside. (493).

Aristocracy.| An Epic Poem.| De Bellare Superbos.| 8vo. pp. [5],-6-17. *[p. □] - 16* A.B.H. (494).
The advertisement is dated Philadelphia, *March* 26th, 1795. Page 17 is misnumbered 18.

Aristocracy. An Epic Poem. Book Second. [Philadelphia: 1795.] 8vo. pp. 18. A. (495).

THE | ASSOCIATION, &c. | of the | Delegates of the Colonies, | at
the | Grand Congress, | Held at Philadelphia, Sept. 1, 1774, |
Versified, and adapted to Music, | calculated | For Grave and
Gay Dispositions; | With a short | Introduction.| By Bob
Jingle, Esq; | Poet Laureat to the Congress, | "I sing the Men,
read it who list, | "Bold Trojans true, as ever p - st. Cotton's
Virg. Trav.| Printed in the Year M,DCC,LXXIV.| 8vo. pp.
[3], iv, [1], 6-22. B. (496).

A | BATTLE! A BATTLE! | A Battle of Squirt, | Where no man
is kill'd, | and no man is hurt! | To the Tune of three blue
Beans, | in a blue Bladder; | Rattle Bladder Rattle.| To which
is added, | The Quaker's Address, | And the | School-Boy's
Answer | To an insolent Fellow | Who accus'd him of Stealing
his Cherries. | . . . | . . . | . . . | . . . | . . . | . . . |
. . . . | Sold by Edward Merefield, at the Corner of | Arch-
Street, and opposite the Church-Burying-|Ground, in Phila-
delphia. 1764.| 8vo. pp. 20. (497).

> The following title is found on page 17:
> King Wampum.| Or Harm Watch,| Harm Catch.| And the Lord
> departed from Is . . . 1,| and behold He went a Whore- | ing after
> his own Invention un- | til his abominable Iniquity was | found out |
> [Printed by Anthony Armbruster.] Sold by Edward Merefield, at
> the Corner | of Arch-Street, and opposite the Church- | Burying-
> Ground in Philadelphia. 1764.

A BATTLE! A BATTLE! a Battle a Squirt; | Where no Man is
kill'd, and no Man is hurt! | To the Tune of | Three new blue
Beans, in a new blue blown Bladder; | rattle Bladder rattle
Bladder! | To which is added, | The | Quaker's Address,
versify'd; | and | King Wampum, on Harm watch Harm |
Catch. | . . . | . . . | . . . | . . . . | [Philadelphia:] Printed
[by Andrew Steuart] and sold at the Blue-Nose, near | Brazen-
Nose-College, Germantown, [1764.] | 12mo. pp. 11, [1],
[Plate]. (498).

> Both of the above rare pieces relate to "The Paxton Boys."
> The Historical Society of Pennsylvania possesses a copy of each.

BATTLE OF BUNKER HILL, Composed by a British Officer the day
after the Battle, June 17, 1775. Sold by Leonard Deming,
Middlebury, Vt. 4to. Broadside containing 24 verses of 4
lines each. [Circa, 1830.] Probably a reprint of an early
issue. (499).

Bloody Indian Battle,

FOUGHT AT MIAMI VILLAGE,

NOVEMBER 4, 1791.

A MOURNFUL ELEGY ON THE OCCASION.

AND

JEMMY and NANCY:

A Tragical Garland.

❧❧❧❧❧❧

NEW-HAVEN:
Printed by Moſes H. Woodward.

Damaris Nettleton
Her Book

THE BIRTH OF COLUMBIA. The Massachusetts Centinel, Extra-ordinary, Dec. 3, 1788. Boston: 1788. Two columns. Folio.
A. (500).

THE | BIRTH, PARENTAGE, AND EDUCATION, | of | Praise-God Barebone.| To which is added, | An Election Ballad, | or | the Lamentation of Mrs . . . . | A true but dole-ful Ditty.| [Philadelphia:] Printed [by Andrew Steuart] for Jack Northwester, at the | Sign of the White-Oak, in Heart of Oak | Street, MDCCLXVI.| 8vo. pp. 16 & [Ibid] 8vo. pp. 17.| (501).
"This ballad refers to Dinckinson's defeat as a Candidate for the Assembly." It was probably written by Isaac Hunt.

BLAZING-STARS | Messengers of God's Wrath: | In a few serious and solemn Meditations upon | the wonderful | Comet: | Which now appears in our Horizon, April, 1759: Together with a solemn | Call to Sinners, and Counsel to Saints; how to be-have themselves When | God is in this wise speaking to them from Heaven.| Boston: Printed and Sold by R. *Draper* in *Newbury*-Street; and by | *Fowle* & *Draper* in Marlborough-Street. 1759.| 1 p. folio. [Curious Cut of several men look-ing through telescopes at the Heavens.] (502).
Another issue, Boston: [1769].

BLOODY INDIAN BATTLE fought in Miami Village November 4, 1791. A Mournful Elegy. And Jemmy and Nancy A Tragic Garland. New Haven: Printed by Moses H. Woodward. [Circa 1792]. Small 8vo. pp. 12. (502B).

A BRIEF | ESSAY | On the Number | Seven: | *Often Occuring in the Holy* | Scripture; | Or of Paradice, lost and found.| By a Well wisher to Truth.| Prov. 9. 1. *Wisdom hath builded her House,* | *she hath hewn out her Seven Pillers.*| Zech. 4. 10. *For who hath dispised the Day* | *of small Things? For they shall rejoyce and shall* | *see the Plummet in the Hand of Zerubbabel with* | *these Seven; they are the Eyes of the* Lord *which* | *run to and fro through the whole Earth.*| New-port: Printed for the Author, in 1735.| [By the Widow Franklin]. 16mo, pp. ii, 16. (503).

BRIEF JOURNAL | of the Taking of | Cape-Breton, | Put in Metre, by L. G. one of the Soldiers in the Expedition [1745]. Broadside. (504).

[CUT.] BRITISH | Lamentation | Together with | Bunker-Hill Ode. [1786]. Broadside. (505).
> The second part is: Ode composed by T. Dawes, Jun. Esq., etc.

BRITISH TAXATION | In North America, | Composed before and during the late War in America-Containing many particu-| lars of the then times.| Folio broadside of 37 verses of four lines each. (506).
> This interesting piece was probably issued in Boston soon after the close of the Revolution.

BRITISH | TAXATION of | North-America.| 35 verses, 4ll. each. Printed in double column. Folio broadside. J.C.B. (506B).

BROADSIDE POEM on the evacuation of Boston. [This part of title only, on copy which I have seen.] Colonies, commanded by the heroic and valiant Major-General Israel | Putnam, Esquire.| By a Daughter of Liberty, living in Marblehead.| [Sold at the Printing-Office, Upper End of M [Milk or Market?] Street, Salem. — 1s. Q. T. for [one word obliterated.] Rags.| 4to. Broadside. 13 verses of 4 lines. Printed in double columns. (507).

BUY THE | TRUTH, | and | sell it not. [cut]. Broadside, probably printed at Boston. Another issue was printed at Providence by William Goddard in 1764. (508).

THE CAMPAIGN, or Dunce Versus Dunce: A Poem, in three Cantos. With Remarks by the Learned Scribblers. [line from Pope] Hallowell—(District of Maine). Printed by Howard S. Robinson, 1795. (509).

[CUT.] CARMEN Miserabile.| A Solemn Lacrymatory for the Grave of | Jonathan Marsh, | Junior-sophister: who Deceas'd at Harvard College in Cambridge: June the 10th, 1708.| Born at Hingham: Aged Eighteen years and Ten Months.| Broadside. (510).

THE | CARRIER of the American Herald's | Congratulation | to his | Customers, | Presenting the following | Balloon Wish! | Dated, Boston, January 1, [*torn.*] [1786]. Broadside. (511).

THE CARRIER of the | Independent Ledger, &c.| Wishes his kind Customers a | Merry Christmas & Happy New-Year | and presents the following: Dated January 1, 1785. Broadside.
(512).

[Royal Arms.] The Carrier of the Massachusetts-Gazette, | and Boston Weekly News-Letter, | humbly presents the following Ode | on the New Year, to all his generous Customers. 1775. Broadside. (513).

THE CARRIER | of the | Massachusetts Magazine, | to | His Patrons and Friends, | Presents the best Wishes of a Good Heart. Dated, Boston, January, 1792. Broadside. Also 1795. (514).

[CUT.] THE CARRIER of | The Massachusetts | Spy, | Wishes all his kind Customers | A Merry Christmas, | and | A Happy New Year. . . . . January 1, 1772.| Broadside. A. (515).

THE CARRIER of Russells' | Columbian Centinel, | Presents the following, to his respected | Patrons. Dated, Boston, January 1, 1792. Broadside. (516).

THE | CATHOLIC REMEDY.| An Excellent New Ballad.| To the Tune of, To all you Ladies Now at Land, &c. America, Printed in the Year 1732. Broadside. (517).

CENSOR | The Carrier of the | Censor, | Wishes all Happiness to his generous | Customers.| Broadside [1786]. (518).

CIVIL WAR; | A | Poem.| Written in the Year 1775.| [3 lines of Greek from Hom. Odyss. Y 351] 8vo. pp. [9], 6-35.
B. (519).

A COLLECTION OF ELEGIAC POEMS devoted to the Memory of the late virtuos Matron and worthy elder of the Church of Christ of the Society of Friends, Martha Thomas, late wife of Rees Thomas of Merion in the County of Philadelphia, in the Province of Pennsylvania, and daughter of William

Aubrey of Llan Elew in the County of Brecknock in Great
Britain, who departed this life on the 7th of 12mo. 1726-27.
Philadelphia: S. Keimer. 1727. (520).

Reprinted by Lydia R. Bailey. Philadelphia, 1837.

A | COLLECTION | OF | POEMS.| By several Hands.| Boston:
Printed and Sold by B. Green and | Company, at their Print-
ing-House in Newbury-street; | and D. Godkin, in Cornhil.
1744.| 8vo. pp. [3], 4-55. A.B. (521).

Mather Byles was one of the contributors to this collection.

COLLECTION OF VERSES. Applied to November 1, 1765, etc., including a prediction that the S——p A——t shall not take
place in North America. Also a Poetical Dream Concerning
Stamped Papers. New Haven: B. Mecom, [1765]. 8vo. pp.
24. (522).

THE | COLUMBIAN MUSE.| A | selection | of | American Poetry, |
from | Various authors | of | established reputation.| New
York: printed by J. Carey, for | Matthew Carey, | Phila-
delphia. | 1794. 12mo. pp. [4] 224, and Carey's Catalogue at
end. pp. 12. A.B. (523).

Poems by Trumbull, Dwight, Barlow, Freneau, Hopkinson and
others.

[CUTS.] THE | COLUMBIAN TRAGEDY: | Containing a particular
and official | Account | Of the Brave and Unfortunate Officers
and Soldiers, who were | Slain and Wounded in the ever mem-
orable and Bloody Indian Battle, [at Miami Village, November
4, 1791.] America: Boston: Printed by E. Russell, | for
Thomas Bassett, of Dun-barton, (New-Hamp.)—[Pr. Six
Pence.] Broadside. (524).

COLUMBIA'S LAMENTATION.| Folio broadside of 14 verses. N. P.
[1800] [Portrait of Washington at top centre, with verse on
each side of the likeness of the Father of his Country.] (525).

THE COMPOSITORS AND DISTRIBUTORS of the Independent Gazet-
teer, | humbly address the following Verses on the New-Year, |
1783, to the Customers.| [Philadelphia: Eleazer Oswald.
1783.] 4to. Broadside. (526).

CONCERNING A MOTHER-IN-LAW, Blinding her Husband, to the undoing of his Son, in Norton, in the year 1760. Broadside, Small folio, Cuts at top. 34 Stanzas of verse. (527).

A | CONGRATULATORY EPISTLE | To the, Redoubtable "Peter Porcupine."| On His | "Complete Triumph | over the | once towering but fallen and despicable faction, | in the United States."| A Poem, | By Peter Grievous, Junr | [Quotation of 2 lines from Swift.] To which is annexed | The Vision, | A Dialogue | Between Marat and Peter Porcupine, | in the Infernal Regions.| Philadeljhia: | From the free and independent | Political & Literary | Press of | Thomas Bradford, | Printer, Book-Seller & Stationer, | No. 3 South Front Street. | 1796.| 8vo. pp. [3] 6-44. B. (528).

THE CONFESSION and Lamentation of a Leper while shut out of the Camp of God's Spiritual Israel, &c. &c. &c. Printed at Northampton by William Butler, 1795. 8vo. pp. 24. (529).

"AURI SACRA FAMES."| Confessional Tears of a Louis d'or.| Giving a short account of his Rise and Progress, and his | Adventures in Europe—with some account of his Po-|litical Campaigns and Adventures as a Spy in the Am-|erican States, under the auspices of Generals G-n-t | and F-ch-t, and his disgraceful retreat and narrow | escape from America.| 12mo. pp. (3),-4-11. B. (530).

CONFLAGRATION. A Poem. New-York: Printed by Hugh Gaine. M,DCC,LXXX. 8vo. pp. [2],-3-8. (531).
Written after the fire at New York, September 21, 1776.

THE | CONTINENTAL KEY | Of The | Liberties | Of | America: | In Three Parts.| Perhaps the critiks of the age, | May find a fault in ev'ry page, | Or yet, perhaps, in ev'ry line, | Well, they have their faults, I have mine.| If any man should ask the price, | One or two shillings take your choice: | Sometimes true whigs have given twenty | But tories think that five is plenty.| New York: | Printed for Elijah Weege, 1776.| 8vo. pp. 15. A. (532).

THE | COUNTERPART | to the | State-Dunces.| By a | Native of New-York.| [Vignette] | London: | Printed for W. Mears, at the Lamb on Ludgate-Hill, | M.DCC.XXXIII.| (Price, Sixpence.) | 4to. pp. 10.   (533).

THE DAGON OF CALVINISM, or the Moloch of Decrees; a Poem, in Three Cantos. To which is Annexed a Song of Reason. By the Same.   N.p.   Printed for the Author, n.d.   12mo. pp. 46.   (534).

THE DEATH OF GENERAL WOLF.| A Song. [1759]. Broadside.
(535).

[CUT.] The *Death* of | Gen. Wolfe | A Song. Broadside [1759].   (536).

[CUT.] The Death of | the brave | General Wolf. [1759]. Broadside.   (537).

[CUT.] The Death of | Brave Wolf. [1759]. Broadside.
(538).

[CUTS.] The Death of the Brave | General Wolf [And] The Death of General Wolf.| A Song. [1759]. Broadside.
(539).

The second poem of this title is by Thomas Paine.

THE DECREE OF THE SUN; | or, | France regenerated.| A Poem, | in three cantos.| The first offering of a youthful Muse.| Printed at | Boston, for the purchasers.| [1793.] 8vo. pp. 21.
A. (540).

THE DEMOS IN COUNCILS | or 'Bijah in Pandemonium.| Being a sweep of the lyre, | In close Imitation of Milton.| [Quotation of 4 lines]. Boston: | Printed by James Cutler, and for sale at the | Bookstores.—April, 1799.| 16 mo. pp. [3] 4-16.
A.B. (541).

[CUT.] Description of the Pope, 1769.| Toasts on the Front of a large Lanthorn.| Love and Unity. The American Whig. . . . [1769.] Broadside.   (542).

A | DIALOGUE, | Between | A Southern Delegate, | and | His
Spouse, | on his return from | The Grand Continental Con-
gress.| A Fragment, | inscribed | To the Married Ladies of
America, | By their most sincere, | And affectionate Friend, |
And Servant, | Mary V. V.| Printed in the Year M,DCC,-
LXXIV.| 12mo. pp. [3], 4-14.   A.B. (543).

A DIALOGUE | on Peace, | an Entertainment, | Given by the Senior
Class at the | Anniversary Commencement, | Held at Nassau-
Hall | September 28th, 1763.| Philadelphia: | Printed by
William Bradford, M.DCC,LXIII.| Sm. 4to. pp. 27.   (544).

DISCOURS de son excellence Monsieur Jean Hancock, President du
Congres de Philadelphia. A Philadelphie: MDCCLXXVI.
8vo. pp. 32.   N.Y.H.S. (545).
     A Satire on John Hancock.

The DYING SPEECH of Old Tenor, | on the 31st of *March* 1750;
being the Day appointed for his Execution.| *With a Word of
Comfort to his disconsolate Mourners.*| Sold next to the
Prison in Queen-Street. Broadside.   (546).

AN | EARNEST EXPOSTULATION | In the Name of the great and
glorious God with the Inhabitants | of this Land, especially
the Rising Generation.| [3 Columns of 3 Verses] | Boston:
Printed and Sold at the Printing House in Queen-Street over
against the Prison. 1739.| 4to. broadside.   A. (547).

AN ECLOGUE | OCCASIONED by the Death of the Reverend | Alex-
ander Cumming, A.M.| On the 25th of August A. D. 1763.|
Ætat. 37.| [Two lines from Psalm 112 with a large black line
above and below] | Boston: Printed by D. & J. Kneeland, for
J. | Edwards, in Corn-hill. MDCCLXIII.| 12mo. pp. [3],-
4-8.   A. (548).

THE EFFIGY [of John Jay] Burning. A Poem. Philadelphia:
1795.   (549).

EFFUSIONS | OF | FEMALE FANCY.| By a Young Lady, Native
of | America: | consisting of | Elegys, | and other original |
Essays in Poetry.| (8 lines from Prior.) | New-York: Printed

for the Author, and sold by all | the Booksellers and Printers in York, Baltimore and Philadelphia.| M,DCC,LXXXIV.| 12mo. pp. [5],-6-59,-[4].   B. (550).

> Evans mentions another edition with a change in title. New York: Thos. Greenleaf, 1790.

EIN DENCKMAHL aufgerichtet zum heiligen andencken der H. Jungfrau and Schwester Melania in Saron, als sie den 11ten September 1784 ein erbauliches Liebesmal vor die Gemein-schaft gehalten. Ephrata, 1784. 4to. broadside.   (551).

EIN SCHON weltlich Lied. Melodie: Ein Soldat bin ich eben und Steh vor meinem Feind. Philadelphia: Anton Armbruster 1764. 4to. pp. 10.   (552).

> "A burlesque on the Quakers taking up arms to protect the Indians in Philadelphia" against the "Paxton boys."

EIN TRAUER GEDICT uber eine Grausame Mordthat. Reading: [Penna.] J. C. Schneider, 1799.   (552B).

AN ELEGIAC POEM on the Death of General George Washington, Commander in Chief of the Armies of the United States. Who died at Mount Vernon, Virginia, 14th December, 1799, aged 68 years. Dedicated to the Citizens of the United States. Folio broadside printed in three columns with engraved ornamented borders, by R. Aitken, Philadelphia, January 1, 1800. (553).

> The copy from which this title was taken was printed on satin.

AN | ELEGY | occasioned by the death of the Late Reverend | Daniel M'Clelin, | Pastor of the Church of Christ in *Colerain*.| By a Neighbour.| [2 lines from Rom. 14, 13.] | Boston: Printed by J. Kneeland, in Milk-Street. 1773.] Folio broad-side.   (554).

AN | ELEGY, | Occasion'd by the Death of Major-General Joseph Warren, who fell | fighting in Defence of the glorious Cause of his Country, at Charlestown, in New-|England, on the Mem-orable 17th Day of June, 1775. Printed and Sold in Water-town, near the Bridge, 1775. [Broadside].   (555).

[Cut.] An Elegy, Occasion'd by the Death of | Mrs. Ruth Edson, | Wife to Mr. Josiah Edson, junr. of Bridgewater; who deceas'd May 31st, 1743, in the 34th Year of her Age; and sent to him upon this sorrowful Dispensation | of Providence,—By a Friend. Boston: 1743. Brodaside. (556).

[Cut.] An | Elegy | Occasioned by the Sudden and awful Death | of | Mr. Nathanael Baker | of Dedham: | A Young Man just upon the point of Marriage.| And Son to Lieutenant John Baker.| He fell from his Horse on Monday night the 7th of May, 1733: and Died | the Wednesday following. Ætat 27. Broadside. (557).

An Elegy on the Death of that ancient, venerable and useful Matron and Midwife, Mrs. Mary Broadwell, who rested from her Labours, Jan. 2, 1730. Aged A Hundred Years and One Day. Sold by David Harry, Printer in Philadelphia. 1730. (558).

An Elegy.| On the Death of that worthy Friend Priscilla Coleman, deceased, Widow of | John Coleman, late of Sherburne, on the Island of Nantucket, who departed | this Life on the 14th Day of the Third Month. 1762. Boston: Printed by Zachariah Fowle & Samuel Draper, at their Pri|nting-Office in Marlboro|-street. 1762. Broadside. (559).

An Elegy, on the Death of Mrs. Anne Belding, late Wife of the Reverend Mr. Joshua Belding, of Newington . . . By a Youth of his Parish. Hartford, E. Watson, 1774. 8vo. pp. 8. (560).

An Elegy, | On the much lamented Death | of | His Excellency Sir Henry Moore, Baronet, Captain | General, and Governor in Chief in and over the Province | of New-York, and the Territories depending thereon in | America, Chancellor and Vice-Admiral of the same; who | departed this Life in Fort George, on Monday the 11th | of September, 1769.| [2 lines from Hor.] | Folio broadside Poem of 46 lines with black borders. Probably printed in N. Y. by Hugh Gaine. (561).

107

An Elegy, On the much lamented Death of Lamson Mitchell, the eldest son of Mr. Peter Mitchel of Woodbury, and for some time a Member of Yale College, who departed this Life March 1, 1774. Folio broadside. (562).

An | Elegy | To the Infamous | Memory | of Sr. F. - - - B- - - - -, | "Auri cæcus Amore, | "Vendidt Hic Patriam." Printed in the Year | 1769.| 8vo. pp. [5] 6-14. (563).
A poem directed against Sir Francis Bernard.

An Elegy, | [   ] the Memory of Mason and Alpheus, sons of Mr. Elisha Hale | of Douglas, who were drowned, July 3, 1790, one in the 22d. | the other in the 17th year of his age. [Printed by] Samuel Webster, Sutton. [1790]. Broadside. (564).

An | Elegy | To The Memory | of | That pious and eminent Servant of | Jesus Christ, | The Reverend Mr. George White-field, | Who departed this Life the 30th of September, 1770 | Ætatis Suæ 56.| [Two lines of Latin and underneath a large black line] | Boston: New-England: Printed by Richard Draper.| MDCCLXX.| 12mo. pp. [2],-3-7,-[1]. [Last page signed B. C. senior.] A. (565).

An Elegy to the Memory of Miss Sarah Hart, Daughter of Rev. William Hart, of Saybrook; Who departed this life, June 24, 1788. Hartford: Printed by Hudson & Goodwin. 1790. 8vo. pp. 7. M.H.S. (566).

[Elegy?] Upon the | Death of that Reverend and Aged Man of God.| Mr. Samuel Arnold, | Pastor of the Church at Marsh-field, who deceased in the 71st Year of | his Age, and of his Ministry the 36th, September 1, 1693.| Broadside. (567).
On same sheet "Samuel Arnold. | Anagram, | &c.

An Elegy | Upon the Death of several | Worthy Pious Persons. [1780] Broadside. (568).

AN | ELEGY | Upon his Excellency | William Burnet, Esq; | Who
departed this Life Sept. 7th. 1729. Ætat. 42.| [Boston:
Printed and Sold by T. Fleet in Pudding-Lane, near the Town-
House, where may be had His Excellencey's Character.] Folio
broadside.   (569).

> Printed within black borders, surmounted by cut of two skulls
> and crossbones, with hour glass. A copy is in the New York Public
> Library, New York.

MEMENTO MORI, Remember Death.|

AN | ELEGY | Upon the much lamented Deaths of two desirable
Brothers, the two eldest sons of | Capt. Joshua and Mrs.
Comfort Weeks, | Of Greenland; | Who departed this Life
in February, 1735, 6. the youngest, whose name was *Ichabod*,
died the 3d Day in | the 22d year of his Age, and the eldest,
whose name was *Joshua*, deceased the 10th Day, in the 24th
year of his age, leaving | his honoured parents and a desir-
able Widow with other near Relations in mournful Tears.
Let us all that are yet spared, improve this | and the many
other warnings that we have had in the year past, remembering
the Command of Christ is *Be Ye Also Ready*.| Folio broad-
side with cut at top.   (570).

AN | ELOGY | On the death of Mr. Nathaniel Burt, Deacon of the
Church of | Christ at Longmeadow, and Lieutenant in his
Majesty's service; who | was killed in the memorable battle at
Lake George, Sept. 8, 1755, | in the 45th year of his age. Broad-
side.   (571).

THE | ENGLISH SOLDIER | Encouraged. Rouse Heroes, Arm
brave Captains take the Field, Great *George* commands, Arm
with your Spear and Shield. [1745] Broadside.   (572).

EPISTLE from Edward an American Prisoner in England, to
Harriet in America descriptive of the treatment of those poor
wretches in English jails during the Revolution. London:
1779. 4to. pp. 12. [With an Ode to Charity.] A. (573).

AN EPISTLE from Titus to Timothy. Quillsylvania. [Philadel-
phia.] Printed for the Author. [1781.] Folio broadside.
                                                              (574).

AN | EPISTLE | To | *Alexander Pope,* Esq; | From South Caro-
lina.| [3 lines in Latin from Horat.] | [Vignette.] | London: |
Printed for J. Brindley, | Bookseller to His Royal Highness |
the Prince of *Wales,* at the *King's-Arms* in *New Bond-|street;*
and C. Corbett, at *Addison's-Head,* over against | St. *Dun-
stans'-Church,* Fleetstreet. MDCCXXXVII.| Small folio,
pp. [5],-6-18. Half title reads. An | Epistle | To | *Alexander
Pope* Esq; | from South Carolina.| (575).

AN | EULOGIUM | on Major General | Joseph Warren, | who fell
in the action at Charlestown, | June 17, 1775.| By a Colum-
bian.| Arma virumque cano. Virgil.| Boston: | Printed by
John Boyle in Marlborough-Street.| 1781.| 12mo. pp. [3]-
4-22. A.B. (576).

THE EVERY THING, or an History of the Late War in America, in
Miniature, in Two Odes, or Poems, to be said or sung. By
Crispianus. Philadelphia: 1784. (577).

> See also *To Perpetuate, Etc.*

THE | EVIDENCE and Import | of | Christ's Resurrection, | versi-
fied, some years ago, | for the Help | of the | Memory.| The
force of Divine Truth which appears in | this plain short Poem,
may well strike a | Total Damp to every favourable thought
of | Deism or Deistical Christianity.| Providence (R. I.) |
Printed by B. Wheeler, for D. Brewer, of Taun-|ton, and sold
at their respective Bookstores.| MDCCXCVII.| 8vo. pp.
[2],-3-12. A.H. (578).

> Copy in Harvard is stitched with "Divine Oracles," the true anti-
> dote to deism, &c. Same imprint.

AN | EXERCISE, | Containing | A Dialogue and Ode | on Peace.|
Performed at the public Commencement in the | College of
Philadelphia, May 17th, 1763. . . . | . . . | . . . |
. . . | . . . . | Philadelphia: | Printed by Andrew
Steuart, at the Bible-in-Heart, | in Second street, M,DCC,-
LXIII.| 8vo. pp. 8. (579).

> The Dialogue was written by Nathaniel Evans, the Ode by Dr.
> Paul Jackson.

AN | EXERCISE, | containing | a | Dialogue and two Odes, | Performed at the Public Commencement in the College | of Philadelphia, November 17, 1767.| [Royal Arms.] | Philadelphia: | Printed by William Goddard, in Market-Street. [1767.] | Sm. 4to. pp. 8. (580).

> The Dialogue was written by Thos. Coombe.

AN | EXERCISE; | Containing, | a Dialogue and Two Odes | Set to Music, | for the | Public Commencement, | in the | College of Philadelphia, | May 17th, 1775.| Philadelphia: | Printed by Joseph Crukshank, in Market-|Street, between Second and Third Streets.| MDCCLXXV.| 8vo. pp. 8. (581).

AN EXERCISE, Containing a Dialogue and two Odes set to Music. Philadelphia: 1776. Sm. 8vo. (582).

THE FALL | OF | LUCIFER, | an | Elegiac Poem | on the | Infamous Deflection | of the late | General Arnold.| Hartford, Hudson & Goodwin, 1781.| 12mo. pp. 18. (583).

> "This poem was composed in October and finished by the First of November," 1780.

A | FAMILY TABLET: | containing | A Selection | of | Original Poetry.| [7 lines from Akenside.] Boston: | Printed and sold by William Spotswood.| 1796.| 12mo. pp. [13], 2-81. A.B. (584).

> Edited by Abiel Holmes.

[CUT.] THE FARMER and his Son's Return from a Visit to | Camp: Together With The | Rose Tree. [1775.] Broadside. (585).

A few Lines Composed on the Dark Day, | May 19, 1780. [Broadside.] (586).

[CUT.] A few Lines on | Magnus Mode, Richard Hodges, & J. Newington Clark.| Who are Sentenc'd to stand one Hour in the Pillory at Charlestown; | to have one of their ears cut off, and to be Whipped 20 Stripes at the public whipping-Post, for making | and passing Counterfeit Dollars, &c. [Boston: Printed by Zachariah Fowle. 1767.] Broadside. (587).

111

A FEW LINES | On occasion of the untimely End of | Mark and Phillis, | Who were Executed at Cambridge, | September 18th for Poysoning their | Master, Capt. John Codman of | Charlestown.| [1775.] Folio broadside of xiv verses, with view of the execution of Mark in upper right hand corner.

(588).

A FEW LINES | Upon the Awful Execution of | John Ormesby & Matth. Cushing, | October 17th, 1734.| One for Murder, the other for Burglary. [Cut.] Printed and Sold at the Printing House in Queen-Street, over against the Prison.| Broadside.

(589).

Printed also with Cushing's "Confession" 1734.

A FEW LINES wrote upon the intended Execution of | Levi Ames, | For Burglary, and being sent to him for his Improvement, are now published at his Desire. [Boston: 1773.] Broadside.

(590).

THE FOLLOWING LINES were Compos'd by the desire of a | friend upon the Death of Mr. Timothy Bacon, | who died 24th of May, A. D. 1794, in the 23d year | of his age.| Small folio. Broadside. (591).

THE FOLLOWING THOUGHTS came from a Youth | scarce 15. [And] The following Lines (Wrote by a Youth 16.) | were designed for the Consolation of the | late Rev. Dr. Mayhew's Spouse. [Boston: Draper.] Broadside. [1766]. (592).

THE FORC'D ALLIANCE; A Dialogue. Or, The News-Boy's Shift for January 1, 1788. [Hartford: *Hudson & Goodwin.*] 1788. Folio broadside. (593).

The Hartford Courants' New-Year's verses for 1788. These verses were written by some of the author's of "The Anarchiad."

FOUR EXCELLENT | New Songs, | Called, | Yankee Doodle.| Death of General Wolfe.| Nancy Dawison.| Guardian Angels.| [Cut.] | New-York: | Printed and Sold by John Reid, at his | Book and Stationery Store, | No. 17 Water Street, 1788.| 12mo. pp. [1],-2-8. (594).

The only copy traced is in the possession of the compiler.

112

FRENCH ARROGANCE; or, "The cat let out of the bag." A Poetical dialogue between the Envoys of America and X. Y. Z. and the Lady. Philadelphia: 1798. 12mo. pp. 31.   (595).

FROM THE VIRGINIA GAZETTE, August 25. [1774]. A Parody on a Late Proclamation. . . . [40 lines of Verse] &c., &c. [16 lines of Verse]. N. P. [1774]. Broadside.   (596).

[CUTS.]   A | FUNERAL ELEGY, | Composed on the Death of the truly Brave and Heroic Captain | James Mugford, | Late Commander of the Franklin Privateer Schooner, lately fitted out from Marblehead, with a few Two Pounders, and Swirvels, and Twenty-one Men, who | was Killed in a disperate Engagement with Thirteen Boats, and Two Hundred Men, belonging to the Ministerial Fleet, near Boston, on Sunday the Nineteenth | of May, One Thousand Seventeen Hundred and Seventy-Six.| Salem: Printed and Sold by E. Russell, in Main-Street: where Shopkeepers, Travelling-Traders, &c. may be Supplied with sundry new Pieces on the Times, very Cheap. [1776.]   Broadside.   (597).

[CUTS.]   A Funeral Elegy, | Occasioned by the | Tragedy, | At Salem, near Boston, on Thursday Afternoon, the 17th of June 1773, at which Time the 10 following Persons . . . were drowned.   [Boston: 1773.]   Broadside.   (598).
  Another issue, Printed and Sold by E. Russell, next the Cornfield, Union Street, near the Market. (Pr. 3. Cop.)

A FUNERAL ELEGY on George Whitefield. [Boston: 1770.] [Cuts of Coffin, &c.]   Folio broadside   A. (599).
  Another issue, Boston: Printed and Sold at the Printing-Office in Milk Street, MDCCLXX. Folio broadside.   (A).

GENERAL | WARREN: | or | the Battle of Bunker Hill.| [4to. broadside, 7 verses in 2 columns]. Printed by Nathaniel Coverly, Jun'r.| Corner Theatre Alley, Boston.| A. (600).

THE | GLASS; | or, | Speculation: | A | Poem.| Containing an account of the | Ancient, and Genius of the | Modern, Speculators.| [Quotation of 4 lines.] New York: Printed for the author.| 1791.| 12mo. pp. [3] 4-12.   B. (601).

A | Good Wife, | God's Gift; | or a | Character | of a | Wife Indeed!| Also, | a poetical description | of the | Chaste Virgin, | of a Good Wife; and a | Pious Widow, etc.| Boston.| Printed by J. White, Neare Charles-river Bridge.| 1796.| 8vo. pp. 44.   A. (602).

The Grand Exploits of one of His Majesty's Generals, viz. John Burgoyne in Anno Domini, 1777. When Israel Forth from Egypt came, The Lord was their Protector. All Nations heard of Israel's Fame, And Moses their Director. [42 4ll. Verses]. Followed by: A Surprising Dream, &c. [100ll. of Verse]. N. P. [1777]. Folio pp. 2.   (603).

Grateful Reflections on the Divine Goodness vouchsaf'd to the American Arms in their remarkable successes in the Northern Department, after the giving up of our Fortresses at Ticonderoga, on the sixth of July, A.D. 1777. With some Account of the Battles fought and the Transactions of that memorable Campaign. Occasioned by he Surrender of the King's Forces by Lieutenant-General Burgoyne to Major-General Gates, on the 23d day of October, in the said Year. In four Parts. Hartford: Printed and Sold by Hudson & Goodwin [1779]. 12mo.
                                                        (604).

By William Wolcott. See 466.

Guillotina, | For January 1, 1797. | *Addressed to the Readers of the* Connecticut Courant.| [Hartford, January 1, 1797.] Folio broadside.   A.B. (605).
    Same: for 1798.

The Hermit of New Jersey; a Collection of Poetical Essays; an Ode to Liberty, and a Dialogue between Lorenzo and the Hermit on Human Happiness. Philadelphia: William Goddard. 1769.   (606).

Hope: | A Rhapsody.| Folio broadside, relating to ante-revolutionary events.   (607).
    The copy in the New York Historical Society has written on it in a contemporary hand, "New York, July 26th, 1774 P. M."

114

THE | HOUSE OF WISDOM | in a | Bustle; | A Poem, | descrip-
tive of the noted | Battle, | Lately fought in C-ng-ss.| By
Geoffry Touchstone.| Philadelphia: | Printed for the au-
thor.| 1798.| [Price 25 Cents.] 8vo. pp. [3] 4-27.

A.B. (608).

> This humorous satire relates to the Lyon-Griswold duel in Con-
> gress. I have known of copies containing a copper plate view of
> the row, but I hardly think that the plate was issued with the
> pamphlet, as it is somewhat larger than the latter and was probably
> inserted at the time of issue by those who possessed copies of the
> work.

HOWE's | Proclamation | Versified. [Boston: 1775.] Broadside.

(609).

JAN. 1, 1796.| Indep. xx.| The Humble Address | Of the Car-
riers of the | Albany Register, | To their Generous Customers,
greeting them with a | Happy New-Year.| Folio broadside
printed in double column, with cut of arms of the State of New
York. [Albany, 1795.] N.Y.P.L. (610).

AN | INDEPENDENT ODE, | Dedicated to the Illustrious President
of the United States, the Governor of this Commonwealth, |
and all true Patriots of Liberty. [1795.] Broadside. (611).

THE INDIAN TALE, interpreted and told in English Verse. Philadelphia: B. Franklin. 1734. (612).

> Advertised in the *Pennsylvania Gazette,* Jan. 16, 1734.

[————] JOURNAL | Of the Taking of | Cape-Breton, | Put
in Metre, by L. G. one of the Soldiers in the Expedition.|
[1745]. Small folio. Broadside. (613).

> The first word has been torn from the copy of this broadside
> which is in the New York Historical Society. This copy is the
> only one which I have seen.

JOYFUL NEWS | TO | AMERICA, | a | Poem.| Expressive of Our
More than ordinary | Joy, on the Repeal of the | Stamp-Act.|
Together-with the | Praise of Liberty, | And | Two Acrosticks.|
[Philadelphia:] Printed [by Andrew Steuart] in the Year
1766.| Sm. 8vo. pp. 8. (614).

115

JUDGE WOLCOTT.| A Funeral | Poem | upon | Roger Wolcott Esq; | Who was One of the Honourable Council | Of The | Colony of Connecticut, | And a Judge of their Superior Court; | Who died October 19th, 1759; in the 56 Year of his Age.| Inscribed To | William Wolcott Esq; | *Quem semper amatum,* | *Semper bonoratum, sic Dii voluistiis, hatebo.*| *Vir.* | *My whole Life tells me, that a just Demand for Esteem is sacred, but* | *rare. We may well afford to pay it, when it is due.*| The Centaur not fabulous.| New Haven; | *Printed by* James Parker, *and* Company, 1760.| 4to. pp. 10.

A. (615).

JUVENILE POEMS, designed especially for the improvement and instruction of Youth. [3 lines from Dent. vi. 6, 7.] Windsor: State of Vermont. Printed by Alden Spooner, 1792. 8vo. pp. 31. B.A. (616).

L'AMERIQUIADE | Poëme, | Pour le benefice de l'auteur.| á Phila-delphie. | MDCCLXXX.| 8vo. pp. [2] 3-22. (617).

THE LADY ERRANT INCHANTED: A Poem, Dedicated to her Most Serene Highness in the Princess Magallia. Philadel-phia: Franklin and Meredith. 1731. (618).

Title from Hildeburn, who evidently never saw a copy.

THE | LAMENTATIONS | OF | MARY MAGDALENE, | On missing the Body of our Lord out of the | Sepulchre.| Together with | Her Exultation on the Angel's appear-|ing, and telling He was risen from the Dead.| Printed for William Glendinning, Preacher of the Gospel.| 1793.| 16mo. pp. [3] 4-11.

B. (619).

THE | LAMENTATIONS | of a | Sow, | on a late Thanksgiving-Day, at | Danbury, in Connecticut, | *Among those who emphatically stile themselves Saints,* | Composed by a Gentleman for his Amusement.| Anno MDCCLXXVIII.| 12mo. pp. 8.

N.Y.H.S. (620).

116

[CUT.] THE | LAST WORDS | of William Huggins and John
Mansfield, | Who are to be Executed this Day, June 19th,
1783, at Worcester, in the Commonwealth of Massachusetts,
for Burglary, committed in October last. Printed and Sold
at the Printing Office in Worcester.| [By Isaiah Thomas.]
Broadside.   A. (621).

LESSONS | FOR | LOVERS; | With some | Tender and Pathetic |
Anecdotes, | taken from | Real Life.| By Ovid Americanus.|
[6 lines from Swift.] | *To which is added,* | The | Thunder-
Storm, | A Poem.| Supposed to be written by the late cele-
brated Miss A * * *, | now Mrs. L * * * *, | Philadelphia: |
Printed and Sold by Robert Bell, in Third Street,| M,DCC,-
LXXXIV.| 8vo. pp. [5],-6-35, [1].   A.B. (622).
  Dedicated to Robert Morris.

LIBERTY.| A Poem | by Rusticus.| Charles-town: | Printed and
sold by T. Powell, at Mr. Timothy's Printing Office in Broad
Street.| M.DCC.LXX.| 4to. pp. 21.   A. (623).
  Second Edition, same date.

LIBERTY. A Poem. In Imitation of Churchill. Philadelphia:
W. and T. Bradford. 1770.   (624).

LIBERTY IN SLAVERY: | Or, | The Idolatrous Christian.| Some |
Political Thoughts, | occasioned by the late | Public Rejoic-
ings | at Hartford, | On the News of the Repeal of the |
Stamp-Act.| [Hartford, Thomas Green, 1767]. 16 mo. pp.
[1],-3-8.   N.Y.H.S. (625).

LIBERTY, PROPERTY AND NO EXCISE.| A | Poem | Compos'd |
On Occasion of the Sight seen on the Great | Trees, (so-called)
in Boston, New-Eng-|land, on the 14th of August, 1765.|
Printed in the Year, 1765. (Price 6 Cop.) 12mo. pp. [3] 4-8.
                                                    B. (626).
  Also as a broadside [1765.]

LINES | Composed *on the Great* Earthquake, *in the Year* 1755.|
1 p. 8vo.   (627).

117

A | Little Looking-Glass | For the Times; | Or, | A brief
Remembrancer | for | Pennsylvania.| Containing | Some
serious Hints, affectionately addressed to People of | every
Rank and Station in the Province: | With an Appendix, by
Way of Supplication to | Almighty God.| By G. C. | . . .
| . . . | . . . | . . . | . . . | . . . | . . . | . . . | Wilmington, |
Printed and Sold by James Adams, 764.| Sm. 8vo. pp. 24.
N.Y.H.S. (628).

Look before ye Loup; | or, | A Healin' Sa' | for the | Crackit
Crowns | of | Country Politicians, | by | Tam Thrum, | an
auld Weaver.| "Twas well, I wish'd to be better, | "And
here I lie."| Epitaph on a Constitution-Mender.| Philadel-
phia: | Printed for Thomas Dobson, at the Stone | House,
No. 41, South-Second Street.| M,DCC,XCVIII.| 16mo. pp.
[3], 4-40. B. (629).

The Loyal Address of the Clergy of Virginia. Williamsburg:
Printed for Fr. Maggot, at the sign of the Hickery Tree, in
Queen Street, 1702. Folio broadside. (630).
> A fictitious imprint. This piece was probably printed in London,
> as no trace of a press in Virginia at this time [1702] can be found.

[Cut.] Major Andre, | Written while he was a Prisoner in the
American Camp. [Also, The Rose]. [1780]. Broadside.
(631).

The | Manners of the Times; | A | Satire.| In two Parts.|
By Philadelphiensis.| [2 lines from Juv.] Philadelphia: |
Printed and Sold by William Dunlap, M,DCC,LXII.| 12mo.
pp. [2], 3-16. A.B. (632).

Meditations on Death.| Composed on the Death of | Mr.
John Pierson, junr. | Of Killingworth, who died April 8th,
A. D. 1776; | In the Thirty-first Year of his Age.| Directed
in Particular to the bereaved Friends.| [New London: 1776.]
Folio broadside. (633).

Meditations | on | Death ⌐and the | Grave | N.P.N.D. 12mo.
pp. [2],-3-8. (634).
> Probably printed about 1780. There is no sign of place of issue,
> but it seems to be of American origin. Probably printed in Con-
> necticut.

118

[CUT.] THE MEMORABLE YEAR 1759. Broadside.   (635).

THE | MERCIES | OF THE YEAR, | Commemorated: | A Song for| Little Children | in New-England.| December 13th, 1720. [And] Psalm CVII—last Part.| Translated | by the Reverend | Mr. Isaac Watts | and by him Intitled, | A Psalm for New-England.| Broadside.   (636).

A MIRROR FOR A PRINTER. [And] A Proclamation. [A Parody on Gage's] "From Salem's Council Chamber I, these wise Instructions give. 1774." N. P. [1774.] Folio broadside.
(637).

A MISCELLANEOUS Collection of Original pieces. Springfield: John Russell: 1686. [1786] 12mo. pp. 182.   A. (638).

MISCELLANEOUS REFLECTIONS.| In Verse.| Mostly written at sundry times, | when under long confinement | by a complication of | nervous disorders.| By a Valetudinary | Printed by Request of Friends of | that Class. | Printed at Greenfield, Massachusetts. | by Thomas Dickman.| MDCCXCII.| 12mo. pp. [2],-3-40.   (639).

MR. W—D'S SOLILOQUY, or a Serious Debate with himself what course he shall take. Boston, 1745.   (640).
> A Poem upon the celebrated George Whitefield.

THE MODERN VENI, Vidi, Vici. [1775] Handbill.   (641).

MONARCHY, a parody on the Eclogue of Pope. Philadelphia: 1795. 8vo.   (642).

THE MONITOR; or a Poem on Dancing. Addressed to Ladies and Gentlemen of the Fayetteville Assembly. Fayetteville: Printed by Sibley & Howard, 1790.   (643).

A | MONODY | In Honor of the | Chiefs | Who have fallen in the Cause of | American Liberty, | Spoken at the Theatre, | in | Philadelphia, December 7, 1784.| With the Vocal Accompanyments: | And | A Rondelay, | Celebrating | American Independency.| . . . . | [Philadelphia:] Printed by Thomas Bradford.| [1784.] Sm. 4to. pp. 8.   (644).
> The vocal parts were sung by a "Lady." It was not delivered until Dec. 14.

119

MONSIEUR RAGOO; or, a Squib for the late F-REW-RKS; in Humorous verse. Broadside. (645).
Advertised in *Boston Evening-Post,* Sept. 4, 1749.

A MONUMENTAL INSCRIPTION | on the | Fifth of March.| Together with a few Lines | On the Enlargement of | Ebenezer Richardson, | Convicted of Murder.| [Boston: Isaiah Thomas, 1771?] Folio broadside with 32 lines of verse, and column of prose relating to the Boston Massacre, the trial of the soldiers, &c. Has a cut of the Massacre at upper left hand corner.
A. (646).

Some of the events noted are dated in the year 1782, and yet a copy in the Emmet Collection [2086] in the New York Public Library has written on it in a contemporaneous hand "Printed 1771 by I. Thomas." A copy is also in the American Antiquarian Society. known as "The Massacre Handbill."

MORAL FOR THE YEAR 1771, with verses upon the Spiritual Gifts. To which is added (By Permission of the author), An acrostic on the memory of the Rev. Mr. George Whitefield. N. P. 1771. 12mo. (647).

A MOURNFUL POEM on the Death of John Ormsby and Matthew Cushing, | who were appointed to be executed on Boston Neck the 17th of October, 1734.| Sold at the Heart and Crown in Boston.| 17 lines and Epitaphs of Ormsby and Cushing. [woodcut at top.] Folio broadside. (648).

MOVING TIMES | and | No Friends.| The Newest Dialogue.| Sold by William Topsyturvy, at the Sign of the Boot | in the County of Restraints, and Province of Mercy | chuse this Bay; Printed in the Year Seventeen Hund-|red and O Terrible ! ! ! ! ! ! ! ! | 12mo. pp. [3] 4-8. B. (649).

MYSTERIOUS NOTHING, a Poem; with an Allegory of Life and Futurity. By [W. S.] the Author of Contempt on Revenge. Philadelphia, for the Author, [By Benj. Franklin.] 1736. 12mo. pp. 16. (650).

The initials "W.S." are supposed to apply to William Smith, not the poet whose works will be found in another part of this book, but a much earlier writer.

A New | Collection | of Verses | applied to the | First of *No-*
vember, | A. D. 1765, &c.| Including a *Prediction* that the
S——p A——t shall not | take place in *North-America.*| To-
gether with | A poetical Dream, | Concerning | *Stamped*
Papers.| [2 lines from Pope's Homer] | [2 lines in Latin from
Cicero] | [6 lines in Latin and English from Agric. Vit.] |
New-Haven: Printed and Sold by *B. Mecom.*| [1765], 8vo.
pp. [5],-4-24.   (651).

New England Bravery. [Cut.] Being a full and true Account
of the taking of the City of Louisbourg, by | the New-England
Forces under the Command of the Gallant General | Pepperell,
on the 17th of June, 1745. Tune of, Chivey Chase. Sold at
the Heart and Crown in Cornhill, Boston. [1745] Broadside.
                                                                 (652).

New-England | Lasses.| 1 p. 4to.   A. (653).
    A rather broad song, with a representation of one of "The Lasses"
    above the verses.

New-England's | Misery, | The procuring | Cause, | And | A
Remedy | proposed.| Composed October, 1758.| [Printer's
ornament] | Boston: Printed and Sold by Z. Fowle and | S.
Draper, opposite the Lion & Bell, in Marl-|borough-Street, |
M,DCC,LVIII.| [Price Half-Piastereen.] | 12mo. pp. [2],-
3-15,-[1].   A. (654).

[Cuts.] A | New Liberty | Song, | Composed at the Camp on
Pros-|pect Hill, August, 1775.| By a Son of Liberty. Salem:
Printed by E. Russell &c. [Broadside.]   (655).

A New Song. Address'd to the Sons of Liberty, on the Con-
tinent of America; particularly to the Illustrious, Glorious
and never to be Forgotten Ninety-Two of Boston. Small
folio composed of 7 verses of 8 lines each, with curious woodcut at the top, of a Man on horseback, probably meant to repre-
sent Paul Revere. [Boston: Green & Russell, 1768.]   (656).

A New Song | Called | Brae and Burn.| A New Song, | the |
Top-Sails.| A New Song | Called | Diana.| A New Song |

121

Called | Father Paul.| Folio Broadside, each song occupying a Separate Column, a crude copperplate cut surmounting each. Without doubt printed in America probably about 1780. The only Copy we have found is in the possession of the Compiler. (657).

[Cuts.] A New Th [anksgiving] Song | Revised, Enlarged and Adapted [to] The Glorious Conquest of Canada.| Fitted to a Live Tune, Called the Grenadiers March, proper for the Fifes and Drums. [Sold at the New Printing-Office, near the Town-House, in Boston.] Broadside. A. (658).

A New Song, | To an Old Tune, viz. "God Save the ———" [God save the People.] 1 p. folio. (659).
Relates to the French Revolution.

A New-Year's Address, | To the Customers, of the Boston Gazette, &c.| For January 1765. Broadside. (660).
Signed "J. T." Also following years.

New-Year's Address of the Carrier of the Independent Chronicle, Respectfully Presented to its Patrons. Boston, January 1, 1806. Folio Broadside, printed in double Column. A. (661).

A New-Year's | Address, which your obedient | Servant the young Shaver | humbly presents to all his Ge-|nerous Customers. [1768.] Broadside. (662).

A New-Year's Present from the Lad that | Carries the Boston News-Letter, to all | Generous Customers, January 1, 1761. [Printed by John Draper.] Broadside. (663).
Also following years, with slight variations.

A New-Year's Ode. [1795.] Broadside. (664).

New-Year Verses of the Carriers of the American Weekly Mercury. Philadelphia: Andrew Bradford, 1741. Folio broadside. (665).
Also issued for a number of years following, the wording each year being somewhat different.
No attempt has been made to include more than a few specimens of the New Year's Verses issued by many of the newspapers during the latter half of the 18th Century as they add but little to the interest of the book.

122

New Year Verses of the Carriers of the Pennsylvania Chronicle. Philadelphia: William Goddard, 1770. (666).
> Also New Year Verses of the Carriers of the *Pennsylvania Ledger,* Philadelphia: James Humphrey, Jr., 1776.

New-Year Verses of the Carriers of the Pennsylvania Evening Post. Philadelphia: B. Towne. 1777. A. (667).
> Also 1776, 1778, 1780, 1781. (A).

New-Year Verses of the Carriers of the Freeman's Journal. Philadelphia: Francis Bailey, 1782. (668).

The New Year Verses of the Carriers of the Pennsylvania Packet. Philadelphia: John Dunlap. 1773. (669).

[Royal Arms.] New Year's Verses, | Addressed to the kind Customers of the | Massachusetts Gazette, &c. [1774.] Broadside. (670).

A New Year's Wish, | A Happy Year to My Generous Customers. Boston, January 1, 1764. Broadside. (671).

A | New-Year's Wish, | From the Baker's Lad. Boston, January 1769. Broadside. (672).

A | New-Year's Wish, | From the Farriers Lad. Boston, January 1769. [Broadside.] (673).

[Cut.] A | New Year's Wish, | from the Lad, who Carries | The Post-Boy & Advertiser. Boston, January 1, 1760. [Boston: Printed by Green & Russell, 1761.] Broadside. (674).
> Carrier's Addresses were issued every year by the several Boston newspapers.

[Cut.] A | New Year's Wish, | from the Carrier of the Post-Boy & Advertiser. Boston, January 1, 1762. [Boston: Printed by Green & Russell. 1762.] Broadside. (675).

A New-Year's Wish, | From the Carrier of the Post-Boy and Ad-|vertiser. [1785.] Broadside. [Boston.] (676).

A New Year's Wish. 1765. Broadside. (677).
> Also 1766.

A New Year's Wish. [1795.] Broadside. (678).

123

THE NEWS-BOYS; | An Eclogue, for January 1, 1787 | Scene— *Hartford Street*—Time of Day; The Morning.| [Also] The News-Boy's Apology | for the foregoing Verses.| Written by Himself.| Folio broadside. (679).

THE NEWS-BOYS | ADDRESS | To the Generous Subscribers of | Woods's Newark Gazette | and | Paterson Advertiser, | *Wishing them* Health, Peace *and* Prospe-|rity, *and* many happy Years.| January 1, 1794.| Folio broadside. (680).

[CUT.] THE | NEWS-BOY'S | CHRISTMAS and New-Year's Verses.| Humbly Address'd | To the Gentlemen and Ladies to whom he Carries the Boston Evening-Post, published by T. & J. Fleet. December 31. 1764. Broadside. (681).

THE | NEWS-CARRIER'S | ADDRESS | To His | Customers | *Hartford, January* 1, 1785.| Folio broadside. (682).

OCCASIONAL ODE, | for 17th of June, 1786.| Narrow folio of one column. Boston: [1786]. (683).

ODE, | Anniversary—June 2, 1794. Broadside. (684).

ODE distributed among the spectators during the federal procession, at New-York, July, 1788. 8vo. (685).

   Printed also in The American Museum. Phila., 1788, vol. 4 pp. 572-574. The original was probably a broadside.

ODE | for the 23d of October, 1792. Broadside. A. (686).

AN ODE for the Thanksgiving Day. By Titus Antigallus, Esq. Boston: Printed and Sold by T. Fleet, 1749. 8vo. (687).

AN ODE on the Prospect of Peace. Philadelphia: Henry Miller. 1756. (688).

ODE ON WASHINGTON and Days of Absence. Ode sung on the arrival of President Washington at the State House, in Boston, October 24, 1789. Broadside. Small. 4to. (689).

ODE, | Sung at the Feast of St. John, June 24, 1795.| To a new Tune—By a Brother. Broadside. A. (690).

ODE, | Sung at the Feast of St. John, | June 24, 1795.| Tune— Rule Britannia. Broadside. A. (691).

ODE, | Sung at the Feast of St. John, | June 24, 1795.| Tune— Attick Fire. Broadside.   A. (692).

ODE | To the President of the Uni-|ted States on his arrival at | Boston. [1789.] Broadside.   (693).

ODES | For the Fourth of July, 1796.| broadside. 2 odes of 5 and 6 verses, respectively. 4to. [Providence?] [1796.]   (694).

THE | OFFICERS BALL.| A new | Dialogue.| Ball-Town.| Printed and Sold by I. T. at the — of Flying-Fame, in Dis-|cretion-Alley, near the Street of —. (Price 6 Coppers.) | 12mo. pp. [3], 4-8.   B. (695).

> In the copy from which the above title was taken, the words designated with a dash are mutilated and cannot be deciphered.

OLD ENGLAND'S TRIUMPH: | Sung at the Second Anniversary Meeting | of the Sons of St. George, | In New-York, April 23d, 1771.| Folio broadside. 10 Verses in 2 columns.
                                                        A. (696).

ON THE DARK DAY. May Nineteenth 1780. Broadside.
                                                        A. (697).

ON THE DEATH of Beulah Warfield.| Who departed this life September 26, 1776, aged 17.| Broadside, 4to.   A. (698).

> The Poem is in two columns of 16 verses each. At bottom are her dying words, in prose.

ON THE | DEATH | Of the Reverend | Benjamin Colman, D. D. | Who deceased August 29. 1747.| An | Eclogue.| Attempted by O - - - E - - - a young Student.| A grateful Mind, not Fancy hath inspir'd | Great Colman's Honour, not his own desir'd.| Boston, Printed and sold by Rogers and Fowle | in Queen-Street next to the Prison.| 12mo. pp. [3], 4-8.
                                                        B. (699).

MEMENTO MORI. Remember Death.| On the Death of the Very Learned, Pious and Excelling | Gershom Bulkley, Esq. M.D.| Who had his Mortality swallowed up of Life, *December* the *Second* 1713. *Ætatis Suæ* 78.| [Cut at top.] Folio broadside. [*New-London*: Printed by T. Green, 1714.]
                                      Photostat in N.Y.P.L. (700).

ON | THE DEPARTURE | of an infamous B - r - - - t.| [Folio broadside. A poem attacking Governor Bernard, and Welcoming his departure from Boston. [Woodcut of "The Tom-Cod Catcher" at top of broadside].   A. (701).

ON THE LANDING of the Troops in Boston, 1758, September 13th. Their March out Sept. 16th. And the Reduction | of Frontenac, August 28. To which is added, The present | State of Europe.| Sold at the Printing-office in Newbury-street.| [By John Draper.] Broadside.   A. (702).

OPPRESSION. A Poem, | By an American.| With Notes, By a | North Briton.| · [6 lines signed Anon.] | [2 lines signed Anon.] | London: | Printed for the Author; | and Sold by C. Moran, in the Great Piazza, Covent Garden.| MDCCLXV.| 4to. pp. [3],-2-34.   (703).
    This is the title of the first edition. Other issues are as follows:

OPPRESSION.| A | Poem, | By An | American.| With Notes, | By A | North Briton.| *Blest harmony of verse! you 'tis command, | The ear of princes, cramp the tyrant's hand, | You Strip Oppression, of her gay disguise, | and bid the hag in native horror rise: | |Strike tow'ring pride, and lawless rapine dead, | And plant the wreath on virtue's awful head.* | Anon.| *To see such crimes, and in so good a reign, | Who hoops of iron can my spleen contain?* | Anon.| London: Printed | Boston: Re-printed and Sold opposite the Probate | Office in Queen-Street. 1765.| Price *Half a Pistereen.*| 8vo. pp. [3], 2-20.   A. (704).
    The following edition has same title-page with exception of the imprint which is:
    London; Printed: | New York Reprinted, and sold by Hugh Gaine, at the Bible | and Crown, in Hanover Square. | M,DCC,LXV. | 12mo. pp. 20.   (A).

OPPRESSIONS | A | Poem. | Or, New-England's Lamentation on the dreadful Extortion and other Sins of the | Times. Being a serious Exhortation to all to repent and turn from the Evil of their Ways, if they would avert the terrible and heavy Judgments of the Almighty that | hang over America at this alarming and distressing Day.| [Two Curious Cuts.] [Boston: 1777.] Folio broadside.   (705).

A | PANEGYRICK.| By Strephon.| . . . | . . . | . . . |. . . . |
Philadelphia: | Printed and Sold by William Dunlap, M,DCC,-
LXII.| 8vo. pp. 11.   (706).

THE PARABLE of the One Talent, Expounded according to Scrip-
ture and Reason: | [line from Matthew xxv, 14th to 25th
Verses.] Small folio broadside.   (706B).
   Probably printed in Connecticut, *Circa* 1780.

THE PATRIOT, | A Poem.| The duration and advantages of a
Free Government, | depend on the wisdom and virtue of "The
People," | By A Mechanic of Charlestown.| Charlestown: |
Printed for the Author.| 1798.| 12mo. pp. [3] vi, vii, [2]
10-24.   B. (707).

THE PAXTONIAD.| A | Poem.| By Christopher Gymnast, Esq; |
With the Prolegomena and Exercitations of | Scriblerus.|
[Philadelphia:] Printed [by Anthony Armbruster.] in the
Year, 1764.| Sm. 4to. pp. 8.   (708).

THE PAXTONIADE.| A | Poem.| By Christopher Gymnast, Esq; |
With the Prolegomana and Exercitations of | Scriblerus.| The
Second Edition.| Printed word for word, from the first Grand
Edition.| Philadelphia: Printed and Sold by | John Morris,
opposite the three Reapers in Third-Street. [1764.] Sm.
8vo. pp. 8.   (709).

A PETITION and Remonstrance to the President and Congress of
the United States. [Written by a North Carolina Planter.]
[Philadelphia? 1791.] Folio broadside.   (710).

PIETAS ET CONGRATULATIO *Collegii Cantabrigiensis apud* Nov-
anglos. Bostoni, Massachusettensium: Typis J. Green & J.
Russell, MDCCLXI. 4to. pp. xiv, [2], 106 and slip of errata.
                                                  A.B. (711).
   A collection of 31 Greek, Latin and English poems by Harvard
graduates, celebrating the Death of Geo. II, and accession of Geo.
III. Among the writers were Benj. Church, Stephen Sewall, James
Bowdoin, Gov. Bernard, and President Holyoke. The above was
the first poetical offering from an American College to an English
Sovereign.

PITCHERO-THRENODIA.| Or, An | Elegiack Poem | Sacred to the Memory | Of the late *Reverend* | Nathaniel Pitcher, | Pastor of the North-Church | in Scituate; | *Who* put off his *Earthly Tabernacle* | on Friday, Septemb xxvii, | MDCCXXIII.| [2 lines in Latin.] | Boston: | Printed by B. Green. 1724.| 8vo. pp. [4],-1-11, [1.]
                                             A. (712).

A | POEM. Medford: Printed and Sold 1771. Broadside. (713).

A | POEM, | Addressed To A Young Lady.| In Three Parts.| Part I. Descriptive and Moral.| 2. On Love and Friendship.| 3. The Caution.| *En ego, cum patriá caream, vobisq; domoq; | Raptaque sint, adimi quae potuere mihi; | Ingenio tamen ipse meo comitorque fruorque*: | Ovid.| Written At Antigua.| Boston: Printed by Green and Russell, 1773.| 8vo. pp. 33.
                                             A. (714).

    By Benjamin Mecom. For the title of the first edition see No. 271 of this bibliography.

A | POEM, | Commemorative | Of | Goffe, Whaley, & Dixwell, | Three of the Judges of Charles I. | Who, | At the Restoration, Took Refuge and Died in | America.| To which is prefixed, | An Abstract | Of | Their History.| By Philagathos.| *Celata* virtus! nou ego te meis | Chartis inornatum filebo, | Totre tuos patiar labores | Obliviones capere lividas. | Hor. | Boston: | Printed and Sold by Samuel Hall, in Cornhill. | MDCCXCIII.| 8vo. pp. 28.
                                             A. (715).

[CUT.] A POEM, descriptive of the terrible Fire, which made such shocking Devastation in Boston, | on the Evening of Friday April 21, 1787, in which were consumed one House of Worship, of which the | Rev. Ebenezer Wight was Pastor, and upwards of One Hundred Dwelling-Houses and other Buildings— | . . . Composed by H. W. Sold at the Office next Liberty-Pole. [1788.] Broadside. (716).

A POEM in Memory of that Pious servant and Faithful Minister of Jesus Christ, Mr. Isaac Cushman. First Pastor of the First Church of Christ in Plymton who deceased Oct. 22, 1732, in the eighty-fourth year of his age, and the thirty-seventh of his ministry. 60 lines and epitaph. Folio broadside. (717).

[Cut.] A | Poem, | occasioned | By hearing the late Reverend George Whitefield preach. Sold over the Auction-Room in Queen-Street. [Boston: 1771.] Broadside. (718).

A Poem | Occasion'd by the late | powerful and awakening Preaching | of the Reverend | Mr. Gilbert Tennent | By some young Lads much effected therewith.| [Boston: 1741.] Broadside. (719).

A Poem | Occasioned by the late sudden and awful Death, of a Young Woman, who | was found drowned, in Medford-River, July 14th, 1771. Medford: Printed & Sold, 1771. Broadside. (720).

A Poem occasioned by the Spreading in this Province the result of a Consocation in a Neighbour Government: &c. &c. Boston: Printed and Sold by Rogers and Fowle. 1742. 18mo. pp .[8]. (721).

A Poem, | Occasioned by the sudden and surprising death of Mr. Asa Burt, of Granville, (Mas-|sachusetts), who was mortally wounded by falling of a Tree, on the 28th of January, 1774, | in the 37th Year of his age, and expired in a few hours after he received the Wound. Tracey & Bliss, Printers, Lansingburgh. [N. Y. *Circa* 1774.] Broadside. (722).

A Poem on the Burning of New York in September, 1766. New York. Printed by Hugh Gaine, 1780. 12mo. (723).

A Poem on Death. Boston: Printed and Sold by E. Russell, near Liberty-Pole, 1793. (724).

A | Poem | On the Death of | Dr. Abraham Howe, | of Shrewsbury, Massachusetts-Bay, who died October 19th, 1779, in the | twenty-second Year of his Age. Printed and sold at the Printing-Office in Worcester. [by Isaiah Thomas.] Broadside. A. (725).

A Poem on the Death of Deacon William Brown, of Groton. Norwich: Printed by John Trumbull, 1794. (726).

A Poem on the Departure of James Davenport from Boston, in the way of a Dream. Boston, 1742. 12mo. pp. 8. (727).

129

[CUT.] A POEM. On the Execution of Samuel Frost, who is to be executed this day, October 31, 1793, for the Murder of Capt. Elisha Allen, of Princeton, Massachusetts. Printed and sold at Mr. Thomas's Printing Office, in Worcester. 1793. Broadside. A. (728).

A | POEM | on reading the | President's Address; | with a sketch of the character | of a | Candidate | for the | Presidency.| Philadelphia: | Printed by Ormrod & Conrad, | No. 41 Chestnut-street, | 1796.| 8vo. pp. [3] 4-7. B. (729).

A POEM | on the Rebuke of God's Hand | In the *Awful Desolation* made by | Fire | In the Town of | Boston, | On the 20th Day of *March,* 1760, | By which, in about 6 or 7 Hours, between *three* and *four hundred Buildings* were Consumed :— To which is added, some brief Hints, | on the *great conflagration* [————] *Consumation of all things.* [one line.] [Boston: Printed and sold at *Fowle & Draper's* Printing | Office in *Marlborough Street.* 1760.| Broadside signed A. F. (730).

> The only copy of this broadside which I have been enabled to trace is damaged and a word or two of the title are missing. A view of the conflagration is in the upper left hand corner.

A POEM on the Rise and Progress of Moor's Indian Charity School, now incorporated with Dartmouth College, its removal and settlement in Hanover, and the founding of a Church in the same. By one of Dr. Wheelock's pupils educated in said school, and now a member of said College preparing for a mission among the Indians. 1771. 8vo. pp. 8. (731).

A | A POEM, | on the | Unsuccessful Measures; | Taken at the | British Army; | In order to Enslave and destroy the Uni-|ted States in North-America: | From the Beginning of the War, 1775, to | the taking of General Burgoyne, and the | the Army under the command of at Syrato | ga, [sic] 1777.| Printed 1782.| 12mo. pp. [2],-3-16. (732).

> The only copy we have seen is now in the possession of Dr. A. S. W. Rosenbach.

A POEM, or, an Hymn of Adoration; with the Messiah's Complaint on the Bleeding Cross, or the Cries of the Son of God. To which are added, a Prayer, The Conclusion and The Supplement. By a Friend and well-wisher to vital Religion. Philadelphia: Printed by Enoch Stony, for the Author. 1788.

(733).

A | POEM | sacred to the Memory of | Mrs. Abigail Conant, | the late amiable Consort of the | Rev. Mr. *Silvanus Conant* | Of | Middleborough; | Who died on *January* 3d. 1759. | in the 28th Year of her Age.| Lo! Soft *Remembrance* drops a pious Tear; | and holy *Friendship* stands a Mourner here.| *Mallet.*| New London: | Printed by Timothy Green. MDCCLIX.| 4to. pp. 7. A. (734).

A POEM upon the Death and Memory of Two Eminent and Faithful Stewards and Servants in Christ. The Reverend Mr. Isaac Cushman, first pastor of the Church in Plympton, who deceased Oct. 21, Anno Domini 1732, and Dr. Caleb Loring, a careful and faithful Physician of said Town, who deceased Dec. 22, A.D. 1732. Composed with an intention to make Plympton and others sensible how liable and obnoxious to the sore Judgment of God a people are when the Righteous are taken away out of the Land of the Living. 2 Epitaphs. Folio broadside.

(735).

A POEM upon the Death of Mrs. Martha Chandler, of North Yarmouth. A very hopeful young woman; who departed this Life, August 4th. 1737. [Boston: 1737.] Broadside. (736).

A POEM, | On the joyful News of the Rev. Mr. Whitefield's visit to Boston.| Dedicated to all the true Friends, etc. Boston, Printed Oct. 1754. Broadside. (737).

A POEM, | Upon the present Times with a brief [and] humble Address to the Almighty, | In behalf of the [justic]e of our Cause.| Composed by Philoleutheros Americanus. [1776.] Broadside. (738).

131

POEMS Moral and Divine etc. by an American Gentleman. To which is added, some account of the Author. London, 1756. 4to. pp. [6], 105, and advertisement on last leaf.   (739).

Contains *The Prince and the Patriot: A Poem in Three Dialogues.* pp. 79-105, which is one of the earliest plays written by an American.

POEMS upon Several Occasions, Viz:—1. A Poem on the Enemy's first coming to Boston; the Burning of Charlestown; the fight at Bunker-Hill, etc. II. The Widow's Lamentation. III. Nebucadnezzar's Dream. IV. Against Oppression. V. An Heroic Poem on the taking of General Burgoyne, etc. Shall every sense of Virtue sleep, and every talent lie buried in the Earth when subjects of such importance call for them to be improved? Boston: Printed for the Author. 1799. 8vo. pp. 16.   B. (740).

POEMS | on | Several occasions.| [4ll. from Cic.] | *By a Gentleman of* Virginia.| Williamsburg: | Printed and Sold by William Parks.| M,DCC,XXXVI.| 8vo. pp. [2],-iii,-iv,-5-30.
                                                                                        (741).

Reprinted in Heartman's Historical Series, No. 33. New York, 1920.

The only copy of the original now known is Washington's copy in the Boston Athenaeum.

POEMS, on Various subjects; written by a Youth. Hartford, 1781. 12mo.   A. (742).

A | POETICAL EPISTLE | to the | Enslaved Africans, | in the Character of an Ancient Negro, | Born a slave in | Pennsylvania; | But liberated some Years since, and instructed in | useful Learning, and the great Truths of Chri-|stianity.| With | A brief historical Introduction, and biographical | Notices of some of the earliest Advocates for that | oppressed class of our Fellow-Creatures.| [2 lines from Psalms lxviii. 31.] | Philadelphia: | Printed by Joseph Crukshank, in Market-Street, between | Second and Third-Streets. MDCCXC.| 8vo. pp. [3], 4-24.   (743).

A Poetical | Sermon | occasioned by a | Disappointment in Love.| Preached in the Parish Church of W——, | by the Clergyman who met with the | Disappointment.| [2 lines of Verse from Phillips.] | Boston: | Printed and Sold at J. Boyle's Printing-Office in | Marlborough-Street. 1778.| 12mo. pp. [5],-6-12, and paper covers. (744).

The | Political Green-House, | for the Year 1798.| Addressed to the Readers of | the Connecticut Courant, | January 1st, 1799.| Published according to act of Congress.| Hartford: Printed by | Hudson & Goodwin.| 12mo. pp. 24.

A.B. (745).

> Contains poems written by Lemuel Hopkins, Richard Alsop and Dr. Timothy Dwight.

Poor Julleyoun's Warning to Children and Servants | to shun the Ways of sin, | and those particularly which | hath brought him to this doleful end. Published at his Deside in Presence of two Witnesses.| Boston: Printed for B. Gray and A. Butler. 19 Stanzas. [Woodcut at top]. Folio broadside. (746).

The | Poor Man's Advice | to his | Poor Neighbours: | a | Ballad, | To the Tune of Chevy-Chace. | New-York: | Printed in the Year M.DCC.LXXIV.| 8vo. pp. 19. (747).

[Cuts.] Predictions | for the | Year | 1783. Sold at the Printing-Office in Essex-Street, near Liberty-Stump. Broadside. (748).

The | Procession, | with the | Standard | of | Faction: | A Cantata, Recitative.| 4to. pp. [1],-2-4. (749).

> This burlesque, written by a Tory, was called forth by the occasion of the planting of the first Liberty Pole in N. Y. Copies of it were found under the front doors of many houses on the morning of March 5, 1770.

Quarter Day Exercises, Yale College, March 28, 1776. Hartford: 1776. 12mo. pp. 31. (750).

> Two dialogue, one of which is entitled *On the success of our Arms and the Rising Glory of America*. The speakers are Count Massilon, a French gentleman, and Narvon, an American.

133

THE REBELS | REWARD | or, | *English* Courage Displayed. | being | A full and True Account of the | Victory obtained over the Indians | at *Norrigiwock,* on the Twelfth | of *August* last, by the English | Forces under Command of Capt. | *Johnson Harmon.*| To the Tune of, All you that love Good Fellows, &c.| [Below in right hand corner] Boston: Printed and Sold by *J. Franklin,* in Union Street. 1724.| folio broadside with curious copperplate cut of the Battle in upper right-hand corner. (751).

THE RELIGIOUS Imposter Unmask'd; A Satirical Poem, in three parts. Part the first. [Ornament.] Charleston: Printed for the author. M,DCC,XCV. 4to. pp. 50, [52]. (752).

Page 25 misnumbered 23 and the error continued to the end.

THE | RETURNED CAPTIVE.| A | Poem.| Founded on a late fact.| [Six lines of verse.] | Hudson: | Printed by Ashbel Stoddard.| M.DCC.LXXXVII.| 12mo. pp. [3],-4-60. (753).

Another edition, Norwich: 1790.

A | RHAPSODY.| A | Poem.| New-York: | Printed by Hodge, Allen, and Campbell.| MDCC.LXXXIX.| 8vo. pp. [3], 4-19.
B. (754).

RHYMES Relating to the present Times, etc. Philadelphia: Printed for the Author and sold by W. Dunlap. 1765.
(755).

SACRED to the Memory of Dr. [E.] Wigglesworth. Boston: 1765. 8vo. Printed on last 5 pages of Nathaniel Appleton's "Faithful and Wise Servants," Discourse on Death of Wigglesworth. Boston: 1765. A. (756).

SAD AND DEPLORABLE NEWES from New England, Poetically Related by an Inhabitant there, and Newly sent over to a Merchant in London; Being a True Narrative of New-England's lamentable Estate at present, occasioned by many un-heard of Cruelties, practised upon the Persons and Estates of its United Colonies, without Respect of Sex, Age, or Quality of Persons by the barbarous Heathen thereof. With Allowance. London: [1675?] 4to. 8ll. (757).

Imprint cut from copy Christie-Miller Sale, August 15-17, 1916.

Saint Clair's *Defeat.* Folio broadside printed in three Columns. N. P. [Circa 1790]. (758).

A | Satyr on the Origin of the *Whale-bone* petticoat. 8vo. pp. 8 dated Boston, Aug. 2, 1714. (759).

A | Satyr | on the | Sweepers Courage | When put to the Test, | or | Military Sweepers Heroism and Pride | Exposed.| "What knows the Stripling of the Soldier's trade, | "Beyond his Regimentals and Cockade?"| By A. & B. Mechanics.| Printed by John Clean, at the sign | of the Water Pot and Broom,| in Sweepers Alley, | 1774.| 12mo. pp. [3], 4-8. (760).

"Saw Ye My Hero George; and The Rosary." Broadside. 4to, [Boston: *Circa* 1779]. [Woodcut Portrait of George Washington]. (761).

Select Essays, | With some few | Miscellaneous | copies of | Verses | Drawn by | Ingenious Hands.| [one line in Latin] | [Boston] Printed in the Year 1714.| 8vo. pp. 47. A. (762).

The Senators, A Poem: Or, A Candid Examination into the Merits of the Principal Performers of St. Stephen's Chapel. Philadelphia: William Goddard. 1772. (763).

Sensibility: A Poem. By a Young Lady. New Haven: 1785. (764).

A Serious Poem. Printed at Concord, by Elijah Russell, 1793. (765).

Serious Reflections on the Times. A Poem. By a Minister of the Gospel. Philadelphia: James Chattin. 1757. (766).

Sibyllæ Americanæ | genethliacum | Ludovico xvii.| Regni Gallici Delphino | Prognosticum.| *Philadelphiæ:* | *Apud* Benjaminum Towne.| M,DCC,LXXXII.| 4to. pp. 16. (767).

The Shop-Keeper, Turned Sailor, or, the folly of going out of our element. Ornamented with cuts. Philadelphia: 1818. 12mo. (768).

A SHORT AND BRIEF ACCOUNT of the Shipwreck of Cap. Joshua Winslow, | who was overset on Carolina Coast in Lat. 35, 30, M. N. on the 23d | Day of July, 1788.| 4to. broadside, 3 columns of verse.　　　　　　　　　　　A. (769).

THE SILVER-KEY: | or | *A Fancy* of Truth, *and a Warning to Youth* : | Shewing the Benefit of Money, and the Contempt of the Poor, under the Term of a | Silver-Key.| [at end *From your Servant,* | *Poor* George *Beverstock.*| [Boston: Printed and Sold in Milk-Street.| Broadside, Sm. folio printed in double column. [1774.]　　　　　　　　　(770).

A | SOLEMN FAREWELL to | Levi Ames, | Being a Poem written a few Days before his | Execution for Burglary, Oct. 21, 1772. Boston: Printed and Sold at Draper's Printing-Office, in N[ewbury-Street.] Broadside.　　　　　　　　　(771).

SOME CONSOLATORY Reflections and Lamentations Occasioned by the premature Death of three of the Children of Captain Joseph and Mr. and Mrs. Mary Hinckley of Barnstable, viz.: Hannah, who departed this life July 7, 1732, in the 18th year of her age; Samuel, who departed this life Oct. 14, 1733, in the 28th year of his age; Elizabeth, who departed this life Oct. 28, 1733, in the 21st year of her age. 164 lines. Folio broadside.
　　　　　　　　　　　　　　　　　　　　(772).

SOME CRITICAL OBSERVATIONS upon a late Poem, entitled, The Breeches, written by James Porterfield, A.B., and printed for the author, 1749. By An Inpartial Hand. New York: Printed and sold by Ja. Parker in Beaver-street. 1750. 8vo. pp. 20.
　　　　　　　　　　　　　　　　　　　　(773).
　　　The Poem by Porterfield was issued in 1749.

[CUT.] SOME EXCELLENT VERSES | on Admiral Vernon's taking the Forts and Castles of Carthagena, | in the Month of March last.| [Boston:] Sold at the Heart and Crown in Cornhill. [1741.] Broadside.　　　　　　　　　(774).

SOME POETICAL Thoughts on the Difficulties our Fore-Fathers endured in Planting Religious and Civil Liberty, In this Western World. With a few Hints on the present State of Affairs. [New Haven: 1774?] Broadside. Small folio. (775).

Some rude and Indigested Thoughts on the Terrible Majesty of God in the Works of Nature, particularly in the Phœnomena of Earthquakes: Occasioned by that Memorable Earthquake October 29th, 1727. New London: T. Green, 1730. 16mo. pp. [2], 12. (776).

Some | Thoughts | On | Education:| With | Reasons for Erecting a College in this Province, | and fixing the same at the City of *New York*: | *To which is added,* | A Scheme for employing Masters or Teachers | in the mean Time: | And also for raising and endowing an Edifice in an easy Manner.| *The Whole concluding, with* | A Poem: | Being a serious *Address* to the *House of Representatives*: | *Non solus is Reipublicae prodest, - - . qui de Pace Belloque censet; sed qui* | *Juventutem exhortaim, qui, in tanta honorum* Præceptorum | *Inopia, virtute in struit Animos, - - - &* ad Luxuriam *cursu ruentes,* | *prensat ac retrahit:* — — | *Nam omnium Regnorum & Populorum felicitas, tum maxime Reipub-|Christiane Salus, a recta Juventutis Institutione pendet; quae* | *quidem rudes adhuc Animos ad Humanitatem flectet; steriles alioquin* | *& infructuosos Reip. Munus idoneos & utiles reddit: Dei Cultum,| in Parentes & Patriam Pietatem, erga Magistratus Reverentiam* | *& Obedientiam promovet.*—| New York: | Printed and Sold by J. Parker, at the New Printing-Office, in | Beaver-Street, 1752.| (Price One Shilling) | 8vo. pp. 32. A. (777).
    The introduction is signed Philomathes.

Some | Thoughts | on Religion.| By a Youth.| Providence: | Printed at Shakespeare's Head, for the Author.| M,DCC,-LXX.| 12mo. pp. 24. A. (778).

A Song | Composed by the British Butchers, after the Fight | at Bunker-Hill on the 17th of June 1775. Sold at the Bible and Heart in Cornhill, Boston. Broadside. (779).
    Another issue probably printed in Chelmsford.

A Song composed for the Fraternity of Steuben | Lodge, No. 18, Newburgh, by G - - - H - - - S - - -.| January 18, 1791.| Tune—"God save the King."| 4to. Broadside. (780).

Song | made on the taking of | General Burgoyne. Broadside. (781).

A Song made upon the Election of | New Magistrates for this City.| To the tune of, To fair Ladies now | on land | [Also] A Song made upon the foregoing Occasion. [New-York: Printed by John Peter Zenger, 1734.]| Broadside. 1 p. 4to. (782).

The two "Virulent, Scandalous and Seditious" songs that were brought into question when Zenger, the New York printer, was arrested. They were ordered to be burnt by the common Hangman, Monday, 21 Nov., 1734. The New York Public Library possesses a copy.

Boston, April 2, 1750.| A Song | on the Remarkable Resurrection of above One Hundred and Fifty Thousand | Pounds Sterling in Dollars and English Copper-Half-Pence, which have | lain bury'd for many Months, attended with a strong Guard of Watchmen.| To the Tune of Jack the Piper, or any other that suits. [Boston: 1750.] Broadside. (783).

A Song | On the Surrendery of General Burgoyne, | Who gave up his whole Army to the brave General Gates, of glorious Memory, | October 17, 1777. Broadside. (784).

South End Forever [Cut] North End Forever.| Extraordinary Verses on Pope-Night.| Or, A Commemoration of the Fifth of November, giving a History of the | Attempt, made by the Papishes, to blow up King and Parliament, A.D. 1588.| Together with some Account of the Pope himself, and his Wife Joan; with several | other things worthy of Notice, too tedious to Mention. [Boston: *Circa* 1768.] Broadside. (785).

The | Speech | of a | Creek-Indian, | against the | Immoderate use | of | Spirituous Liquors.| Delivered | In a National Assembly of the Creeks, upon | the breaking out of the late War.| To which are added, | 1. A Letter from Yariza, an Indian | Maid of the Royal Line of the Mohawks, to | the principal Ladies of New York. 2. Indian | Songs of Peace. 3. An American Fable.| Together with | Some Remarks upon the Characters and | Genius of the Indians, and upon their Customs | and Ceremonies at Making War and Peace.| [Quotation of 4 lines] | London: | Printed for R. Griffiths, Bookseller, in St. Paul's | Church-Yard. M.DCC.LIV.| 8vo. pp. [3], iv, [1], v-viii, [1], 10-68. B. (786).

THE SPEECH of Death to Levi Ames. Who was Executed on Boston-Neck, Oct. 21, 1773, for the Crime of Burglary. 4to. [Boston. 1773] [Curious cut.] (787).

THE | SPUNKIAD: | or | Heroism Improved.| A | Congressional Display | of | Spit and Cudgel.| A Poem, | in Four Cantoes.| By An American Youth.| Newburgh: | Printed and Sold by D. Denniston. | 1798.| 12mo. pp. [3] 4-23. B. (788).

THE SQUABBLE, | a | Pastoral Eclogue.| By Agricola.| The Second Edition.| [Philadelphia:] Printed [by Anthony Armbruster] in the Year MDCCLXIV.| 4to. pp. 8. (789).

THE SQUABBLE; | A | Pastoral Eclogue.| By Agricola.| With a curious and well-designed Frontispiece.| Printed (from The First Edition.) By Andrew Steuart, in Second-street, Philadelphia. [1764.] 8vo. pp. 8. (790).

> The frontispiece, which will be found on page 4, is a rude cut representing "Thyrsis, with a Pr*sy*t*rian Nose," and "Corin, with a Q**k*ronian Nose."

THEATRE.| [On the reverse side appears the following:] Argument.| *The Town being collected in Faneuil Hall, Reso|nus addressed them on the subject of a Theatre, | greatly disapproving of one; and is answered by Mu|sacus. Parties growing high, Crites gets up, with an | intention to settle the affair, when Jove hangs out | his scales, to balance the parties, and both parts uprising, the multitude saw nothing but a blank.| n.p., n.d. 8vo. pp. 7. A. (791).

[CUT.] THEFT AND MURDER!| A Poem on the Execution of | Levi Ames, | Which is to be on Thursday, the 21st of October inst. | for robbing the House of Mr. Martin Bicker, and was convicted of | Burglary. Sold near the Mill-Bridge: and at the Printing Office near the Market. [Boston: 1773.] Broadside. (792).

THIS | POEM, | Humbly dedicated to Sir Q — C —o. at his Study over a | Pot of Charcole.| [Philadelphia: Anthony Armbruster. 1765.] Folio broadside. (793).

> A Lampoon on Isaac Hunt.

THE | TIMES, | A Solemn and Pathetic Elegy, | Addressed to the Inhabitants of | Newburyport, &c. Broadside.　　　　(794).

To ALL CHRISTIAN PEOPLE; | More especially those who take the | Connecticut Courant.| [Hartford, January 1, 1795.] Folio broadside.　　　　(795).

To MRS. MARGARET DUBOIS on the Death of her late vertuous Father, John Nicoll, M.D. 8vo. pp. 4.　　　　(796).

　　Signed "W. S." Published with *A Sermon on the Death of John Nicoll, M.D.* by Ebenezer Pemberton. New York: James Parker, 1743. The poem is found on pp. 29-32.

To THE MEMORY of that Faithful Minister of Christ, Thomas | Lightfoot, who fell asleep in Jesus, *November* 4. 1725.| [One line from Psal. xxxvii. 37.] | [Philadelphia: Printed for the Author, and sold by *Samuel Keimer,* in Market-street.] | Folio broadside.　　　　(797).

　　A copy of this scarce broadside is in the New York Historical Society.

To PERPETUATE THE MEMORY OF PEACE.| The Triumphal Arch, and | Looking Glass, or the Continent-| Al Mirror, humbly hop'd without an error.| Setting forth to view, [8 lines of verse] | [Rule] | [6 lines of verse] | [Rule] | [3 lines of verse] | [Rule] | [5 lines of verse] | [Rule] | [2 lines of verse] | [Rule] | [4 lines of verse] | [Rule] | [10 lines of verse, signed Crispianus] | [Rule].| 8vo. pp. [1],-2-8.
　　　　　　　　　　　　　　　　　　　　　　　B. (798).

　　In a short note at end the author relates that "In or about the year before the British took Philadelphia, the Author of the fore-going lost (out of a bad pocket) in manuscript, about an hundred Hymns of Praise to the antient of Days." And asks that if they were found that the finder "return it to any of the Printers in this City." He would "return grateful Thanks for the Favour done him."
　　This piece was undoubtedly printed at Philadelphia, Pa., about 1785. It seems to have escaped the notice of all bibliographers, although an important item relating to the American Revolution. In it are mentioned Washington, Wayne Greene Clinton, Carleton Arnold, George Third, Bute, North and others.

A | TOKEN FOR CHILDREN.| That they may know to avoid the Evil, | and chuse the Good.| Boston: Printed and Sold at the Heart and Crown in Cornhill.|　　　　A. (799).

The Tom-Cod Catcher. [Cut.] On | The Departure | of the infamous B[a]r [one]t. [1769.] Broadside. A. (800).

Tom Paine's Jests; | Being an entirely | New and Select Collection | of | Patriotic Bon Mots, Repartees, Anecdotes, | Epigrams, Observations, &c. | on | Political Subjects.| By Thomas Paine, | and other | Supporters of the Rights of Man.| To which is added, | A Tribute to the Swinish Multitude, | Being a choice Collection of | Patriotic Songs | Speak truth and shame the devil.| Seria Mixta jocis.| Philadelphia: | Printed for Matthew Carey, No. 118, | Market-Street. | 1796.| 8vo. pp. [3], 4, [1], 6-72. B.A. (801).
    Also 1794. ¦A.

The | Tragedy | of Louis Capet | Being a True and Authentic Narrative of the horrid and barbarous Execution of the late | unfortunate Monarch Louis XVIth of *France,* who was beheaded, on the Twenty-first of January, | 1793, conformably to a Decree of the National Convention on Suspicion of Treason.—Which bloo-|dy Transaction (it is thought by every true friend to American Revolution) will eternally disgrace the Annals of the | French Nation: And may his Death be as sincerely lamented by every *honest* and *grateful* American, as it is by the | Majority of the Citizens of *France.*—This Narrative, with the Poetry annexed, is puplished [*sic*] in this Form at the | Request of many true Republicans, and recommended to be preserved as a Memorial of that shocking and Melan-|choly Event.| Folio broadside [Springfield: Printed and Sold by Edward Gray, 1793.] A. (802).

    Contains the following poems: Occasioned by the Death | of Louis XVIth.; On the Decolation of Louis 16.; The | Queen's | Lamentations | For the Death of her | beloved Louis. | 17 Verses.

    Cuts of Louis XVI; French Woman of the Revolution, holding Musket; and Coffin of the unfortunate King.

    Other issues are, Boston: E. Russell, [1793.] Also Boston: Sold next Stump, of Liberty-Tree, [1793.]

A Tragical Account of the defeat of Gen. St. Clair by the Savages.| [Also] Battle of Bunkers Hill.| No place. Folio broadside. [Circa 1791.] (803).

141

[20 Coffins] A True and Particular Narrative of the late Tremendous Tornado, or | [view of Ship with all Sails set.] Hurricane, | [view of Sloop with all sails set] At Philadelphia and New-York, on Sabbath-Day, July 1, 1792 When Several pleasure-boats were lost in the harbor of the | *latter,* and Thirty Men, Women and Children (*taking their* pleasure *on that* Sacred Day) were unhappily *drowned* in Neptune's raging and Tempestuous *Element! ! ! ! ! ! !* —— *Tell* this *not in* | Massachusetts! *Publish it not in the Streets of* Connecticut! *lest their sober-minded young Men and Maidens should bitterly reproach thee in the Day of thy* Calamity, *and triumph over thee when* thy Deso- | lation *Cometh; and ask of thee, Where art thy* Magistrates? *Or do they bear the* Sword *of the* Lord *in vain? Where art thy* Watchmen?—*Have they deserted their* Watch-Tower? *Or have they* | *fallen asleep?*| [here follow 24 lines giving an account of the Disaster] [2 lines of Notes to the latter, followed by the Poem entitled, The New-York | Tragedy.| *Being a Relaion of the drowning of* Thirty | Men, Women and Children, *in the late* | *shocking and tremendous Tempest,* in | *that City* on Lord's Day, *July 1, 1792,* | *when taking their* Pleasure *on the Water! !* | —O Tempora! O Mores! [*The Serious reader may, perhaps, do himself a favor by turning to* Exodus, *Chapter* XX. V. 1, 2, 8, 9, 10, 11, 18, 19. Deut. V. 15.| Folio broadside. (804).

A True Copy of an Inimitable and Incomprehensible doggrel poem, sent by Parson All-Sense, alias Smallsense, alias Nonsense, to D. J. Dove, at Germantown-School. [Philadelphia:] Printed by Black-Beard, [Andrew Steuart.] 1763. Folio broadside. (805).

A True | Description | Of | A Number of tyrannical | Pedagogues, | A | Poem.| Dedicated to the Sons of H - - - - - d.| By Clementiæ Amator.| Printed in the Year 1769.| 8vo. pp. 8. A. (806).

[Cut.] Two Favorite New Songs at the American Camp.| Exhortation | To the Freemen of America.| [and] The | American Liberty Song. [1776.] Broadside. (807).

[CUT.] TWO FAVORITE SONGS, | made on the Evacuation of the Town of Boston, | by the British Troops, on the 17th of March, 1776. [Broadside.]   (808).

There are several issues of the above.

TWO POEMS. First, On a Soul pleading with God under a Sense of its Necessities. Second, Thoughts for a Lord's-Day Morning. Norwich: Robertsons & Trumbull, 1775. 16mo. pp. 12.
                                                                                          (809).

TWO SONGS | For the Celebration of the 4th of *July,* 1799: | Broadside, In double column of 12 Verses and Choruses. N.P. [Circa 1799.]   (810).

[TWO CUTS.] TWO SONGS on the Brave General | Montgomery, | and others, who fell within the Walls of Quebec, Dec. 31, 1775, in attempting to Storm that City. Prined and Sold next the Bell-Tavern, in | Danvers: Where Travelling-Traders, &c.| May be supplied with sundry Pieces on the Times.—Cash paid for Linnen Rags. [1776.] Broadside.   (811).

TYPOGRAPHIA.| An | Ode, On Printing.| Inscrib'd to the Honourable | WILLIAM GOOCH, Esq; | His Majesty's Lieutenant-Governour, and Commander in | Chief of the Colony of VIRGINIA.| .... | .... Pleni sunt omnes Libri, plenæ sapientum voces, | plena Exemplorum vetustas; quæ jacerent in Tenebris | omnia, nisi Literarum Lumen accederet.| Cic. Orat. pro. Archia.| ....| WILLIAMSBURG: | Printed by WILLIAM PARKS. M,DCC,XXX.| 4to. pp. [2],-iv,-5-15.   J.C.B. (812).

The first volume of verse printed in Virginia. It was written to celebrate the introduction of a printing press into the Colony by William Parks, and is one of the earliest books printed in the Old Dominion.

THE UNEQUAL CONFLICT. A Poem. Dedicated to the Honourable Memory of the Brave Officers and Privates who fell, nobly, in defence of their Country, in the Late Engagement with the Indians under the Command of his Excellency General St. Clair, November 4th, 1791. Carlisle: Printed by George Kline. 1792.   (813).

143

The Unfortunate Hero; A | Pindaric Ode.| Occasion'd by the lamented Fate of | Viscount *George Augustus Howe,* Baron of *Clenawley,* &c.| who was Slain in the Battle near *Carillon, July* the 6th, 1758.| [1 line from David.] | Together with an Ode, | on the | Reduction of Louisbourgh, | *July* 7, 1758.| [line from Virg.] | [4 lines from Horace.] | [line from Virg.] | New-York: Printed by *Parker* and *Weyman,* 1758.| 4to. pp. [3],-4-15.   (814).

[Wood Cut.]   Upon the Death of the Virtuous and Religious | Mrs. Lydia Minot, | [The wife of Mr. John Minot of Dorchester;] | The Mother of Five children, who Died in child-Bed of the Sixth; and together therewith was | Interred January 27, 1667.| Cambridge: Samuel Green, 1667.] Broadside.   (815).

A Valedicion, | For New Year's Day. 1763. Signed "Philanthropos." [Broadside.]   (816).

Verses | addressed by the | Carrier | to the | Subscribers | of the | New-York Morning Post, | and | Daily Advertiser.| *January,* 1, 1790.| 4to. Broadside.   (817).

Verses addressed to Mr. Elisha Thomas, Together with a brief account of his execution, &c. Portsmouth: Printed by George Jerry Osborne, 1788.   (818).

Verses *for the* Year 1790, | Addressed to the *Generous Subscribers* of the | New-York Weekly Museum, | *Wishing them a* Happy New Year.| 4to. Broadside.   .   (819).

Verses | Made on the sudden Death of Six Young Women and one Boy, who were | Drowned at Jamestown, Rhode-Island, July 13, 1782.| [Newport:] [Printed by H. & O. Farnsworth.] Broadside [3 cuts at top].   (820).

The Verses of the Printer's Boy that | carries about the Pennsylvania Jour-|nal, 1743-4.| [Philadelphia: W. Bradford. 1744]. Folio broadside.   (821).

New Year's Addresses, of the above and other papers were issued from year to year, to the time of the Revolution, the wording each year being different.

144

SALEM, June 25, 1773.| Verses on the sudden and awful Death of Mrs. Rebecca | Giles, Mr. Paul Kimball and his Wife, Mrs. Desire Holman, Mr. William Ward and his Wife, Miss Esther | Masury, Mr. Nathaniel Diggadon and his Wife, and Mrs. Sarah Becket, all of Salem, who were drowned | all together off this Harbour on the 17th Day of June, 1773. Boston: Printed and Sold in Milk-Street. Broadside. (822).

> Another edition with slight variation in lining of title. The first issue noted was printed by John Kneeland.

[CUT.] THE VIRTUOUS, Faithful and Loving | Wife's Garland: | Being a serious and solemn Warning and Caution to all false and treache-rous Husbands, &c. Sold near Liberty-Pole, 1795. Broadside. (823).

THE VOLUNTIER's March; being a full and true Account [of] the bloody Fight which happen'd between Capt. Lovewell's Company, and the Indians at Pigwoket. An excellent new Song. [Boston: J. Franklin, 1725.] (824).

> Probably the original issue of the ballad of "Lovewell's Fight." No copy can be located. Mr. George Lipman Kittredge in his Contribution to *A Tribute to Wilberforce Eames,* 1924, hazards the conjecture that the author was James Franklin himself. Joseph Jewett of Groton, also wrote a poem on this subject, and may be the author of the above.

VOX POPULI.| Liberty, Property, | And No Stamps. [Cut.] The News-Boy | Who Carries the Boston Evening-Post, with the | greatest Submission begs Leave to present the | following Lines to the Gentlemen and Ladies to | whom he carries the News. [Boston: Printed by T. & J. Fleet. 1766?] Broadside. (825).

[CUT.] THE WAGES OF SIN; | or, | Robbery justly Rewarded: | A | Poem | Occasioned by the untimely Death of | Richard Wilson, | Who was Executed on Boston Neck, for Burglary, | On Thursday the 19th of October, 1732. Boston: Printed and Sold at the Heart and Crown in Cornhill. Broadside. (826).

WAR, Temporal and Spiritual, Considered, dated Rowley, May 18th. 1762. 12mo. pp. 16. (827).

145

A WARNING PIECE.| A Poetical Thought, or Paraphrase, | Occasioned by that stupendous Dark-|ness or interposing Cloud, which obscured the | light of the Sun on the 19th day of May in the | present year 1780, which happened about the same time of the year, and on the | self-same day of the Week, as did the | supernatural Eclipse of the Sun, | at the Crucifixion of the Messiah: | A circumstance worthy of Notice. Broadside. (828).

Printed with "Bold Conscience and Old Self."

WASHINGTON. A Poem on the President's Farewell Address; with a sketch of the Character of his Successor. Philadelphia: n.d. 8vo. (829).

THE WIDOWED MOURNER. Advertisement.| [To The Widowed Mourner.] The Author of the following Lines, for some time after the | Decease of the truly excellent Lady, whose virtues he now at|tempts to delineate, fully intended, (as far as in him lay) to do | Justice to her very dear Memory; but the desultory state he has | constantly been in, since that melancholy event took place, has hi|therto prevented his carrying such his inentions into execution.—| In the beginning of the present month he composed the following | Lines, which are only a very small part of the intended Poem.—| To *three* amiable Ladies of his Acquaintance he had given copies | of what he had so composed; the contents whereof were soon com|municated, and applications for other copies were made, which he | could not find time to write out. He has, therefore, caused a *few Copies* | to be *printed,* for the gratification and amusement of the | Circle of Ladies he has the Honour to be known to; each of whom | he entreats not to permit any Copy to be taken from their printed | Copy; as the Poem is at present in an unfinished and incomplete | state. J. G.| Boston, 21st December, 1791.| (830).

On the reverse side of the advertisement the following headline precedes the text:

The Widowed Mourner. | *Ipse cava solans aegrum testudine amorem,* | *Te dulcis conjux, te solo in littore secum,* | *Te veniente die, te decedente canebat.*| *Virgil.*| "He on the desart shore all

146

lonely 'griev'd,| "And with his concave shell his love-sick heart reliev'd;| "To thee, sweet wife, he pour'd the piteous lay,| "Thee sung at dawning, thee at closing of day."| Warton's Translation.| *Oh Name for ever sad! for ever dear!* | *Still breath'd in sighs, still usher'd with a tear.*| Pope's *Abelard* to *Eloisa.*|

   t. p. w. 7 pages not numbered. Signature J. G. at end of lines on page 7.   A.

A YANKEE SONG. Printed and Sold at the Bible and Heart. [1775.] Broadside.   (831).

[Two WOODCUTS.] | Yankee Song.| Broadside, 4to. 18 stanzas and two choruses. Printed in double column. n.p. [Circa 1790].   A. (832).

THE YEARLY | VERSES | Of the Printer's Lad, | who Carrieth a-|bout the Pennsyl-|vania Gazette, | to the Customers | thereof.| Jan. 1, 1741.| [Philadelphia: B. Franklin, 1742.] Folio broadside.   (833).

   By Benjamin Franklin.

   The American Antiquarian Society has the issues for 1739, 1740, 1741, 1743, 1748, 1749 and 1752.

ZUM 29 STEN AUGUST 1773. [Memorial Verses.] Philadelphia: Gedruckt bey Henrich Miller, 1773. 4to. pp. 4.   (834).

The DAY of
DOOM:

OR,
A Poetical Description
OF
The GREAT and LAST
Judgement.

WITH
A Short DISCOURSE about
Eternity.

By Michael Wigglesworth, Teacher of the
Church at Malaon in N. E.

The Fifth Edition, enlarged with
Scripture and Marginal Notes.

Acts 17. 31. Because he hath appointed a day in the which he
will Judge the world in Righteousness, by that Man whom
He hath Ordained. ------
Mat. 24. 30. And then shall appear the Sign of the Son of
Man in heaven, and then shall all the Tribes of the earth
Mourn, and they shall see the Son of Man coming in the
clouds of heaven with power and great glory.

BOSTON: Printed by B. Green, and J. Allen,
for Benjamin Eliot, at his Shop under the
West End of the Town-House. 1701.

EARLY
AMERICAN POETRY

A COMPILATION OF THE TITLES OF VOLUMES
OF VERSE AND BROADSIDES BY WRITERS
BORN OR RESIDING IN NORTH AMERICA
NORTH OF THE MEXICAN BORDER

BY

OSCAR WEGELIN

VOLUME II
1800-1820

"Sweet are the pleasures that to verse belong,
And doubly sweet a brotherhood of song."—*Keats.*

SECOND EDITION, REVISED AND ENLARGED

NEW YORK
PETER SMITH
1930

EARLY AMERICAN POETRY
1800-1820

[AGG, JOHN.] The | Ocean Harp: | A Poem; | in two Cantos: | with | Some Smaller Pieces; | and | A Monody | on the death of John Syng Dorsey, M.D.| By the author of | Lord Byron's Farewell to England," "Pigrimage to | the Holy Land," and other pieces.| Philadelphia: | Published by M. Thomas.| J. Maxwell, Printer.| 1819.| 16mo. pp. [5],-vi-xii,-[1],-xiv,-xxiii,-[5],-xxviii,-[1],-30-182.   B.A. (835).

[ALLEN, BENJAMIN, JR.] Miscellaneous | Poems, | on | Moral and Religious | Subjects | By Osander.| [4 verses.]   Hudson: | Printed by Wm. E. Norman | No. 2 Warren St.| 1811.| 18mo. pp. [4],-7-180.   A.B. (836).

> Another edition. Hudson, New York: 1811. 12mo.
> Also New York: 1812. 16mo. pp. [4],15-180.   A.

[ALLEN.] United We Stand: | Divided We Fall.| A Poem.| By Juba.| [3 lines from "Cicero against Cataline."] | New-York: | Printed by D. & G. Bruce, | 29 Slote-Lane.| 1812.| 16mo.   Pp. [5],-6-52,-[1],-56-74.   A.B. (837).

[ALLEN.] The | Death | of | Abdallah.| An Eastern Tale.| Founded on the Story of Abadallah and | Sabat, in Buchanan's Christian | Researches.| New York: | Published by W. B. Gilley, No. 92 Broadway | Gould and Van Pelt, Printers.| 1814.| 24mo. pp. [5],-VI-192.   A.B. (838).

ALLEN. Urania, | or | The True Use of Poesy; | A Poem | By B. Allen, Jun.| New York: | Published by A. H. Inskeep, and | Bradford & Inskeep.| Philadelphia.| 1814. 16mo. pp. [7],-8, [1],-10-192.   A.B. (839).

> Page 8 is misnumbered 5.

ALLEN. The Phoenix; | or the | Mattle of Valparaiso.| A Poem | By B. Allen, Jun.| New York: | Gould and Van Pelt, Print-ers, 9 Wall-Street.| 1814.| 16mo. pp. [5],-viii,-[3],-10-37,- [1]. B. (840).

[Picture of eagle at top of title-page holding in its mouth a pennant, which reads: "Honour to the Brave."]

ALLEN, BRASSEYA. Pastorals, | Elegies, Odes, | Epistles | And Other Poems | by Mrs. Allen.| [Two lines from first pas-toral] | (Copy Right Secured.)| Abingdon, (Md.) : | printed by Daniel P. Ruff | 1806. 16mo. pp. [11],-10-163.

A.B. (841).

ALLEN, JOHN. Thoughts | on | Man's Redemption, | as exhibited by Christ; | Displayed on the plan of Grace reveal-|ed in the Gospel, for the hope of | Pardon, Peace and Salvation, to | the Guilty and Miserable | of the fallen race.| *Also.*| Deism and Eternal Decrees, | taken up and particularly noticed.| The subject concluding with an | Invitation of the Gospel Call, to all the ends of the Earth.| [2 lines from Isaiah] | By John Allen.| Utica: | *Printed by Merrell & Seward, for the Au-thor.*| 1805.| 12mo. pp. [3],-4-16. A. (842).

ALLEN, JONATHAN. A | Poem, | on the Existence of | God.| An Ode on Creation.| To which are Added | Several Hymns, | And an Eulogy on | General George Washington.| By Jona-than Allen, A.M.| [3 verses from Milton.] | Haverhill, | Printed by Galen H. Fay, for the Author.| 1803.| 18mo. pp. [5],-6-36. A.B. (843).

ALLEN, PAUL. Original Poems, | Serious | and | Entertaining.| By Paul Allen, A.M.| *Published according to Act of Con-gress.*| Printed by Joshua Cushing, Salem.| 1801.| 12mo. pp. [5],-v-vii,-[2],-x-xi. [2],-3-141. A.B. (844).

ALLISTON, WASHINGTON. The | Sylphs of the Seasons, | with | Other Poems.| By | W. Allston.| First American from the London Edition.| Boston: | Published by Cummings and Hilliard, | *No. 1, Cornhill.*| Cambridge . . . . Hilliard & Metcalf.| 1813.| 12mo. pp. [5],-vi-168. A.B. (845).

The First edition was issued in London, 1813. 16mo.

ALSOP, RICHARD. A Poem; | Sacred to the Memory | of | George
Washington, | Late President of the United States, and Com- |
mander in Chief of the Armies of the | United States.|
Adapted to the 22d of Feb. 1800.| By Richard Alsop.| [4
lines from "Charms of Fancy."]| Hartford: | Printed by
Hudson and Goodwin.| 1800.| 8vo. pp. [5],-6-23.
                                            A.B. (846).

    There are two editions.

[ALSOP.] The | Enchanted Lake | of the | Fairy Morgana.|
From the Orlando Inamorata of | Francesco Berni.| New-
York: | Printed and Published by Isaac Riley and Co. |
Lexitypographic Office.| 1806.| 8vo. pp. [3],-iv-vii,-[1],-
2-67. [Frontispiece engraved by Leney.]   B. (847).

AMES, JANE. Compositions, | Original and Selected | By Jane
Ames | Part Second.| Boston: | Printed by Lincoln & Ed-
mands, | No. 53 Cornhill, 1808.| 16mo. pp. [5],-6-106,-[2].
                                            A. (848).

ANDREWS, EDWARD W. An | Address | before the | Washington
Benevolent Society, | in | Newburyport, | on the | 22d. of
Feb. 1816, | by Edward W. Andrews, A.M.| Published by
request of the Society.| Newburyport: | Published by Wil-
liam B. Allen & Co. | No. 13 Cornhill. 1816.| 8vo. pp. [3],-
4-15.   A.B. (849).

ARMSTRONG, PRICE. A | Theatrical Elegy | on the death of |
George F. Cook, Esq.| By Price Armstrong | [Two verses
from Dr. Johnson.] | New-York: | Printed by Samuel Marks.|
1812.| 16mo. pp. [3],-4-8.   B. (850).

    This elegy was written on the death of George Frederick Cooke,
the celebrated actor.

[BADGER, JOSEPH.] The following lines were compos'd | by Mr.
Joseph Badger, a Day | or two before his Death.| [8vo. broad-
side. 5 verses, about 1800.]   A. (851).

BAILEY, ISAAC. A | Poem, | Delivered Before | The Philermenian Society | of | Brown University, | on their Anniversary, | September, A.D. 1812.| By Isaac Bailey, Esq.| Published by Request of the Society.| Providence: | Printed by David Hawkins, Jun.| 1812.| 8vo. pp. [3],-4-14. A.B. (852).

BALL, JONATHAN. Spiritual Experience | of | Jonathan Ball, | of | Millford, (N. H.) | (Caption title only.) 12mo. pp. [1],-2-12. A. (853).

BARLOW, JOEL. The | Columbiad | a poem, | by Joel Barlow.| [8 lines from Gierus. Lib. Can, xv.] | Printed by Fry and Kammerer | for C. and A. Conrad and Co. Philadelphia; Conrad, Lucis and Co. Baltimore.| Philadelphia: | 1807.| 4to. pp. [3],-iv, [1],-vi-xvi, [1],-2-454. [Portrait of Barlow and eleven plates.] A.B. (854).

> This edition, one of the finest Specimens of early American book-making, was issued at the expense of Robert Fulton, the Inventor.

BARLOW. The | Columbiad | A Poem.| By Joel Barlow.| In Two Volumes.| [8 verses from Gierus.] | Vol. I. | Philadelphia: | Published by C. and A. Conrad and Co. Philadelphia; Conrad, | Lucas and Co., Baltimore.| Fry and Kammerer, Printers.| 1809.| 2 volumes. 12mo. pp. [3],-iv-xiv,-[1],-2-258; [5],-6-218. A. (855).

BARLOW. The | Columbiad, | A Poem | By Joel Barlow.| [8 verses from Gierus.] | London: | Printed for Richard Phillips, Bridge Street, | Blackfriars. | 1809.| 8vo. pp. [3],-iv-xxxiii,-[4],-2-426. A.B. (856).

> Another edition. Paris: Printed for S. Schoell, Booksellev (sic), 1813. 4to. pp. [5],-xxii-xl, [3],-ii-,xx [1],-2-448. [Frontispiece.]

BARRY, GARRETT. Poems, | on | Several Occasions | By Garrett Barry, *Esq.* | [line in Latin]. | Baltimore: | Printed for | Cole & I. Bonsal and John Vance & Co. | In Market-Street: | 1807.| 12mo. pp. [3],-iv, [1],-6-101, 10 pp. Subscribers' names and 2 pp. of adv. A.B. (857).

Beauchamp Ann. The | confession | of | Jereboam O. Beau-
champ.| who was executed at Frankfort, Ky.| on the 7th of
July, 1826, | for the Murder of | Col. Solomon P. Sharp, |
*A member of the Legislature, and late Attorney General of
Ky.*| Written by Himself, | And containing the only authentic
account of the Murder, and | the Causes which induced it |
To which is added, | Some Poetical Pieces, | Written by |
Mrs. Ann Beauchamp, | *Who voluntarily put an end to her
existence, on the day of the* ex-|ecution of her husband, and
was buried in the same | grave with him.| Bloomfield, Ky.|
Printed for the Publisher.| 1826.| 8vo. pp. [3],-4,-[1],-6-
130,-[1],-132-134.   (858).

Benedict, David. A | Poem, | Delivered in | Taunton, | Sep-
tember 16th, A.D. 1807, | at the | Anniversary Election | of
the | Philandrian Society.| By David Benedict.| Boston: |
Belcher & Armstrong, Printers, | No. 70, State-Street.|
1807.| 8vo. pp. [3],-4-19.   A.B. (859).

[Benedict.] The | Watery War: | or, | A Poetical Description |
of the Existing | Controversy | Between the | Pedobaptists
and Baptists, | on the | Subjects and Mode of Baptism | By
John of Enon.| And so they Wrap it up . . . Micah | Bos-
ton: | Printed and sold by Manning & Loring, No. 2, Cornhill.|
1808.| 12mo. pp. [5],-6-34.   A. (860).

Bigelow, Jacob. A | Poem | on | Professional Life, | Delivered
by Appointment | of the Society of | Phi Beta Kappa, | at
their Anniversary | August 29, 1811.| By Jacob Bigelow,
M.D.| Boston, | Published by J. Belcher.| 1811. | 8vo. pp.
[3],-4-15.   B. (861).

    Another edition. Salem, 1811.

Biglow Samuel. The True Christian Delineated, in Plain and
Homely Verse. Boston: E. Lincoln, [Circa 1805.] 16mo.
                                                    A. (862).

[BIGELOW, WILLIAM.] Commencement, | A Poem: | or Rather | Commencement of a Poem.| Recited Before the | Phi Beta Kappa Society, | In Their Dining Hall, in | Cambridge, | Aug. 29, 1811.| By A Brother | [2 verses *one in Latin*] | Salem: | Printed By Thomas C. Cushing.| 1811.| 8vo. pp. [3],-4-8.

A. (863)

[BIGLOW.] Re-Commencement Commencement, again, Commencement in earnest, Commencement indeed, etc. Called also Censure, Scandal, Vague Report, Common Paine, Matter and Things in General, or What you please, recited before the associated teachers of Youth in the Town of Boston, October 30, 1811, by a Brother. Boston: J. Belcher, 1812. 8vo. pp. 11.
A.B. (864).

[BIGLOW.] Re-Re-Commmencement: | A Kind of a Poem: | Calculated to be recited before an "Assemblage" of New-England Divines, of all the various De- | Nominations; but which never was so re- | cited, and in all human probability | never will be.| By a Friend of Every Body and Every Soul.| [Line from Commencement] | [Line from Night Thoughts].| Salem: | Printed by Thomas C. Cushing.| 1812.| 8vo. pp. [3],-4-8.
B.A. (865).

BIGLOW. Sawney, | Redivivus et Restauratus; | or, | Micellaneous verses.| by William Biglow.|
> *"Obliged by * * * — * * * request of friends"* |
> Pope.
> *"Made, quoth the fellow with a smile, to sell."* |
> Peter Pindar.|

16mo. pp. [1],-2-36.
A.B. (866).

No general title, the above is printed on the first page. No. 2, Boston: Printed for the author. 1816. 12mo. pp. [1],-2-36.

BIGLOW. Select Odes | of | Anacreon.| Translated | Into English Verse, From the Greek, | as Published in | Dalzel's Collectanea Minora.'| By William Biglow | Cambridge: | Univ-Press . . . Hilliard and Metcalf.| 1817.| 16mo. pp. [5],-6-18.
A. (867).

[BLAUVELT, SAMUEL.] Fashion's Analysis; | or, The | Winter in Town.| A Satirical Poem | By Sir Anthony Avalanche, | With | Notes, Illustrations, Etc.| By | Gregory Glacier, Gent. | Part 1 | New York: | Printed for J. Osborn | No. 13 Park.| 1807.| 16mo. pp. [5],-6-84. A.B. (868).

BLISS, HENRY. The | Genius of Federalism, | A | Poem, | in | Three Cantos.| By Henry Bliss.| [Copy-right secured.] | Pittsfield: | Printed by Phinehas Allen.| 1813.| 12mo. pp. [3],-4-24. A.B. (869).

BLISS. Thanksgiving, | A. | Poem | In Two Parts | By Henry Bliss | [Copy-Right Secured, By the Author] | Pittsfield: | Printed by Phinehas Allen, | May, 1815.| 8vo. pp. [3],-4-24. A. (870).

BOLTON, NATHANIEL. A | Poem: | on | Infidelity.| By Nathaniel Bolton.| [4 lines of verse] | John Howe, *Printer*.| Greenwich, *February*, 1808.| 16mo. pp. [3],-4-16. A. (871).

[BOTSFORD, EDMUND.] Sambo & Toney, | A | Dialogue | in | Three Parts,| Georgetown, (S. C.) | Printed by Francis M. Baxter.| 1808.| 16mo. pp. [3],-4-17,-20-46. B. (872).

[BOTSFORD, MARGARET.] Viola | or | The Heiress of St. Valverde, | An Original Poem, | in Five Cantos.| To Which is Annexed, | Patriotic Songs, Sonnets, &c.| By a Lady of Philadelphia, | *Author of Adelaide*.| Louisville, Ky. | Printed by S. Penn, Jr. | 1820.| 18mo. pp. [3],-4-96. B. (873).

[BRACKENRIDGE, HUGH HENRY.] An Ode in honor of the Pennsylvania Militia, and a small band of regular troops under the Command of General George Washington, who in the depth of Winter in the year 1776 turned the tide of fortune against Britain, and repulsed her forces to the banks of the River Delaware. Albany, 1800. 12mo. pp. 10. (874).
Originally issued in *"The Death of General Montgomery, A Tragedy."* Phila.: R. Bell, 1777.

BRACKET, JOHN. A Hymn composed by John Bracket of Dudley, Mass. on the Death of his Wife. Sutton: 1810. 12mo. pp. 12. A. (875).

157

BRACKETT, J. WARREN. The | Ghost of Law, | or | Anarchy and Despotism.| A Poem, | Delivered Before The | Phi Beta Kappa, Dartmouth College, | at Their Anniversary | August 23, 1803.| By J. Warren Brackett.|—And this I know, that, where law ends, tyranny begins.| Chatham.| [3 lines from Virgil.] | Hanover; | Printed by Moses Davis, | 1803.| 12mo. pp. [3],-4-24. A.B. (876).

[BRADFORD, JOHN.] The Poetical Vagaries | of a Knight of the Folding-Stick | of | Paste Castle.| To which is annexed, the | History | of the Garret, &c., &c. | translated | from the Hieroglyphics of the Society.| By a Member of the Order of the Blue-String.| I neither write for fame or Pelf, | But merely do't to please myself.| Gotham: | Printed for the author.| 1815.| 12mo. pp. vi,-[7],-62. [Copper plate of binder's tools grouped together to suggest a human figure, "Knight of the Folding-Stick.."]

(In the same volume:)

The | History | of the | Garret, &c., &c., | translated | from the Hieroglyphics of the Society.| By a Member of the order of the Blue-String.| Gotham: | Printed by order of the society, in the land of Mosquitos, | Year of the Garret, Eleven Thousand Five Hundred.| 12mo. pp. [63],-143. [Folding copper plate, "The Garret in full Session."] (877).

> Probably printed in Newark, New Jersey. The first part contains poems on the binder's art, incidents of the War of 1812, and personal experiences, in a humorous view. The second part is a history of Newark, attempted somewhat in imitation of Diedrich Knickerbocker.

BRANAGAN, THOMAS. Avenia: | or, | A Tragical Poem, | on the | Oppression of the Human Species, | and | infringement | on the | Rights of Man | in Six Books, | with notes explanatory and miscellaneous.| Written in imitation of Homer's Iliad.| By Thomas Branagan, | Author of A Preliminary Essay on Slavery.| [2 lines from Pope.! | Philadelphia: | Printed for Silas Engles, No. 248 South Third- | Street; and Samuel Wood, No. 362, Pearl- | Street, New York.| S. Engles, Printer.| 1805.| 12mo. pp. [5],-vi-x,

[5],-16-358 and leaf of errata. [Frontispiece engraved by D. Edwin, Barralet, Del.] A.B. (878).
A New Edition. Philadelphia: 1810. 16mo. pp. [4],-5-324. [Frontispiece engraved by Edwin.]

BRANAGAN. The | Penitential Tyrant; | A Juvenile Poem, | In Two Cantos.| To Which is Prefixed, | Compendious Memoirs of the | Author.| By Thomas Branagan. | Author of "Preliminary Essay on Slavery," | "Avenia," &c.| [5 lines of biography.] *Bold in the Lord, I know his grace is free | Free for the vile, or it hath pass'd by me!!*| Philadelphia: | Printed for the Author | 1805.| 18mo. pp. [3],-iv-122. [Plate.] 2d enlarged, New York, 1807. 18mo. pp. [5],-vi-xii,-[1],-2-290,-[9]. [Plate.] A.B. (879).

BRANAGAN. The | Excellency | of | The Female Character | Vindicated; | Being | An Investigation Relative to the | Cause and Effects | of | The Enroachments of Men Upon | The Rights of Women, | and | The Too Frequent Degradation and | Consequent Misfortunes | of | The Fair Sex.| By Thomas Branagan.| New York: | Printed by Samuel Wood | For the Author.| 1807.| 18mo. pp. [5],-vi-xii,-[1],-2-308. A. (880).

BRANAGAN. The | Excellency | of | Virtue, | Contrasted with | The Deformity of Vice: | or, | The Armonitions of a Loving Father to his | Only Son, | On the most useful, entertaining, and interesting sub- | jects. Intended to inspire adults, as well as children, | with suitable detestation at the destructive practices | and delusive opinions of the slaves of superstition, | the votaries of fashion, and the vices of the present | age.| To which is Added, | A Terrestial Paradise, Displayed, | or, | The Road to Happiness and Heaven, strewed with | Flowers, and carpeted with Roses, &c.| By Thomas Branagan, | Author of "Flowers of Literature," "Political and Theological | Disquisitions," &c., &c., &c.| Printed for the Author by J. Rakestraw, | No. 190, North Third Street.| 1808.| 18mo. pp. [3],-4-228. [Portrait of the Author.] A.B. (881).

159

BRANCH, WILLIAM, JR. Life, | A Poem in Three Books; | Descriptive of the various Characters in life; the different | passions, with their moral influence; | the good and evil | resulting from their sway; and of the perfect man. | dedicated to the | Social and Political Welfare | of the | People of the United States. | by William Branch, Junior, | *Of Prince Edward, Virginia.*| [Line from Virgil's Geo.] | Richmond: | From the Franklin Press. | W. W. Gray, Printer.| 1819.| 12mo. pp. [3],-iv-xii, [2],-3-218 and leaf of errata.
A.B. (882).

BRASHEARS, NOAH. Political Poems, | by | Noah Brashears.| [4 lines from Churchill.] | Washington City: | 1816.| 16mo. pp. [7],-8-24.   (883).

[BROOKS, MARIA GOWAN.] Judith, Esther, | And | Other Poems.| By a Lover of the Fine Arts.| [8 verses in Italian from Metastasio.] | Boston: | Published By Cummings and Hilliard.| 1820.| 16mo. pp. [3],-iv-112.   A.B. (883B).

BROWN, ERASTUS. An Elegy | on the Death of Esther Brown, who died at Alford, Mass. April | 17, 1806 [torn] Erastus Brown, her husband.| 8vo. broadside, 29 verses in 3 columns.
A. (884).

BROWN. The Trial | of | Cain the First Murderer, | in Poetry, by Rule of Court, | in which a Predestinarian, a Universalian, | and an Arminian argue as attorneys at the | bar, | the two former as the Prison | er's Council, the latter as Attorney-| General.| Succeeded by hymns | and Spiritual songs, the meas- | ures of which are adapted to | some very pleasing and har|monious tunes, calcula-|ted for the entertain-|ment of Youth and | other serious | minded persons.| Composed by Erastus Brown.| [line from St. Paul] | Printed at | Stockbridge, (Mass.) | *For the author.*| 1815.| 12mo. pp. [7],-8-90.   (885).

Same, Bridgeport: Stiles Nichols, 1819. 12mo. pp. 32.   A.

BROWN, SAMUEL. Days of Seventy-Six.| By Samuel Brown, |
A Revolvolutionary Soldier, Chelmsford.| 26 verses of 4 lines
each, and one verse of 5 lines. [Also] Republicanism.| By
the same.| Poem on 36 lines. Small folio broadside, n.p.
[*Circa* 1809]. (885B).

BROWN, SOLYMAN. An | Essay | on | American Poetry, | with
several | Miscellaneous Pieces | on a | Variety of Subjects, |
Sentimental, Descriptive, Moral, and Patriotic.| By Solyman
Brown, A.M.| "To you, Americans! the Muse appeals; |
"For you she labours, and for you she feels"| New Haven: |
Published by Hezekiah Howe.| Flagg & Gray, Printers.|
1818.| 12mo. pp. [3],-4-191. A.B. (886).

BROWN, FREDERICK W. A. S. A | Valedictory Poem; | Addressed
to | The Inhabitants | of | Rainsford's, George's, Gallop's,
Light House, and Deer | Islands, | In Boston Harbor.| By
Frederick W. A. S. Brown.| Boston: | Printed by True &
Weston.| 1819.| 16mo. pp. [5],-6-52. B. (887).

BRUCE, D. Poems | Chiefly in | The Scottish Dialect, | Origi-
nally Written | Under the Signature | Of the Scots-Irishman, |
By | A Native of Scotland.| With | Notes and Illustrations.|
Washington: | Printed By John Colerick, | And Sold by the
Booksellers.| 1801.| 12mo. pp. [3],-iv-xii,-[1],-2-126-[11].
A.B. (888).

BRYAN (DANIEL). The | Mountain Muse; | comprising | The
Adventures | of Daniel Boone; | and | The Power | of |
Virtuous and Refined Beauty.| By Daniel Bryan. | Of Rock-
ingham County, Virginia.| Harrisonburg: | Printed for the
Author: | By Davidson and Bourne.| 1813.| 12mo. pp.
[15],-252, [1],-12. A.B. (889).

[BRYANT, WILLIAM CULLEN.] The | Embargo, | or | Sketches
of the Times; | A | Satire.| By a Youth of Thirteen.| Bos-
ton: | Printed for the Purchasers.| 1808.| 12mo. pp. [2],-
3-12. A. (890).

Bryant's first book.

161

BRYANT. The | Embargo; | or, Sketches of the Times. | A Satire.| The Second edition, Corrected and enlarged.| Together with the | Spanish Revolution, | and | other poems.| [dotted line] | by William Cullen Bryant. | [dotted line] | Boston: | Printed for the author, by E. G. House, | No. 5, Court Street. | [dotted line] | 1809.| Small 12mo. pp. [5],-6, [1],-8-35, [1]. A. (891).

[BUFFUM, GASKILL.] The | Surrejoinder; | or | A Short Remonstrance, | in | behalf of the Public, | against | Balance-Masters and Beam-Kickers, | for | intruding into the Balance-Masters play their pranks | and catch the applause of the multitude; | "shewing" | that both "scales" are too much incumbered | with vanity and ignorance, to weigh augu- | ments to any advantage.| By Rt. Hon. Gaskill Buffum, P. C. S.| [1 line from Job, xxxi, 6] | [2 lines from Prov. xxvi, 3.] | [line from Eccl. iii, 4.] | [line from Prov. xxvi. 5.] | Providence.| 1819.| 12mo. pp. [5],-6-11. A. (892).

BURGES, TRISTAM. An | Address | to the | *Washington Benevolent Society,* | Delivered to them | On their Anniversary, | Holden at | Providence, February 22d, A.D. 1811.| By Tristam Burges, Esq.| Providence: | Printed at the Office of the American, by Dunham & Hawkins.| 1811.| 8vo. pp. [3],-4-8. B. (893).

BURTT, JOHN. Horae Poeticae; | or, the | Transient Murmers of a Solitary Lyre.| Coinsisting of | Poems and Songs, | in | English and Scotch.| By John Burtt.| [4 verses from Gray.] | Bridgeton, N. J. | William Schultz, Printer.| 1819. 24mo. pp. [3],-iv-183, [1]. (894).

CADY, EUNICE. A Poem, in four parts. Composed by Eunice Cady, of Torrington. Printed for the Publisher. Newtown: 1819. 12mo. pp. 35. (895).

CALDWELL, CHARLES. An | Elegaic Poem | on the | Death | of | General Washington.| By Charles Caldwell, A.M. M.D.| Philadelphia: | Printed at the office of | "The True American."| 1800.| 12mo. pp. [5],-2-12. B. (896).

CAMPBELL, JAMES. [Cut.] Written and corrected by | James Campbell, | late of the Constitution: | in behalf of the brave Capt. James Lawrence, and Lieut. C. Ludlow, | on the Chesapeake.| Together with—Lines on the Death of Lt. Ludlow— Tune "Disconsolate Sailor." ☞ N. Coverly, Jr., Printer, Milk-Street, Boston. Broadside. A. (897).

CAMPBELL. [2 cuts.] Glorious Naval Victory, | obtained by Commodore Bainbridge, of the United States Frigate Java.| By James Campbell, a Boatswain's Mate on board the Constitution. Boston: | ☞ Printed, and sold by Nathaniel Coverly, jnr.| Corner Theatre-Alley. [1813.] Broadside.
A. (898).

CARPENTER, FREDERIC. American Freedom; answer to a poem by Charles Prentice of Brimfield. [Palmer, Mass., 1810.] 12mo. (899).

CARTER, BERNARD M. Miscellaneous Poems, | By | Bernard M. Carter.| [3 lines from Edinburgh Review, No. 63 p. 119.] | Philadelphia: | Printed for J. Maxwell, Walnut Street.| 1820.| 12mo. pp. [9],-6-95. B. (900).

CHANDLER, DAVID. The | Miscellaneous | Works, | of | David Chandler, | Elizabeth-town, | New-Jersey.| [Center rule.] | Schenectady: | Published by Jonathan Price.| Briggs & Stevens, Printers.| 1814.| 12mo. pp. 21. (901).

CHARLTON, JOHN K. M. Tales | and | Miscellanies | In Prose and Poetry.| By John K. M. Charlton. | *Author of several Dramatic Works.*| No. 1 | [10 verses from Creech]. | Washington, Geo. | Published By P. C. Guien, | 1820.| 12mo. pp. [5],-2-28. B. (902).

[CLARK, ASAHEL.] A Poem spoken before the Philomathian Society of Middlebury College. Middlebury: 1807. 12mo. pp. 12. A. (903).

CLARK, ISAAC. Clark's | Miscellany, | in | Prose and Verse; | By Isaac Clark, of Sumner | County, Ten.| Price one Dollar.| Nashville, (Ten.) | Printed for the author, | By T. G. Bradford.| 1812.| 16mo. pp. [17],-10-120. (904).

CLARK, VICTORIANUS. A | Rhyming Geography; | or, a | Poetic Description | of the | United States of America, &c. | Prefaced by | A Prose Introduction to Geography in General: | And Concluded with an | Appendix of Questions.| By Victorianus Clark.| Hartford: | Printed by Peter B. Gleason & Co.| 1819.| 12mo. pp. [3],-4-167 and leaf of errata.
A.B. (905).

CLIFTON, WILLIAM. Poems, | Chiefly Occasional, | By the Late | Mr. Clifton | To which are Prefixed, Introductory Notices | of the Life, Character and Writings, | of the Author, | and | An Engraved Likeness.| [12 verses of Latin Poetry.] | New York: | Printed for J. W. Fenno, | By G. & R. Waite.| 1800.| 18mo. pp. [5],-6-82-85-119,-[1]. [Portrait of Author engraved by D. Edwin.] A.B. (906).

COFFIN, ALEXANDER, JR. The | Death | of | General Montgomery, | or, the | Storming of Quebec, | A Poem, | By Alexander Coffin, Jun.| New York: | Printed for the Author.| 1814.| 18mo. pp. [3],-4-69, [2]. A.B. (907).

COFFIN, ROBERT STEVENSON. The | Printer, | and | Several Other Poems: | By R. S. Coffin.| [6 verses of poetry.] | Boston: | Printed by Farnham and Badger, Congress Street.| 1817.| 12mo. pp. [3],-iv-84. A.B. (908).

[COFFIN.] The | Miscellaneous Poems | of the | Boston Bard.| Philadelphia: Printed for the Author, | By J. H. Cunningham.| 1818.| 16mo. pp. [3],-iv-156. [Portrait.] B. (909).

Some copies contain frontispiece of "Barry" [a St. Bernard dog] saving a boy.

164

[COLE, JOHN.] The | Minstrel; | A Collection | of | Celebrated Songs, | Set to Music | Copy Right Secured.| Baltimore: | Published by F. Lucas, Jun. 138 Market St. | G. Dobbin & Murphy . . . Print.| 1812.| 16mo. pp. [5],-vi-x-[3],-6-316.
B. (910).

[COX, HENRY H.] Metrical Sketches by a Citizen of the World. Philadelphia: Printed for the Author. 1817. 16mo. pp. 60.
(911).

[CRAFTS, WILLIAM.] The Raciad and other occasional poems. Charleston: E. Morford; Wilmington & Co. 1810. 12mo. pp. 32. (912).

[CRAFTS.] (Sullivan's Island, | the | Raciad, | and | Other Poems, | Reprinted.| *"Quis novus nostris successit sedibus hospes?"*| Charleston: | Printed by T. B. Stephens, 8, Tradd St.| 1820.| 8vo. pp. [3],-4-100. B. (913).

CRAM, NANCY GOVE. A collection of hymns and poems. Designed to instruct the inquirer, and furnish the public with a small variety. Schenectady, 1815. 16mo. pp. 104. (914).

CROSWELL, ANDREA. Carmina Lugubria. In Memoriam Dominæ Rebeccæ Croswell, Domini Croswell Uxoris, nuper denetæ: Cum Hymno Laudis ad Redemptorem. Autore Andrea Croswell, V.D.M. in Bostonio. Broadside, folio. [Boston: Circa 1810.] (915).

CURRIE, HELEN. Poems, | By | Helen Currie.| [6 verses from Burns.] | Philadelphia: | Printed by Thomas H. Palmer.| 1818.| 18mo. pp. [5],-vi-viii,-[3],-8-150. B. (916).

DABNEY, RICHARD. Poems, original and Translated. By Richard Dabney. Philadelphia: M. Carey, 1814. 18mo. (917).

DABNEY. Poems, | Original | and | translated.| By Richard Dabney.| [3 lines from Antiphanes, apud Antholog., in Greek.] | Second Edition.| Philadelphia: | Published by M. Carey, | No. 121, Chestnut Street.| 1815.| 16mo. pp. [3],-iv,-[1],-vi-viii,-[3],-8-9,-[4],-14-172. B. (918).

165

D'ARCY, URIAH DERICK. The | Black Vampyre; | A | Legend
of St. Domingo.| By Uriah Derick D'Arcy.| (3 verses from
Bombast, Furios.) | Second Edition, With Additions.| New
York: | Printed for the Author.| 1819.| 12mo. pp. [5],-6-72.
B. (919).

DAVIDSON, (ROBERT.) Geography | Epitomized; | or, a | Tour
Round the World: | Being | A Short but Comprehensive |
Description | of the | Terraqueous Globe; | attempted in
Verse, | (for the sake of the Memory;) | and Principally de-
signed for the Use of Schools.| By Robert Davidson.| Stan-
ford: | Printed and sold by Daniel Lawrence, and Henry |
Hull, and John F. Hull.| M.DCCC.V.| 16mo. pp. [3],-iv,-
viii,-[1],-10-72. (920).
Stanford, (Now Stanfordville) is in Dutchess Co., N. Y.

[DAVIS, JOHN.] The Life Boat.| A Poem.| By a Member of
the Humane Society.| [1 line from Job xxix., 13.] | 8vo.
pp. [3],-4-8. A.S. (921).
N. p. n. d., but issued in connection with a Discourse before the
Humane Society. Boston: 1806.

DAVIS, MARTHA ANN. Poems | of | Laura; | An | Original
| American Work.| By Martha Ann Davis.| Petersburg |
1818.| 16mo. pp. [3],-2,-[1],-2-106,-[3],-ii-iv. B. (922).

DAVIS, RICHARD BINGHAM. Poems | By Richard B. Davis; |
with | A Sketch of His Life |—"A simple, solitary Bard was
he."| *New York*: | Printed and sold by T. and J. Swords |
1807.| 12mo. pp. [7],viii-xxxi,-[4],-2-145,-[3],-151-152,-
[1],-150,-153-154. A.B. (923).

DEANE, E. An | Oration, | Pronounced | At | Tivertown, | July
the Fourth, 1804.| By *E. Deane,* Esq | Published By Desire.|
Dedham: | Printed by H. Mann.| 1804.| 12mo. pp. [3],-
4-23. B. (924).

DEANE, SAMUEL. *Pitchwood Hill.* A Poem | Written in the
year | 1780.| By Samuel Deane, D.D. Printed at Port-
land.| 1806.| 12mo. pp. [5],-6-11. B. (925).
Originally printed in the Cumberland [Maine] Gazette, March 5,
1795.

D'ELVILLE, RINALDO. The | Hermitage; | or, | Alphonso and Agnes, | in two Cantos; | With | the Nun, | and other poems.| by Rinaldo D'Elville, | *author of Spanish Tales, Naval Discipline, &c., &c.*| New-York: | Printed for the author.| 1813.| 16mo. pp. [5],-6-44. (926).

[DENISON, EDWARD.] The | Lottery, | A Poem, | In Two Parts, | And | An Ode to War.| By St. Denis Le Cadet.| [Five verses, the first of which is in Latin.] | Baltimore: | Printed by J. Robinson, | For the Author.| 1815.| 12mo. pp. [3],-4-71,-[1]. A. (927).

[DENNIE, JOSEPH.] The | Poetry | of | the Port Folio.| Collected | by Oliver Oldschool.| Philadelphia: | Published by Harrison Hall.| J. Maxwell, Printer.| 1818.| 16mo. pp. [3],-4-144. B. (928).

Contains 3 Poems by Croaker & Co. [Drake & Halleck].

[DE PEYSTER, ARENT SCHUYLER.] Miscellanies, | by | An Officer.| Volume 1.| Dumfries.| *Printed at the Durfries and Galloway Courier Office,* | by C. Munro.| 1813. 4to. pp. [5],-6-277. (929).

All issued. Reprinted with additions. New York: 1888. 2 parts.

DEVEREUX, RACHEL. Poetical Pieces | Written on several occasions | of Unfortunate and Unhappy | Facts.| On the drowning of Mr. John Beers, and Mr. | Mulford Sweezy of Brookhaven, | Long-Island.| On the unhappy occasion of two brothers being | drowned in the south-bay of Long-Island.| An elegy to the memory of a friend who com- | mitted suicide in New York.| On the fate of the war: occasioned by an incident | which occurred in Great Britain.| An Elegaic to Mrs. Elizabeth Ketcham | To which is added | An Essay on Masonry | and an | Address to Spring | By Rachel Devereux.| Also the Portrait of Masonry | Composed by Brother Devereux.| New York: | Printed by L. Beach, No. 358 Pearl-Street | [1803]. 12mo. pp. [5],-6-29,-[1]. B. (930).

[DEWITT, SUSAN.] The | Pleasures of Religion | A Poem.|
(4 verses from Cowper.) | New York: | Published by Wiley
and Halsted | C. S. Van Winkle, Printer.| 1820.| 16mo.
pp. [5],-6-72. B. (931).

DINMORE, RICHARD. Select and Fugitive | Poetry.| A Com-
pilation:| [3 verses, anon.] | With Notes | Biographical and
Historical.| By Richard Dinmore.| Washington City: |
Printed at the Franklin Press | 1802.| 16mo. pp. [4],-v-288.
B. (932).
    Dinmore was the editor of the National Magazine. This volume
    contains a few poems by American Writers.

[DOW, HENRICUS.] A Poem, | in | Two Letters.| Middlebury: |
1803. 12mo. pp. 11. A. (933).

DOWNS, WILLIAM. A New Kentucky Composition of Hymns
and Spiritual Songs; together with a Few Odes, Poems, Ele-
gies, &c. Frankfort, Ky., 1816. 12mo. A. (934).

[DUER, W. A.] The | Pilgrims of Hope: | An Oratorio |
For the Clintonian celebration of the New Year.| Re-pub-
lished from "The American" | *of January* 1, 1820.| With
additional Notes and an Appendix, containing | "The Coal-
ition," | A political Tract, occasioned by the nomination of |
DeWitt Clinton | *As a Candidate for the Office of* | Presi-
dent of the United States, | *In the year* 1812.| [Line from
Dict. of Quot.] | Albany: | Reprinted by Richard & Van
Benthuysen.| 1820.| 12mo. pp. [3],-iv-40,-[5],-4-10.
A. (935).

DUNN, SAMUEL. A Poem, | on the last | Sickness and Death
of Mrs. Nancy Williams, | first wife of Capt. Zuri Williams
of Dana, and elder daughter of Mr. Joshua | and Mrs. Nancy
Chamberlain of Petersham.| Mrs. Nancy Williams died Feb.
23, 1815, aged 19 years, 6 months, and 12 days, and left an
infant son of four weeks old.| Composed at the request of
her friends.| Folio broadside of 43 Verses in 3 Columns,
signed by Samuel Dunn, Newsalem, January 1817.
A. (936).

DURFEE, JOB. The | Vision of Petrarch, | a Poem.| Delivered Before the | United Brothers' Society | of | Brown University, | on Their Anniversary, September 6, 1814.| By Job Durfee, A.B.| Providence: | Printed by Miller, Goddard & Mann.| 1814.| 8vo. pp. [5],-6-17. A.B. (937).

DUTTON, TIMOTHY. A | Christmas Hymn: | Composed and Written By | Timothy Dutton | of Northfield. | December 25-1810.| (2 quotations: the first prose in six lines; the second poetry in 4 verses.) | Brattleborough: | Printed by William Fessenden, | For the Author.| 1811.| 12mo. pp. [3],-4-22. B. (938).

DUTTON, WARREN. The Present State of Literature; | A | Poem, | Delivered in New-Haven, | at the | Public Commencement | of | Yale-College, | September 10, 1800.| By Warren Dutton.| [One line of Latin.] | Hartford: | Printed by Hudson and Goodwin: | 1800.| 8vo. pp. [3],-4-16.
A.B. (939).

DYSTER, JOSEPH JOSHUA. Five Odes, Written by Joseph Joshua Dyster. Philadelphia: Hall & Atkinson, 1817. 12mo. pp. 14.
(940).

EASTBURN, JAMES WALLIS, AND [SANDS, ROBERT C.] Yamoyden, | A tale | of the Wars of King Philip: | in six Cantos. | by the late | Rev. James Wallis Eastburn, A.M. | and his friend.| [12 lines from Wordsworth.] | New-York: | Published by James Eastburn.| Clayton & Kingsland, Printers.| 1820.| 12mo. pp. [5],-vi-xii,-[3],-4-339,-[1]. [Engraved title and Front by A. B. Durand.] A.B. (941).

EATON, THEOPHILUS. Review | of | New York, | or | Rambles Through the City.| Original Poems.| Moral, Religious, Sarcastic, and | Descriptive.| By Th. Eaton.| New York: | Printed for the Author, By John Low, | No. 17 Chatham-Street.| 1813.| 12mo. pp. [3],-iv-144. A.B. (942).
  The Same. Second Edition. New York: John Low, 1814. 16mo. pp. [3],iv, [1], 6-144.

EDMERTON, JOSEPH. A Frontispiece for a Meeting House. By Jonathan Edmerton of Malden. 8vo. pp. 12.   (943).

EUSTAPHIEVE, ALEXIS. Reflections, | Notes, and Original Anecdotes, | Illustrating the Character | of | Peter The Great.| To which is added, | A Tragedy in Five Acts. | Entitled, | Alexis, The Czarewitz.| By | Alexis Eustaphieve, | Boston.| The second edition, corrected and enlarged.| Boston: | Published by Munroe and Francis, No. 4 Cornhill.| 1814.| 12mo. pp. [3],-4-272.   A.B. (944).

EUSTAPHIEVE. Demetrius, | The Hero of the Don.| An Epick Poem, | by | Alexis Eustaphieve.| Boston: | Published by Munroe & Francis, | No. 4 Cornhill. | Sold also by E. T. Goodrich & Co., New-York; and | Edward J. Coale, Baltimore.| 1818.| 12mo. pp. [5],-6-256.   A.B. (945).

[EVANS, OLIVER.] Patent Right Oppression | Exposed; | or, | Knavery Detected.| In an Address, To Unite all Good People to | Obtain a Repeal of the | Patent Laws.| By Patrick N. Elisha, Esq., Poet Laureat.| To Which is Added, | An Alarming Law Case; | Also, | Reflections on the Patent Laws.| Illustrated with | Notes and Anecdotes, | By the Editor.| Philadelphia: | Published by R. Folwell, No. 38, Market Street, and G. Allchin, | No. 262, Arch Street.| 1813.| 12mo. pp. [9],-x,-xi,-[2],-189,-[1].   A.B. (946).

> Also attributed to L. Byllesby. The Second edition has imprint, Philadelphia: | Published by the Booksellers.| 1814.| Same pagination.

[EVERETT, EDWARD.] *Mr. E. Everett presents his respects to* | [Rev. Presidt. Kirkland] *and begs* [him] | *to accept a Copy of his Poem.** | American Poets. | n. p. n. d. [Cambridge 1812]. [No general title-page, the words in brackets are written in ink, and are different in each copy.] 8vo. pp. [1],-2-11.   B.A. (947).

> Another issue with two additional lines on first page and printed on heavier paper.   A.

FARMER, HENRY TUDOR. Imagination; | The Maniac's Dream, | and | other poems; | by | Henry T. Farmer, M.D. | Member of the Historical Society of New-York.| New-York: | Published by Kirk & Mercein, | and | John Miller, Covent Garden, | London. | William A. Mercein, Printer.| 1819.| 12mo. pp. [5],-viii,-[1],-x-xi,-[2],-14-163.   A.B. (948).

FELCH, WALTON. The | Manufacturer's | Pocket-Piece, | Or The | Cotton-Mill Moralized.| A Poem, | With Illustrative Notes.| By Walton Felch.| [4 verses of poetry.] | Published | For Samuel Allen | And sold by him and the Author Medway,—*Price 25 cts. single—2 D.* | *per doz.—and* 12 D. *per hundred.*| 1816.| 12mo. pp. [3],-iv-23.   A.B. (949).

FENN, JAMES. Hymns | and | Poems | on Various subjects, | Never Before Published; | Designed to promote | Religion and Social | Virtue in | Society.| By J. Fenn.| [2 lines of Verse.] | Printed by Van Vechten & Son—Schenectady.| 1808.| 12mo. pp. [5],-6-76.   (950).

FENN. A | Poem | On | Friendship And Society | *To which is added,* | Remarks on the British and French Nations, in | Relations to the Late Wars in Europe.| *With a number of short pieces* | In | Prose and Verse | By James Fenn.| [4 verses of poetry in italics.] | Schenectady: | Printed for the Author by Riggs and Stevens.| 1815. 12mo. pp. [3],-4-50,-55-132.   B. (951).

FENNELL, James. A New Year's gift; presented to the youth of both sexes. By James Fennell. Boston: John West & Co., 1810. 16mo. pp. 72, and paper covers.   (952).
    The printed cover is dated 1812. In some copies it is dated 1810. A.

FENNELL, JAMES. The | Hero of the Lake: | or | the Victory of | Comomdore Perry.| By James Fennell.| Philadelphia: | Published by Moses Thomas, No. 52, Chestnut Street. | J. Maxwell, printer.| 1813. 8vo. pp. [1],-2-7, and printed covers.   (953).

FENNO, JENNY. Original Compositions | In | Prose and Verse. | on | Subjects Moral and Religious | By Miss J. Fenno, of Boston.| Wrentham, (Mass.) | Printed by Nathaniel Heaton, Jr.| 1803.| 12mo. pp. [5],-6-116. A.B. (954).

"Jr" in the printer's name is blurred in the copy which I have seen, the first letter only being distinguishable.

[FESSENDEN, THOMAS GREEN.] A | Poetical Petition | against | Tractorising Trumpery, | and the | Perkinistic Institution.| In four cantos, | most respectfully addressed to | The Royal College of Physicians, | by | Christopher Caustic, | M.D. LL.D. ASS. | Fellow of the Royal College of Physicians, Aberdeen, | and Honorary Member of no less than nineteen | Very learned Societies.| [4 lines of Verse.] | London: | Printed for T. Hurst, Paternoster Row; and | J. Ginger, Piccadilly; | By J. Bensley, Bolt-Court, Fleet-Street.| 1803.| 8vo. pp. [5],-2-92. (955).

FESSENDEN. Original | Poems | By | *Thomas Green Fessenden,* A.M. | Author of | Terrible Tractoration; | or, Caustic's Petition to the Royal College of Physicians | [2 verses from Gifford,] | *Albion Press:* | Printed By J. Cundee, Ivy Lane | For T. Hurst, Paternoster Row.| 1804.| 12mo. pp. [5],-vi-xiii,-[4],-2-197,-[3]. B. (956).

[FESSENDEN.] Democracy Unveiled; | or, | Tyranny | stripped of the | Garb of Patriotism.| By Christopher Caustic, L.L.D. | Etc. [9 lines] | [1 line Latin | 4 lines English Poetry] | Boston: | Printed by David Carlisle, | For the Author.| 1805.| 8vo. pp. [5],-vi-viii,-[1],-2-220. A.B. (957).

Second edition same as the first in all respects. Third edition, with large additions. New York: Printed for I. Riley & Co. 1896. 2 vols. 8vo. pp. [3],-iv-xxiv, [1]-2-179; [3],-4-238, [1]. A.

FESSENDEN. Original | Poems. | by | Thomas Green Fessenden, Esq. | Author of Terrible Tractoration, or Caus- | Tick's Petition to the Royal College | of Physicians, and Democracy unveiled.| [2 lines from Gifford.] | Philadelphia: | Printed at the Lorenzo Press of E. Bronson.| 1806.| 12mo. pp. [5],-vi-xii,-[1],-2-203. A. (958).

[FESSENDEN.] The | Modern Philosopher; | or | Terrible Trac-
toration! | In four cantos, | most respectfully addressed to the
Royal Col- | lege of Physicians, London.| By Christopher
Caustick, | M.D. A.S.S. | Fellow of the Royal College of
Physicians, Aber- | deen, and Honorary Member of no less
than | Nineteen very learned societies.| Second American
Edition. | revised, Corrected, and Much enlarged | by the
Author.| Philadelphia: | From the Lorenzo Press of E.
Bronson.| 1806.| 8vo. pp. [5],-vi-xxxii, [1],-2-271. [Two
Plates.] A. (959).

[FESSENDEN.] Pills, | Poetical, Political, | And | Philosophical.|
Prescribed | For the Purpose of Purging the Public | of |
Piddling Philosophers, of Puny Poetasters, | of Paltry Poli-
ticians, And | Petthy Partisans.| By Peter Pepper-Box, |
Poet and Physician | [4 verses from Paracelsus] | Phila-
delphia: | Printed for the Author.| 1809.| 12mo. pp. [3],-
iv-xviii,-[3],-2-136. B. (960).

FESSENDEN. The | Ladies Monitor. | A Poem. | by Thomas G.
Fessenden. | [2 lines from Young.] | Bellows Falls, Vt. |
Printed by Bill Blake & Co.| 1818.| 12mo. pp. [3],-iv-xii,-
[1],-14-180. A.B. (961).

FIELD, SAMUEL. The | Miscellaneous Productions | In | Poetry
and Prose | of the Late | Samuel Field, Esq. | with | A
Sketch of his life and Character | By Rodolphus Dickinson |
Greenfield, Mass. | Published By Clark and Hunt | *Denio and
Phelps, Printers* | 1818.| 12mo. pp. [5],-6-205,-220,-207-287.
A.B. (962).

[FISHER —— ?] Poems.| O sweet, to stray an' pensive ponder
| a heart-felt sang. | Burns | Boston, | February | 1820.|
Note on opp. page reads: "Supposed to have been written by
Mr. Fisher, an Englishman, editor of the Albion News-paper,
New York. Feb. 1, 1824." 12mo. pp. [3],-4-63 p.
B. (963).

Foster, William C. Poetry | on | Different Subjects, | written under the signature of | Timothy Spectacles. | by William C. Foster. | [3 lines of verse] | Copy-right Secured.| Salem, | (N. Y.) | Printed by John M. Tooker, | for the | Author.| 1805.| 12mo. pp. [3],-iv-v,-[2],-viii-xii,-[1],-2-144.

A.B. (964).

Fowler, Benjamin. The | Lamentation | of | Benjamin Fowler; | Who has served faithfully in the American | Army eight years & four months—in which | service he lost one eye—and is otherwise so dis- | enabled in his health, as to claim the attention | of the generous public. Broadside.

(965).

Fowler. The lamentation of poor Benjamin Fowler, | who served faithfully in the American | Army, &c. Printed for the Author, who in a short time must have one | of his legs cut off on account of a Cancer that is on it. Broadside.

(966).

Fraser, D. The | Mental Flower-Garden, | or | Instructive and Entertaining | Companion | for the | Fair-Sex. | Containing (8 solid lines of contents) | By D. Fraser, *Teacher in New York:* | *Author of the* Young Gentleman and Lady's Assistant, | Columbian Monitor, Select Biography, &c. | (4 *verses*) | [Copy-Right Secured] | Danbury: | Printed by Douglas & Nichols | M.DCCC.| 12mo. pp. [7],-8-208,-[4]. [Plate.]

B.A. (967).

Freneau, (Philip). A Laughable Poem; | or | Robert Slender's | Journey | from | Philadelphia to New York, | by | way of Burlington and South Amboy.| By Philip Freneau, | Author of Poems Written during the American Revo- | lutionary War, and lately published in this City | by Lydia R. Bailey, in two Volumes, duodecimo. | Persons of the Poem.| [Nine lines for nine Characters.] | Philadelphia: | Printed for Thomas Neversink. | December 20, 1809.| 8vo. Title, pp. [3],-24.

B. (968).

Page 20 is unnumbered. The text varies slightly from the 1787 edition.

FRENEAU. Poems | Written and Published during the | American Revolutionary War, | And now | republished from the Original Manuscripts; | interspersed | with translations from the ancients, | and other pieces not heretofore in | Print. | by Philip Freneau.| [4 lines of Poetry.] | The Third Edition, in two volumes. | Vol. 1.| Philadelphia: | From the Press of Lydia R. Bailey, No. 10, | North-Alley.| 1809.| 2 volumes, 12mo. pp. [3],-ii-iv,-[1], p. numbered 4, [1],-6-280; [2],-3-302,-xii. [Front in volume one, Portrait of an Indian Chief [Tammany] engraved by Joh. Eckstein. Front in volume two, Perry's Victory, engraved by Joh. Eckstein.] B.A. (969).

FRENEAU. A | Collection of | Poems, | on | American Affairs, and a variety of other Subjects, | Chiefly Moral and political; | written between the Year 1797 and the pre- | sent Time.| By Philip Freneau, | Author of Poems written during the Revolutinonary | War, Miscellaneous, &c. &c. | In two Volumes.| [Four lines of Verse.] | Vol. 1. | New York: | Published by David Longworth, | At the Dramatic Repository, | Shakspere-Gallery.| 1815.| 2 volumes. 12mo. pp. [4],-v,-[vi],-viii; 13-188,-[4]; [4],-[9],-176. B. (970).

GENIN, THOMAS HEDGES. The | Fatal Disunion | and other | Poems | By T. H. Genin, Esq.| New-York: | Printed for the Author.| 1816.| 16mo. pp. [5],-6-24. B. (971).

[GILMAN, SAMUEL.] Monody | on | the Victims and Sufferers | by the | Late Conflagration | in | the City of Richmond, Virginia.| Boston: | Published by Charles Williams. | . . . | T. B. Wait and Co. | Printers.| 1812.| 8vo. pp. [5],-6-24.
B.A. (972).

[GIRARDIN, (L. H.)] Lines, | on Duelling | addressed | to the | Legislative Assemblies of America.| Translated, | From the Latin | By | L. H. G. | originally published in the Visitor.| Richmond: | *Printed by Lynch & Davis.*| MDCCCX.| 8vo. pp. [7],-8-23 and leaf of errata. (973).
Printed in English and Latin on opposite page.

175

GODDARD, SAMUEL. From the | Dead to the Living.| By Samuel Goddard, jun.| Agreeable to the discourse of Sally Metcalf, before her | Death.| [4to broadside, 20 verses in 2 columns. About 1803.] A. (974).

[GREEN, G.] The | Shunammite. | Recommended | to the | Candid perusal of all denominations | of | Christians | by G. G.——, M. M. M. | [Cut to represent the Sun] | New-York: | Printed by Southwick and Pelsue, | No. 3, New-Street.| 1810.| 8vo. pp. [3],-6-16. (975).

[HALLECK, FITZ-GREENE.] Fanny. | [4 lines of Poetry] | New-York: | Published by C. Wiley & Co. No. 3 Wall-Street. | Clayton & Kingsland, Printers.| 1819.| 8vo. pp. [5],-6-49.
B.A. (976).

[HALLECK.] Poems, | By | Croaker, Croaker & Co. | And | Croaker, Jun. | As published | In the Evening Post | [2 quotations from Shakespeare] | *Published for the Reader.*| New York— 1819.| 16mo. pp. [3],-4-36. B. (977).
<blockquote>Halleck was assisted in the composition of these poems by James Rodman Drake.</blockquote>

HALLING, SOLOMON. The | Messiah, | A Poem; | attempted in English Blank Verse; | from the German of the Celebrated Mr. | Klopstock. | by Solomon Halling, A. M. | *Rector of Prince George's Parish, Winyaw* | [3 lines from Holy Writ.] | Georgetown, (S. C.) | Printed by Francis M. Baxter.| 1810.| 8vo. pp. [5],-2-37. (978).

[HARNEY, JOHN M.] Crystalina; | a fairy tale. | by An American.| [4 lines from Collins.] | New-York: | Printed by George F. Hopkins.| 1816.| 12mo. pp. [5],-2-112.
A.B. (979).

HARWOOD, JOHN EDMUND. Poems | By | John Edmund Harwood | [2 lines from Juv.] | New York: | Published by M. & W. Ward, No. 4 City-Hotel | For Joseph Osborn | 1809.| 12mo. pp. [5],-4-107. A.B. (980).

HASLETT, ANDREW. Original Poems | By | A. Haslett | Author of | Various Miscellaneous Pieces | Baltimore: | Printed by R. Gamble,— No. 12 Light-street | 1812.| 12mo. pp. [4],-ii-ix,-[1],-14-95. B. (981).

HASTINGS, SALLY. Poems, | on | Different Subjects | To Which is Added, | A Descriptive Account | of a | Family Tour to the West; | In the year, 1800 | in a | Letter to a Lady | By Sally Hastings | [13 lines of verse] | Lancaster, | Printed and Sold, By William Dickson, For | The Benefit of the Authoress.| 1808.| 12mo. pp. [3],-4-220. A.B. (982).

HAYES, JOHN. Rural Poems, | Moral and Descriptive; | to which are added, | Poems On Several Subjects.| By John Hayes, A.B. | Proffessor of languages, Dickinson College, | Carlisle.| [2 lines of latin.] | Carlisle: | From the Press of A. Loudon, | (Whitehall,) | 1807.| 12mo. pp. [3],-iv-182. B.A. (983).

HAZARD, JOSEPH. Poems, | On Various Subjects.| By Joseph Hazard.| Brooklyn, N. Y. | Published by the Author, | [A. Spooner, Printer.] | 1814.| 16mo. pp. [5],-6-187.
B.A. (984).

Probably the earliest volume of original verse printed in Brooklyn, New York.

HEAD, JOSEPH, JR. Enthusiasm, | An Occasional Poem, Written by | Appointment of the Society of Φ B. K | And Delivered at Cambridge, | On the Anniversary of their Institution. | August 31st. 1809 | By Joseph Head Jr.| Monthly Anthology, | And | Boston Review | Vol. VII. No. IV. | For October, 1809.| Boston | Published by Thomas B. Wait & Company | Proprietors, Court Street | 1809.| 8vo. pp. [2],-239-245.
A.B. (985).

HEARSEY, FREEMAN. Miscellaneous Pieces in Verse. By Freeman Hearsey. N.P.N.D. Title on Cover. [Circa 1805] 12mo. pp. 36. A. (986).

HESTON, JAMES FRANKLIN. Moral & Political Truth; | or | Reflections Suggested | By Reading | History and Biography.| By James Franklin Heston.| [6 lines of solid matter] | Philadelphia: | Printed for the Author.| 1811.| 12mo. pp. [3],-2-401,-[1]. A.B. (987).

HILLARD, ISAAC. A Short | Poetical History | of | Fragments, | Collected from past and present times. | by Isaac Hillard.| Danbury: | Printed for the Author.| 1808.| Sm. 8vo. pp. [3],-4-12,-[1],-14-84. A.B. (988).

HITCHCOCK, DAVID. The Knight and Quack, or a Looking Glass for imposters in philosophy, physic and Government, an Allegorical poem. By David Hitchcock. Hudson: 1805. 4to. pp. 27. A. (989).

HITCHCOCK. The | Shade of Plato: | or, | A Defense of | Religion, Morality & Government. | A Poem, | In Four Parts | By David Hitchcock.| To Which is Prefixed, | A Sketch of the Author's Life | [2 verses from Pope] | [*Published according to Act of Congress*] | Hudson, | Printed at the Balance-Press. . . . 1805.| 18mo. pp. [3],-iv-107. A.B. (990).

HITCHCOCK. The Poetical Works | of | David Hitchcock | Containing, | The Shade of Plato, Knight and | Quack, And the Subtlety | of Foxes.| Boston: | Published by Etheridge and Bliss, | No. 12, Cornhill. | 1806. | Oliver & Munroe, Printers.| 12mo. pp [3],-iv-xvi,-[1],-18-164 and leaf of adv.
B.A. (991).

HITCHCOCK. A | Political Dictionary; | or Popular terms illustrated in | Rhyme; | With explanatory remarks. | for the use of Society in General, and | Politicians in Particular. | Part First. | by David Hitchcock, *Author of* the "Shade of Plato," &c.| [1 line from Pope.] | From Lewis's Press, | Lenox. | Henry Starr, Printer.| 1808.| 16mo. pp. [3],-iv-vi, [1],-8-113, and leaf of errata. A.B. (992).

HITCHCOCK. The Social Monitor; | or, a Series of | Poems, | on some of the most important and | interesting subjects; being a Contin- | uation of a former work, entitled | "A Poetical Dictionary, or | Popular terms illustrated in Rhyme."| By David Hitchcock, | *Author of the "Shade of Plato."*| [line from Hesiod.] | Stockbridge: | Printed for the Author.| 1812.| H. Willard, Printer.| 12mo. pp. [3],-iv-xvi,-[1],-18-155. A.B. (993).

[HOLDEN, OLIVER.] Sacred Dirges, Hymns, and Anthems.| Commemorative of the Death of | General George Washington | The Guardian of his Country, and | The Friend of Man | [Cut of Urn with 7 lines of text] [8 lines of Verse in double Column] | An Original Composition | by a Citizen of Massachusetts.| Printed at Boston, by I. Thomas & E. T. Andrews, No. 45 Newbury-Street.| [1800]. 4to. pp. [5],-6-24. A.B. (994).

HOLLAND, EDWIN C. Odes, | Naval Songs, | and other | Occasional Poems, | (never before published,) | by Edwin C. Holland, Esq. | *Author of several Communications under | the signature of "Orlando."*| (4 lines of verse) | Charleston, S. C.| Printed for the Author by J. Hoff, 117, Broad-St.| 1813.| (*Copy-right Secured*) 16mo. pp. [5],-vi,-[3],-10-40. B. (995).

HONEYWOOD, ST. JOHN. Poems | by | St. John Honeywood, A.M. | With | Some pieces in Prose.| Copy-Right Secured.| New-York: | Printed by T. & J. Swords, No. 99 Pearl-Street.| 1801.| 12mo. pp. [7],-viii. [1],-2-159,-[1]. A.B. (996).

[HOOPER, ROBERT.] An | Oration, | and | Poem, | Delivered Before the Government and Students | of | Harvard University, | At the Departure of the | Senior Class, | July 31, 1811.| [2 verses in Latin.] | Cambridge: | *Printed by* W. *Hilliard* & E. W. *Metcalf* | 1811.| 12mo. pp. [3],-4-24. B.A. (997).

   The Oration is by John T. Cooper, and the Poem by Hooper occupies pages 18-20.

[HOPKINS, JOSEPH R.] Hamiltoniad: | or, | The Effects of Discord.| An Original Poem. | In Two Books. | With | An Appendix. | Containing | A number of interesting Papers relative to the | Late unfortunate duel. | By a Young Gentleman | of Philadelphia | [10 lines of verse] | Philadelphia: | Printed for the Author.| Published and Sold by D. Hogan, No. 51, South Third Street. | August 3, 1804 | 8vo. pp. [5],-vi-40,-[1],-34-55. B. (998).

[HOWE, SOLOMON.] An Elegy | on the Departure of | General George Washington.| [Signed S. Howe, Greenwich, Mass., Feb. 22, 1800.] Sold by E. Larkin, Cornhill, Boston.| Folio broadside of 20 Verses in 2 columns. A. (999).

Contains also Howe's Poems, *The Divine Fair* and *The Beautiful Infant.*

[HOWE.] An Elegy | on the Departure of | General George Washington.| Sold by E. Larkin, Cornhill, Boston. [1800] [20 Verses in 2 columns.] Includes also Howe's poems "The Divine Law" and "The Beautiful Infant." Folio broadside. A. (1000).

HOWE. Divine Hymns. Greenwich: 1805. pp. 96. A. (1001).

HUGGINS, JOHN RICHARD DESBORNE. Hugginiana; | or, | Huggins' Fantasy, | Being | A Collection of the Most Esteemed Modern | Literary Productions.| Exposing the art of making a noise in the world, without | beating a drum, or crying oysters; and shewing how, | like Whittington of old, who rose from nothing to | be Lord Mayor of London, a mere *Barber* may | become an Emperor, | if he has but spirit | enough to assume, and talents enough, to support the title.| By John Richard Desborne Huggins, | *Empereur du Frisseurs, Roi du Barbieres,* &c. &c, &c | Trifles, light as air. | *Shakespeare* | New York: | Printed by H. C. Southwick, | *No. 2 Wall-Street.* | Most Excellent printer to his Barber-ous Majesty | 1808.| 12mo. pp. [7],-viii-288. B. (1002).

[HUMPHREY, ASA.] A Personal Satire: or Satirical Epistle written by a Schoolmaster in the Eastern Country to his Competitors, with a Short account of the occasion thereof. Boston: 1804. 12mo. pp. vi, 12. A. (1003).

HUNN, (ANTHONY). Sin and Redemption. | a | Religious Poem, | by Anthony Hunn.| Lexington: | Printed by W. W. Worsley. . . . "Reporter" Press.| 1812.| 8vo. pp. [5],-6-25. (1004).

The author was a resident of Harrodsburg, Ky. *Vide* note on title of Copy in New York Public Library, N. Y.

HUNTINGTON, DANIEL. A | Poem, | on the | Pleasures and Advantages | of | True Religion: | Delivered Before the | United Brother's Society, | in | Brown University, | on their Anniversary, August 31, 1819.| By Rev. Daniel Huntington, A.M. | Published By Request.| Providence: | Printed at the Rhode-Island American Office | 1819| 12mo. pp. [9],-10-23. B.A. (1005).

HUTTON, JOSEPH. Leisure Hours; | or | Poetic Effusions.| By Joseph Hutton, | Author of the Heiress of Sobeiski, Ardennis | School for Prodigals, | Castle of Althenheim | Fashionable Follies, &c. | [4 lines of verse] | Philadelphia: | Published by Hellings and Aitken | No. 40 North Second Street. | *D. Heartt, Printer.*| 1812 | 18mo. pp. [5],-6-305. B. (1006).

[HUTTON.] The | Field of Orleans. | A Poem | By the Author of Several | Fugitive Pieces | [6 lines of verse] | Philadelphia: | Published by W. Anderson, | 102, Cherry-street | 1816 | 12mo. pp. [7],-8-31,-[4]. B. (1007).

HYDE, ANDREW, JR. A Short Narration, | Respecting some | *Extraordinary Supernatural Operations* | seen and experienced in Lenox, | and its vicinity, | *Between the years* 1806 *and* 1811.| [double rule] | Also, | A Poem, *in Five Parts,* | on predestination, depravity, free- | grace, perfection, and formal wor- | ship.| [6 lines from 2 Cor. xi. 14, 15.] | By Andrew Hyde jun. [Rule] | *The* profits to be applied to missionary | purposes.| [double rule] | Pittsfield: | Printed by P. Allen, for the Author.| [1811] 12mo. pp. [2],-3-36. B. (1008).

The poem is found on pp. (20),-36.

JACKSON, SAMUEL. Poems. | By | Samuel Jackson, Esq. | [2 lines of verse] | Philadelphia: | Printed by A. Bowman.| 1816.| 12mo. pp. [3],-10. (1009).

Contains poem on *Lewis and Clarke's* Expedition.

[JANSEN, LEWIS B.] Ethick Diversions. | In | Four Epistles | to | Emphasian, R. T. | To Which is Added | The Convent | By Restore Estlack | *New York:* | Printed by T. and J. Swords, | No. 160 Pearl-Street. | 1807 | 12mo. pp. [5],-6-60,-64,-62-79. B. (1010).

JOHNSON, THOMAS. The Kentucky Miscellany. Lexington, Ky., 1789. (1011).

There were several editions of this title, the fourth appearing at Lexington, 1821.

JOHNSTON, ARCHIBALD. The | Mariner; | a | poem | in two Cantos.| By Archibald Johnston. | [4 lines in Greek] | Philadelphia: | Published by Edward Earle, Corner of Fourth and Library Streets.| William Fry, Printer.| 1818.| 12mo. pp. [9],-10-152. [Engraved title.] A.B. (1012).

JONES, ELIZABETH C. Poems | on different Subjects, | Original and Selected, | by | Elizabeth C. Jones.| [4 lines of Poetry.] | Providence: | H. H. Brown, Printer.| 1819.| 12mo. pp. [3],-4-48 and paper covers. A.B. (1013).

JONES, WALTER. A | Masonic Poem, | delivered at Mansfield, | (Conn.) | before | Trinity Chapter of Royal Arch Masons; | and | Eastern Star and Uriel Lodges; | on the Anniversary Festival of | St. John the Evangelist.| To which is added a | Eulogy pronounced at the grave | of | Brother Austin Stowell, | of Pomfret, (Conn.) Feb. 22, A. L. 5814.| Together With an Address | delivered June 30th, A. L. 5819, at the interment of | Brother Stephen Lewis, | of Ashford (Conn.) | by Walter Jones, T. I. G. M. | of Ashford Council of Select Masters.| Published by Request.| Brookfield: | Printed by E. Merriam & Co.| 1819.| 12mo. pp. 24. [cover title.] B. (1014).

JULAP, GILES. The Glosser; | A Poem | in Two Books | By
Giles Julap. | of Chotank, Virginia | Copy-right Secured |
March, 1802 | 18mo. pp. [3],-4-72.   B. (1015).

KENNEDY, THOMAS. Poems | by | Thomas Kennedy.| [8 lines
from Miss H. M. William's Julia.] | Washington City: |
Printed by Daniel Rapine, | For the Author.| 1816.| 12mo.
pp. [3],-4-7, [2],-1, [1],-12-334.   A.B. (1016).

KENNEDY. Songs | of | Love and Liberty | By Thomas Ken-
nedy | [8 verses from Moores legacy] | Washington City |
Printed by Daniel Rapine | 1817| 12mo. pp. [3],-4-98.
                                                 B. (1017).

[KILTY, WILLIAM.] The | Vision | of Dan Crocker | A Poem |
In Three Parts | [Quotation in Latin, Apertum] | Baltimore: |
Printed for the Author.| G. Dobbin and Murphy, Print.|
[1814.] 12mo. pp. [3],-4-20,-23-24,-21-22,-25-71.
                                                 B. (1018).

KIMMENS, HUGH. The | Number | of the | Beast | By | Hugh
Kimmens, | *Author of "The Latter Day Glory, or, Man of
Sin | made manifest.*| [2 verses] | New York | Printed for
the author | Southwick and Hardcastle, printers. | No. 2,
Wall-Street.| 1806.| 8vo. pp. [3],-6-31,-[1].   B. (1019).

KNIGHT, HENRY COGGSWELL. The | Cypriad | in two cantos: |
with other | Poems and Translations.| By Henry C. Knight.|
[1 line from Ovid.] | Boston: | J. Belcher, Print.| 1809.|
8vo. pp. [7],-8-68.   A.B. (1020).

[KNIGHT] TWILIGHT; | a Poem, | spoken at Litchfield, July 4th,
1812. | by a student at Law.| [2 lines from Milton] | New-
York: | Printed by Collins and Co.| No. 189, Pearl-Street.|
1813.| 12mo. pp. [5],-6-48.   A. (1021).

KNIGHT. The | Broken Harp; | Poems | By H. C. Knight |
Philadelphia: | Published by J. Conrad and Co.| 1815.|
18mo. pp. [5],-vi-176.   A.B. (1022).

183

[KNOX, M.] THE | CLERICAL CANDIDATES.| A Poem.| [4 lines from Churchill] | [one line from Hor.] | *Washington City, Nov.* 14, 1801.| 8vo. pp. [5],-6-32.   (1023).

> A Poetical Skit, satirizing the scramble of Clergymen for the positions of Chaplains to Congress.

LADD, JOHN. Lyric Poems, | Chiefly in Two Books, | Never before published.| [9 lines] | By John Ladd.| [3 lines from Apocalypse.] | Schenectady: | Printed for the Author.| 1814.| 12mo. pp. [3],-iv,-[1],-6-127,-[5]. N.Y.P.L. (1024).

LAKE, WILLIAM. The | Parnassian Pilgrim; | or the | Posthumous Works | of the late | Mr. William Lake. | with a Sketch of | His Life. | [4 lines of Verse] | Printed at the Balance-Press. | Hudson. . . . . 1807.| 12mo. pp. [5],-6-184.
                                              A.B. (1025).

LAMB, NEHEMIAH. Hymns and Poems, | on | Various Subjects.| by Nehemiah Lamb.| [12 lines of Verse] | Utica: | Printed for the Author, by T. Walker.| January-1807.| 12mo. pp. [3],-4-36.   (1026).

LAMONT, ENEAS. Poems and Tales in Verse by Mrs. Eneas Lamont. New York: 1819.   (1026B).

[LARD, REBECCA HAMMOND.] Miscellaneous | Poems | on | Moral and Religious | Subjects | By a Lady | Woodstock | Printed by David Watson | 1820.| 12mo. pp. [3],-iv-143.
                                              B. (1027).

LARD. The | Banks | of | The Ohio.| A Poem.| By Mrs. Lard.| Albany: | Printed by John C. Johns [rest of line destroyed] | 1823.| 8vo. pp. [3],-4-16.   B. (1028).

> Copy seen lacked part of first [title] leaf and also parts of last 2 leaves.

LATHROP, JOHN. The | Speech | of | Cannonicus, | or an | Indian Tradition: | A Poem | with Explanatory notes | [3 verses in Latin from Ovid] | By John Lathrop, A.M.| Calcutta: | Printed by Thomas Hollingberry | Hircarrah Press | 1802.| 4to. pp. [5],-iv-xi,-[2],-2-24,-[17].   A.B. (1029).

Same, Boston: 1803. pp. 40.   A.

LATHROP. A Monody, sacred to the memory of the Rev. John Lovejoy Abbott . . . who died October 17, 1814, by John Lathrop, Jun. Boston: Monroe, 1815. 8vo. pp. 16.

A. (1030).

[LAW, THOMAS.] Ballston | Springs. | [line in Latin.] | [4 lines of Verse.] | New-York: | Printed by S. Gould, opposite the City-Hall.| 1806.| 12mo. pp. [6],-7-48. Additions | to | Ballston Springs.| [5],-6-46. B. (1031).

LAWSON, JOHN. The Maniac and other Poems by John Lawson. Philadelphia: 1811. 16mo. pp. 101. A.B. (1032).

LEE, CHAUNCEY. The | Trial of Virtue, | A | Sacred Poem; | being | a paraphrase of the whole | Book of Job, | and | Designed as an explanatory Comment upon the | Divine Original, |interspersed with Critical Notes upon a Variety | of its passages. | in Six parts. | To which is annexed, | A dissertation upon the Book of Job. | by Chauncey Lee, A.M. | Pastor of a Church in Colebrook.| [2 lines from James.] | Hartford: | Printed by Lincoln and Gleason.| 1806.| 12mo. pp. [3],-iv-v, [2],-8-226. A.B. (1033).

LEWIS, ELDAD. An | Eulogy, | on the | Life and Character of His | Excellency | George Washington, Esqr. | Late President of the United States | Delivered at Lenox, February, 22, 1800 | By Eldad Lewis, Esquire | Published at the request of the Audience | [1 verse from Young]. | Pittsfield: (Mass) | Printed by Chester Smith, | March, 1800 | 16mo. pp. [3],-4-20. B. (1034).

[LINCOLN, ENOCH.] The | Village; | A Poem. | with an appendix.| Portland: | Published by Edward Little and Co.| 1816.| C. Norris & Co., printers.| 16mo. pp. [9],-10-180.

B.A. (1035).

LINN, JOHN BLAIR. The | Death of Washington. | A Poem. | in imitation of the Manner of Ossian. | by Rev. John Blair Linn, A.M. | Minister of the First Presbyterian Congregation of | Philadelphia.| [10 lines from Mason.] Philadelphia: | Printed by John Ormrod, No. 41 Chestnut-Street.| 1800.| 8vo. pp. [3],-iv,-[1],-6-24. 2 L A. (1036).

LINN. The Powers of Genius, | A Poem, | in Three Parts. | by John Blair Linn, A.M. | Co-Pastor of the First Presbyterian | Church in the City of Philadelphia. | [4 lines from Horace] | Philadelphia: | Published by | Asbury Dickens, opposite Christ-Church: | H. Maxwell, Printer, Columbia-House. 1801.| 12mo. pp. [5],-6-127.   B. (1037).

    Second edition. Philadelphia: 1802. 12mo. pp. [5], 6-191. [3 plates.]   A.

    Another edition. London: 1804. 12mo. pp. [5],-IV-XV, [2], 2-26-155. [3 plates.]

LINN. Valerian, | A Narrative Poem: | intended, in part, to describe | the Early Persecutions of Christians, | and rapidly to | illustrate the influence of Christianity | on the | Manners of Nations. | by John Blair Linn, D.D. | Late Pastor of the First Presbyterian Congregation, in Philadelphia. | With a Sketch | of the | Life and Character of the Author.| Phila-delphia, | Printed by Thomas and George Palmer, | 116, High Street.| 1805.| 4to. pp. [3],-iv-xxvi, [3],-2-97. [Sketch of Author is by Cr. Brockden Brown.] [Portrait Silhouette of the author eng. by B. Tanner.]   A.B. (1038).

[LISLE, HENRY M.] Milton Hill. A Poem. Boston: E. Lin-coln, 1803. 4to. pp. 15.   (1039).

LITTELL, WILLIAM. Festoons of Fancy, Consisting of Compo-sitions Amatory, Sentimental and Humorous, in verse and Prose. Louisville: From the Press of William Farquar, 1814. 12mo. pp. 179, [1].   (1040).

[LITTLEFORD, MRS. ——?] The Wreath; | or | Verses on Vari-ous Subjects | By a Lady of Richmond | Second Edition— Enlarged.| *"For gain, not glory, wing thy daring flight."*| Richmond: | *Printed by Samuel Shepard & Co.*| 1828.| 16mo. pp. [11],-8-132.   B. (1041).

LIVINGSTON, ANN HUME SHIPPEN. Sacred Records | abridged in verse. | Consisting of | *Some of the Parables and Miracles,* | *The Life, Death, Resurrection and Ascension* | of the | Blessed

Saviour.| By Ann Hume Shippen Livingston.| Philadelphia:
| printed and published for the author, | By J. S. Manning,
No. 13 South Sixth street.| 1817. 12mo. pp. [3],-iv-124.

A.B. (1042).

[LOCHART, HAMILTON.] The | True Republican; | or, a Dialogue
between | The King and the Farmer, | by way of argument; |
in which both their Justifications are Maintained | and their
objections formed to their different Attachments. | in which
also is discovered, | The Early, the Present, and distressed
situa- | tion of Great Britain and Ireland.| Together with |
The rise and progress of the great | Antichrist: | Who, and
where he is: as also distinguishing | the names and characters
of the principal | Members who help to complete that great |
Body. Likewise, briefly discovering a com- | phrensive view
of his Bride the Church to | whom he is espoused.| The Vol-
unteer's Address to the Irish Parlia- | ment before the Union.|
The return of their | Answer, and Form of Redress. With |
The Hint of Prejudice, | The Sinner's Poem, | And, a Second
Dialogue between the Farmer | and his wife, after his escape
from the King | and his Nobles.| *Carefully Considered and
duly composed in Verse.*| By Hamilton Lochart, *School-
master.*| *Sadsbury township, Chester County.*| Printed for
the author, 1806.| 12mo. pp. [2],-iii,-vi,-[1],-2-153.

(1043).

LOMAX, JUDITH. The | Notes | of an | American Lyre. | By
Judith Lomax, | A Native of the State of Virginia.| "Vive
La Bagatelle."| Richmond: | Printed by Samuel Pleasants, |
near the Market Bridge.| 1813.| Sm. 12mo. pp. [8],-9-70.
[p. 54 misprinted 34.]   B. (1044).
        Dedicated to Thos. Jefferson.

[LONGSTREET, AUGUSTUS BALDWIN.] Patriotic | Effusions; | By
Bob Short | New York: | Published by L. and F. Lockwood |
No. 154 Broadway.| 1819.| 12mo. pp. [3],-6-46,-[1].

B. (1045).

LOVE, CHARLES. A | Poem | on the | Death of General | George
Washington. | Late President of the | United States | in two
books.| By Charles Love | [1 verse in Latin] | [Copy-right
secured according to law.] Alexandria, Virginia, | A.D.
M, DCCC.| 12mo. pp. [7],-8-60.   B. (1046).

[LOVELAND, SAMUEL C.] A | Plain Answer | to | "A Sermon, |
Delivered at Rutland, West-Parish, | in the Year 1805;"|
Entitled, | "Universal Salvation: | A Very Ancient Doctrine;
With | Some Accounts of the Life, And | Character Of Its |
Author, | By Lemuel Haynes, A.M." | In Prose And Poetic
Composition.| [Quotation from the Bible] | Weathersfield,
Vt.| Printed by Eddy and Patrick.| 1815.| 12mo. pp. 27.
                                                  A. (1047).

LOVELAND. A Short poem, Containing a Descant on the Universal
Plan. Also, The Wrestler, who found an Evil Beast, Con-
tended with him and threw him, being an answer to Peck's
Poem on the Universal Plan. By Samuel C. Loveland.
Weathersfield, Vt. Eddy and Patrick, [circa 1815] 16mo.
pp. 16.   (1048).

[LOVETT, JOHN.] A | Tribute | to | Washington, | for | Febru-
ary 22d, 1800 | [5 lines in Latin from Horace] | Troy |
Printed by R. Moffitt & Co. | 1800.| Lg. 12mo. pp. [5],-6-15.
                                                  B. (1049).

[LOVETT.] Washington's Birthday: | an | Historical Poem, |
with | Notes and Appendix | [5 lines in Latin from Horace
and translations] | By a Washingtonian | Albany: | Printed
and Published by E. and E. Hosford. | 1812 | [Copy-Right
Secured.] | 12mo. pp. [3],-iv-55,-[1],-5-6,-1-4,7--11
                                                  A.B. (1050).

LOW, SAMUEL. Poems, | By | Samuel Low. | [3 lines] | In Two
Volumes | vol. 1.| New York: | Printed by T. & J. Swords,
No. 99 Pearl-Street. | 1800 | 2 volumes. 12mo. pp. [9],-10-
168; [15],-16-168.   A.B. (1051).

[Low.]   An | Oration, | Delivered | In St. Paul's Church, | on |
The Fourth of July, 1800: | Being | The Twenty-fourth anni-
versary of our independence: | Before | The General Society
of Mechanics & Tradesmen, | Tammany Society or Columbian
Order, | and other | Associations and Citizens | By M. L.
Davis, | *Of the General Society of Mechanics & Tradesmen* |
New-York: | Printed By W. A. Davis, Greenwich-Street |
1800 | 12mo. pp. [5],-6-21,-[3].   A.B. (1052).
  Poem by Samuel Low is on the last 3 pages.

LYON, THEOPHILUS.   A | Poem, | on the | Lord's Day: | together
with | acrostics | on | General Washington | and | President
Adams.| By Theophilus Lyon, of Hopkinton, | Massa-
chusetts: | Printed-1801.| 12mo. pp. 8.   A. (1053).

LYON.   Written by Theophilus Lyon, of Hopkinton, County of
Mid- | dlesex.| Remember the Sabbath Day and keep it holy,
&c.|. [folio broadside, 35 verses in 2 col.].   A. (1054).

[McCoy, JOSEPH.]   The | Frontier Maid; | or, | A Tale of
Wyoming: | A Poem, | In five cantos.| Wilkesbarre, *Penn.* |
Printed by Steuben Butler & Samuel Maffet.| 1819.| 12mo.
pp. [5],-6-208,-[1].   B. (1054B).

M'KINNON, JOHN D.   Descriptive Poems, | By | John D. M'Kin-
non. | Containing | Picturesque Views | of the | State of New-
York | New-York: | Printed by T. & J. Swords, No. 99 Pearl
Street | 1802.| 12mo. pp. [9],-4-79.   B. (1055).

McKISSEN, ROBERT.   Poems, | on | Various Subjects.| By |
Robert McKissen.| [4 lines from Hor.] | Pittsburgh: |
Printed by | Butler & Lambdin: | 1820.| 16mo. pp. [7],-8-113,
and leaf of contents.   (1056).

MACOMBER, JOB.   A | Poem, | delivered in Bowdoinham, |
to a | respectable audience, | on the | Fourth of July, 1806 | it
being | the anniversary of | American Independence.| By
Rev. Job. Macomber.| Third Edition.| Exeter: | Printed
for J. Richardson.| 1814.| 8vo. pp. [3],-4-12.   (1057).
  First edition.   Exeter, 1806.   16mo, pp. 16.

MANSFIELD, JOSEPH. Hope, | A Poem | Delivered in the | Chapel of Harvard University, | At a Public Exhibition, | July 8th, 1800 | By Joseph Mansfield, | A Junior Sophister | Cambridge | Printed by William Hilliard | 1800 | 18mo. pp. [3],-4-15. A.B. (1058).

MARSDEN, JOSHUA. Leisure Hours | or | Poems, | Moral, | Religious, & Descriptive. | By Joshua Marsden, | Missionary | [6 lines from Cowper.] | New York: | Published for the Author, And Sold by Griffin and Rudd, | 189 Greenwich-Street.| *Paul & Thomas, Printers* | 1812| 12mo. pp. [3],-4-160. [PORTRAIT.] B. (1059).

MARSTON, BENJAMIN. The Poor Cripples | New-Year's Address, | to the kind and charitable | Gentlemen and Ladies of Boston.| Broadside of 13 Verses in two Columns. Signed Benjamin Marston, Jan. 1, 1817. A. (1060).

MATTHEWS, ARTHUR. Paraphrase | on the | Book of Genesis; | A Poetical Essay. | by Arthur Matthews.| Providence: | Printed at the American Office, | by Goddard & Mann.| 1816.| 8vo. pp. [3],-4-76. A. (1061).

MAXWELL, WILLIAM. Poems | By | William Maxwell, Esq | Philadelphia: | Printed By William Fry | 1812 | 24mo. pp. [3],-iv-144. B. (1062).
    Another edition. Philadelphia, 1816. 18mo. [5]-vi-vii-[9]-9-168. [Engraved title page.]

MEAD, CHARLES. Mississippian Scenery; | A Poem, | Descriptive of the Interior | of | North America | By Charles Mead | [2 lines!] | Philadelphia: | Published by S. Potter and Co. No. 55, Chestnut Street. | W. Fry, Printer. | 1819 | 12mo. pp. [5],-vi-113 [plate]. A.B. (1063).

MILLS, JOHN HENRY. Poetic Trifles, | by | John Henry Mills. | Comedian. | [5 lines from Shakspeare, | LLL.] | [6 lines from R. Burns.] | Baltimore: | Printed by G. Dobbin & Murphy, 10 Market-Street. | for Cole & J. Bonsal.| 1808.| 12mo. pp. [5],-8-116 and 7 leaves of Contents and subscribers' names. A.B. (1064).

[MURDEN, ELIZA CRAWLEY.] Poems, | By a Young Lady | of | Charleston | [verse from Beattie] | Charleston, (S. C.) | Printed by J. Hoff, No. 6, Broad Street.| 1808.| [*Copy-Right Secured.*] | 12mo. pp. [6],-6-17,-[2],-6-112 [plate].

B. (1065).

[NEAL, JOHN.] Battle of Niagara | A Poem, | Without Notes | and | Goldau, | or | The Maniac Harper. | "Eagles! and Stars! and Rainbows!" | By Jehu O'Cataract, | Author of Keep Cool, &c | Baltimore: | Published by N. G. Maxwell.| From the Portico Press. | Geo. W. Crater, printer.| 1818 | 12mo. pp. [5],-iv,-vii-143. 12mo. pp. [5],-vi-143. Second Edition. Baltimore, 1819. 16mo. pp. [7],-viii-272. [Engraved title.]

A.B. (1066).

In some copies of the first edition page VI is misprinted IV, in others it is correctly printed, hence the two collations as given above. The second edition contains a new preface and several additional poems.

B.

NEUVELLE, M. J. LA. Elégie | sur | La Mort | de | George Washington | Par M. J. La Neuvelle | Membre de La Loge L'Aménité.| A Philadelphia | Chez Thomas & William Bradford, Libraires, | Premiere Rue Sud, No. 8 | 1800.| 8vo. pp. [3],-4-6. [Plate.]

B. (1067).

[NICHOLSON, J.] J. Nicholson. | Street Sweeper General, | Presents his most grateful compliments to his | kind Patrons, wishing them health, pros- | perity, and a Happy New Year.| [Octavo broadside, 7 verses.] Boston, Jan. 1, 1819.

A. (1068).

[NILES, AARON.] A | Controversy | between the | Four Elements.| Wrentham: | Printed by N. Heaton.| 1812.| 12mo. pp. [2],-4-23,-[1].

A.B. (1069).

The author's name is given in an acrostic on last page.

NUGENT, HENRY. The | Orphans of Wyoming, | or, | The Fatal Prayer.| A Moral Poem.| By the Late Henry Nugent.| *With* Memoirs of the Author.| First Edition.| City of Washington, | Apollo Press, | Printed and Published by H. C. Lewis. 1814.| 12mo. pp. [5],16-24,-[5],-30-42,-[3],-46-54,-[2]. N.Y.P.L. (1070).

The title is on the cover, which is included in the pagination.

OLDFIELD, J. " 'Tother Side of Ohio;" or a Review of a Poem. Hartford: 1818. 16mo. (1071).

OLIVER, ISABELLA. Poems, | on | Various Subjects. | by Isabella Oliver, | *Of Cumberland County, Pennsylvania.*| [4 lines from Beattie's Minstrel.] | Carlisle: | From the Press of A. Loudon, | (Whitehall.) | 1805.| 12mo. pp. [3],-4-5,-[2],-vii-ix,-[1],-12-220. A.B. (1072).

PAIGE, JOHN, JR. An Elegy, Composed on the sudden deaths of Lydia Page Sanborn, who died December 9th, | and Rebecca Sanborn, who died December 11, 1814, daughters of the Jonathan | Sanborn, of Gilmanton, N. H.| By John Paige, Jun. Gilmanton,| Folio broadside, 39 verses in 2 Columns.
A. (1073).

Includes also poem "On the same" by Elder Joseph Ladger of Gilmanton William Poit, jun, Typographer.

PAINE, ROBERT TREAT, JUN. Spain, | Commerce, and Freedom.| A National Ode.| . . . at a Public Festival, | Given in Honour of the Spanish Patriots, By the Citizens of Boston.| January 24th, 1809.| Written by Robert Treat Paine, Jun.|
A. (1074).

Printed and Sold by Russell and Cutter, | for the Author.| 12mo. pp. 4.

PAINE. Ode | For the Fourth of July, 1811.| By Robert Treat Paine, Esq.| [Folio broadside.] A. (1075).

PAINE. A | Monody | on the Death of | Lieut. General Sir John Moore. | with | Notes, | Historical and Political. | by | R. T. Paine, Jun, Esq. | To which is prefixed, A Sketch of the Life of General Moore | [2 lines from *Shakespeare*] | Boston, | Published by J. Belcher.| 1811.| 8vo. pp. [3],-4-32.

A.B. (1076).

PAINE. The | Works, | in | Verse and Prose, | of the Late | Robert Treat Paine, Jun. Esq | with Notes. | to which are prefixed, | Sketches | of his | Life, | Character and Writings.| [2 verses in Latin from Milton.] | Boston: | Printed and Published by J. Belcher.| 1812.| 8vo. pp. [3],-vi-lxxxiv,-[11],-6-454,-[1]. [Portrait.] A.B. (1077).

PARDEE, BENJAMIN D. Two | Orations, | and | Poetry | on different Subjects; | by Benjamin D. Pardee.| [9 lines from Virgil, Æneid, 1, iii, v. 443.] | Plattsburgh, N. Y. | Printed by Samuel Lowell, | for the Author.| 1810.| 8vo. pp. [4],-5-79.

(1078).

[PATTERSON, ROBERT.] The | Art | of Domestic Happiness, | and | other poems: | by | The Recluse, | *Author of The Independency of the Mind, affirmed.*| [7 lines in French from Gresset.] | Pittsburgh: | Published by Robert Patterson.| 1817.| 16mo. pp. [5],-vi,-[3],-10-316 and leaf of errata.

B.A. (1079).

[PAULDING, JAMES KIRKE.] The | Lay | of the | Scottish Fiddle: | A Tale | of | Havre De Grace. | *Supposed to be written | By* Walter Scott, *Esq.* | First American, from the Fourth | Edinburgh Edition.| New-York: | Published by Inskeep & Bradford, | and Bradford & Inskeep, | Philadelphia.| 1813.| 16mo. pp. [3],-4-11,-[1],-14-262. A.B. (1080).

PAULDING. The | Backwoodsman. | A Poem. | by J. K. Paulding.| Philadelphia: | Published by M. Thomas, 52 Chestnut St. | J. Maxwell, Printer.| 1818.| 12mo. pp. [11],-8-198, and 12 pages of Adv. preceding title. A.B. (1081).

PAYNE, JOHN HOWARD. Juvenile Poems, principally written between the age of thirteen and Seventeen Years; by John Howard Payne. Communicated to the publisher for the Literary Visitor. Baltimore: Edward J. Coale, 1813. 12mo. pp. 20.

(1082).

PAYNE. [Half title.] Lispings of the Muse: | a | Selection | from | Juvenile Poems. | [verso of half title.] London: | Printed by Richard and Arthur Taylor, Shoe Lane.| [Regular title.] Lispings of the Muse: | a | Selection | from | Juvenile Poems, | Chiefly written at and before the age of sixteen, | by John Howard Payne. | [Line or rule] | "He lisp'd in Numbers, for the Numbers Came." | [Line or rule] | Printed as a testimony of regard | from the Author | to his personal friends. | [Short line] | 1815.| 8vo. pp. [5],-vi-viii,-[1],-2-30 and leaf containing printer's name and name of place of issue. [London.]   B. (1083).

PECK, JOHN. A Short Poem, on the Universal Plan. Second Edition. Keene, N. H., 1802. 12mo.   A. (1084).

    Another edition. Boston. 1818. 12mo. Also Palmer: Ezekiel Terry, 1817. 16mo. pp. [2],-3-20.

PECK. A Short | Poem, | Containing | a Descant on the | *Universal Plan:* | Also, | Lines on the Happy End of the | Righteous, | and | *Prosperity and death of the Rich Man, spok-* | *en of in St. Luke's Gospel, Chap. xvi* | By John Peck | [Quotation from Job.] | Third Edition | Printed and Sold, April, | 1813.| 16mo. pp. [2],-3-23.   B. (1085).

    The same. Boston: 1823. 12mo. Also several other editions.

[PECK.] The | Devil's Shaving Mill, | Or Poem | In Which the Devil is personated: inter- | sperced with various queries and observ- | ations.| With a Paraphrase on | Mr. Devil's Wonderful Mill, | &c. | Ye shall not surely die | The serpent | View ev'ry line, let justice have its due: | You'll be convinc'd, | before that you get through.| Taunton: | Printed By A. Danforth.| 1815.| 12mo. pp. [3],-4-44. B. (1086).

PECK. Description | of the Last | Judgment, | And Reflections Thereon: | Also a Poem on | Death | And One on the | Resurrection | By John Peck.| Palmer: | From E. Terry's Press.| 1817.| 12mo. pp. [3],-6-34. A.B. (1087).

PERRIN, WILLIAM. The Accident, or Henry and Julia; a tale. With original poems. Montpelier: 1815. 12mo. (1088).

PERRIN. Hebrew Canticles | or A | Poetical Commentary, or Paraphrase, | on the | Various Songs of Scripture; | Including | Solomon's Song, Lamentations, &c | And a few Miscellaneous pieces | By Rev. W. Perrin | Philadelphia: | Printed and published by J. Maxwell. | *For the Author* | 1820.| 18mo. pp. [5],-6-126. A.B. (1089).

[PERRY, R.] A Poem on the Destruction of Sodom, by Fire; or The Day of Judgment. Transcribed by R. Perry. Middletown: M. H. Woodward. N. D. 16mo. pp. 32. (1090).

[PIERCE, THOMAS.] An | Ode to Science, | read before the | Western Museum | Society, | at the second Anniversary of that | Institution, | June 10, 1820. [Cincinnati: 1820.] 12mo. pp. [3],-4-8. A. (1091).

PIERCE, WILLIAM LEIGH. The Year: | A | Poem, in three Cantos.| by William Leigh Pierce, Esq. | [2 lines from Shakespeare.] | New-York: | Published by David Longworth, | *At the Shakspeare Gallery.*| 1813.| 16mo. pp. [7],-8-191. Notes pp. 75 and leaf of Adv. A.B. (1092).

PIERPONT, JOHN. The Portrait. | A Poem | delivered before the | Washington Benevolent Society, | of Newburyport, | on the evening of October 27, 1812. | by John Pierpont, Esq.| Boston: | Published by Bradford and Read. | T. B. Wait & Co. Printers.| 1812.| 8vo. pp. [3],-4-36. A.B. (1093).

PIERPONT. Airs of Palestine; | A Poem | By John Pierpont, Esq | [6 lines] | Baltimore: | Published for the Author | B. Edes, printer.| 1816.| 8vo. pp. [9],-viii-xxvi,-[1],-2-56.
A.B. (1094).

> The same. Second edition. Boston: Wells and Lilly, 1817. Sm. 12mo, pp. [5],-6-58. [Engraved title.]   A.
>
> Third edition, Revised. Boston: 1817. 12mo, pp. 66.   A.

PITMAN, JOHN, JR. A Poem | on the | *Social State and its Future Progress:* | delivered before the | Philermenian Society | of | Brown University, | on its | Anniversary, | September 3d, A.D. 1811. | By John Pitman, Jun. Esq.| Providence: | Printed by Jones & Wheeler.| 12mo. pp. [3],-4-14.
B.A. (1095).

PLUMMER, JONATHAN. An Ode and Sermon, | on the Subject of Studying to be Quiet.| Occasioned by a difference between the Rev. Dr. Dana and his consort.| Written by Jonathan Plummer, an independent travelling preacher, and poet laureat to his excellency Sir Timothy Dexter.| [1806.] Folio broadside.   A. (1096).

PLUMMER. An | Elegiac Ode, and a Funeral | Sermon | On the death of Mr. George Hooker, who was drowned at Newburyport, on the 30th of October, 1807, and | on the death of a number of other persons who died suddenly, very lately. Sold by the Author, at his baskets, Market-Square, | price four pence half penny. Also new Almanacks. Broadside. (1097).

PLUMMER. An Elegiac Ode and Funeral Sermon on the death of three persons who killed themselves. Broadside. (1098).

PLUMMER. [Cut] Elegy | on the death of His Excellency Sir Timothy Dexter, | together with a sketch of his Character & a few reflections.| By Jonathan Plummer a travelling preacher, & | poet laureat to his Lordship. Printed for & Sold by the Author. Price Four | pence half penny. [1807?] Broadside.
(1099).

PLUMMER. Parson Pidgin, or Holy Kissing. Verses and a Sermon on the subject of Holy Kissing. . . . . . Newburyport: 1807. Broadside. (1100).

PLUMMER. Great and dreadful Fire at Newbury- | port. Fire, Fire, Fire.| An Ode and a Sermon concerning a tremendous Fire at Newburyport, which commenc | ed on the Evening of the thirty-first of May, 1811: Written by Jonathan Plummer, a lay | Bishop Extraordinary; and a travelling preacher, Physician, Poet, and Trader. Printed for the Author, and sold by him at various | places. Broadside. (1101).

[PLUMMER.] [Twenty-five coffins and cut.] Murder: | Death of | Miss Mack Coy, | and the | Young Teazer. ☞ Sold corner Theatre-Alley, Milk-St. Boston. Broadside.
A. (1102).

PLUMMER. Death of [cut] Tamar Harn! | For the unmarried ladies of America. Composed by Jonathan Plummer. Printed for the Author and Sold by him. 1816. Broadside. (1103).

PLUMMER. Plummer's Alarm to the Unconverted: | being a new funeral Sermon, and a new Funeral Psalm, on the death of thousands! [Coffins.] Printed for the Author: and sold by him at his | Basket. Broadside. (1104).

PLUMMER. The second Ode, | And a second and concluding part of a | Sermon, | On the subject of Studying to be Quiet; occasioned by a difference between the Rev. Dr. Dana and his Consort.| By Jonathan Plummer, an independent travelling Preacher, and Poet Laureat to the Excellency Sir Timothy Dexter. Broadside. (1105).

Plummer also wrote several other "Sermons" with funeral Songs and Odes. See Ford 3300.

POPE, HENRY. An | Elegy | on | Mrs. Elizabeth Lobb, | who died in Child-Birth, December 1810, | Leaving six small children and a disconsolate husband | to deplore her loss.| Humbly Inscribed | to the Reverend Rich'd C. Moore, D.D. | Rector of St. Stephen's Church, | of which she was for many years a pious member, | by his most sincere, and most obliged humble servant, | Henry Pope.| New-York: | Printed by Largin & Thompson, | No. 189 Water-Street.| 8vo. pp. [8]. [four unnumbered ll.]. (1106).

PORTER, JACOB. Poems, | By | Jacob Porter | [2 verses from Gifford] | Hartford: | Printed by Peter B. Gleason and Co.| 1818.| 8vo. pp. [5],-6-27. A.B. (1107).

The same. Second Edition. Hartford: 1819. 8vo. pp. 27.

[PRENTISS, CHARLES.] The Reporter. A Partial Imitation of Horace. [Alexandria:] S. Snowden, 1812. pp. 14.
A. (1108).

PRENTISS. A | Poem | delivered at Brookfield. | July 5th, 1813, | before the Washington Benevolent Societies | of that and the adjacent Towns. | by Charles Prentiss. | Published at the request of the audience.| [2 lines from Ovid, Met.] | [2 lines of Prose.] | Brookfield: | Printed by E. Merriam & Co.| 8vo. pp. [3],-4-14 [mispaged 44]. A. B. (1109).

PRENTISS. New England Freedom: | A | Poem | Delivered Before the Washington Benevolent Society, | In Brimfield, February 22d, 1813 | By Charles Prentiss | [6 verses in Latin verse from Juvenal and translated in prose] | Brookfield: | Printed By E. Merriam & Co | *March* . . . . 1813 | 8vo. pp. [3],-4-28. A.B. (1110).

PRICE, JAMES H. Miscellany, | in | Verse and Prose | By | James H. Price, Esq. | [4 verses] | Albany: | Published by H. C. Southwick.| 1813.| 12mo. pp. [7],-8-168. B. (1111).

QUINCEY, VERNON H. A | Parody | on Some of the Most Striking passages | in a late pamphlet, entitled | "A Letter to a Federalist," with *Large Additions & Improvements,* | by Vernon H. Quincey, Esq. | [4 lines from Buckingham] | [2 lines from Chatham.] | 2 lines from Pope.] | Portsmouth, N. H. | Printed at the Oracle Press, 1805.| 8vo. pp. [3],-vi-viii, [1], 10-47. A. (1112).

RALLING, JOHN. The | Time Piece. | Tempus Fugit | Multum in Parvo | [8 lines and a quotation from the Bible] | The Third Edition, Corrected and Enlarged. | By John Ralling | Philadelphia: | Printed By Jane Aitken, No. 20, North | Third Street.| 1803.| 8vo. pp. [3],-iv-170. B. (1113).

RAND, THOMAS. The Voice of the Turtle; a Collection of pieces in prose and Verse. [Wrentham, Mass.] 1802. 12mo.
A. (1114).

REYNOLDS, TERTIUS. A | Poem, | Spoken on the Summit | of | Wamaug Mountain, | August 16, 1820, | To | A Party of | Ladies and Gentlemen, | Who had Ascended to the Pinacle of This Lofty | Mountain for the Purpose of Enjoying | A Prospect of the Romantic | Scenery Around.| Suggested by the Author's First Visit to That | Place a Short Time Previous.| By Tertius Reynolds.| New Haven, | Printed for the Publisher. | 1820 | 18mo. pp. [3],-4-12. B. (1115).

[RICHARDS, GEORGE.] Hymns and Odes | Composed | On the Death of | Gen. George Washington: | Adapted | to the 22d Day of February | and Dedicated to | Those Who Please to Sing them] | [7 lines of solid matter] | *Many of them are pure Originals, never published | before.|* Portsmouth, (N. H.) January, 1800 | Printed at the United States Oracle Office | By Charles Peirce, sold by him, at the | Columbian Bookstore, By Groce (*sic*) Dozen, or Single. 12mo. pp. [4],-5-12. A.B. (1116).

RICHMOND, WILLIAM E. Mount Hope, | An Evening Excursion. | by William E. Richmond, | Barrister at Law. | Providence: | Printed by Miller & Hutchens.| 1818.| 12mo. pp. [5],-6-69, [1] and leaf of Copyright. A.B. (1117).

[RITSON, ANNE.] A Poetical Picture | of | America, | being | observations | made during a residence of several years, at | Alexandria, and Norfolk, in Virginia; | illustrative of the Manners and Customs | of the Inhabitants: | and interspersed with | Anecdotes, | Arising from a general Intercourse with Society in that Country, | from the year 1799 to 1807.| By a Lady.| London: | Printed for the Author; | and sold by Vernor, Hood, and Sharpe, 31, Poultry.| 1809.| 12mo. pp. [17],-4-177. (1118).

ROGERS, DANIEL. A Poem, | on | Liberty and Equality. | by Daniel Rogers, | Student at Union College.| [One line from Schrevelli.] | Published by Special request. | Printed for the Author, | at the Office of the Albany Centinel, Court-Street.| 1804.| 8vo. pp. [3],-iv, [1],-6-29. B. (1119).

[ROSE, R. H.] Sketches in Verse | [2 lines in Latin] | Printed for C. & A. Conrad & Co. Philadelphia, | By Smith & Maxwell.| 1810.| 8vo. pp. [5],-vi-184. [Engraved title.]
B. (1120).

ROWELL, NATHANIEL. The | Village Church: | a | Poem. | By Nathaniel Rowell.| Sag-Harbor: | Printed by Alden Spooner.| 1809.| 16mo. pp. [3],-4-11. (1121).

> Dated at end "February 15th, A. D. 1809." "The Village" is *Miller's Place* in the town of *Brookhaven, Long Island, N. Y.*

ROWSON, SUSANNA. Miscellaneous Poems; | by Susanna Rowson, | Preceptress of the Ladies' Academy, Newton, Mass. | Author of | Charlotte, Inquisitor, Reuben and | Rachel, etc. etc.| [2 quotations of 4 and 2 lines respectively from Johnson's Rambler.] | Printed for the Author, by Gilbert and Dean, | State-street, Sold by them, | and by *W. P.* and *S. Rlake,* (*sic*) Cornhill, | Boston. —— 1804.| 8vo. pp. [3],-iv-227. A.B. (1122).

[SANDS, ROBERT CHARLES.] The | Bridal of Vaumond; | A Metrical Romance. | [2 verses in Latin from Auson & 4 verses (translated) from Goethe] | New York: | Published By James Eastburn And Co. | Literary Rooms, Corner of Broadway and | Pine Street | *Abraham Paul, Printer.*| 1817.| 16mo. pp. [5],-6-186. A.B. (1123).

> For another title by Sands, seè Eastburn, J. W.

SARGENT, LUCIUS MANILUS. CÆLII Symposii | ÆIGMATA.| Hanc Novam Editiomem, | Juxta | Lectiones Optimas | diligenter Congestam, | Curavit. | Lucius M. Sargent.| Bostoniæ, Nov Angl: | Prelo | Belcher et Armstrong. | MDCCC-VII.| 8vo. pp. [3],-iv, [1],-6-35. A.B. (1124).

SARGENT. The | Culex | of | Virgil; | with | A Translation | into | English Verse, | by | Lucius M. Sargent.| [2 lines Latin.] | Boston: | Printed at the Emerald Press, | by Belcher and Armstrong, | No. 70, State Street.| 1807.| 8vo. pp. [3],-iv-144. A.B. (1125).

SARGENT. Hubert and Ellen. | with | Other Poems | The Trial of the Harp . . . Billowy Water . . . The Plunderer's grave . . . | The Tear-Drop . . . The Billow | By | Lucius M. Sargent | Boston: | Published by Chester Stebbins.| 1812.| 8vo. pp. [3],-4-135. A.B. (1126).

> Also eleven copies on large paper. Boston: 1812.
> Another edition. Boston: 1813. 8vo, pp. 3,-4-135.
> The same. Boston: 1815. 16mo, [5],-6-96.

[SARGENT, WINTHROP.] Boston.| A Poem.| Boston: [5 lines from Horace] | Printed for Joseph Nancrede, No. 49 Marlboro' Street. | 1803. 8vo. pp. [3],-4-16. A.B. (1127).

SARGENT. Boston. | A Poem. | by Winthrop Sargent. | Second edition.| Corrected and enlarged. | [5 lines from Horace] | [6 lines of Verse.] | Boston: | Printed by Hosea Sprague, | Sold at No. 49, Marlboro' Street.| 1803.| 12mo. pp. [5],-vi, [1],-8-23. A.B. (1128).

SCALES, WILLIAM. The | Quintescence | of | Universal History; | or, | An Epitomial History | of the | Christian Era: | A Poem | By Wm. Scales, A.M. LL.D. F.R.S. | Massachusetts: Printed for the Purchasers.| 1806.| 8vo. pp. [3],-iv-22.

A.B. (1129).

SCHOOLCRAFT, HENRY ROWE. Transsallegania | or the | Groans of Missouri | A Poem | [2 verses from Pope's letters] | New-York | Printed for the Author, By J. Seymour | 1820.| 16mo. pp. [3],-4-24.

B. (1130).

SCOTT, JOHN W. The | Poetical Recreations | of | John W. Scott.| Philadelphia: | Collected and Printed, | June, 1809.| 12mo. pp. [3],-4-6,-[3],-99,-[5],-2-20,-[3],-4-16.

(1131).

SCOTT, JONATHAN M. Blue Lights, | Or | The Convention. | A Poem | In Four Cantos | By Jonathan M. Scott, Esq.| [4 verses] | New York: | Printed and Published by Charles N. Baldwin, Book- | seller, Chatham, corner of Chamber-street | 1817.| 16mo. pp. [7],-vi-150.

A.B. (1132).

SCOTT. The | Sorceress, | or | Salem Delivered. | A Poem, | In Four Cantos. | By Jonathan M. Scott, Esq.| [Quotation from King Lear and a line from Horace.] | New York: Printed and Published by Charles N. Baldwin, Book- | seller, corner of Chamber and Chatham-street.| 1817.| 16mo. pp. [7],-viii-120.

A.B. (1133).

SCOTT, MOSES Y. The | Deaf and Dumb; | A Poem, | By. | Moses Y. Scott. | Written and Published for the Benefit of | "The New-York Institution for the Instruction of the Deaf and Dumb."| New-York: | Published by Elam Bliss, 208 Broadway | J. Seymour, printer | 1819.| 8vo. pp. [5],-6-23.

B.A. (1134).

SCOTT. Fatal Jest, | A tale: | and | other poems. | by Moses Y. Scott.| New-York: | Published by Elam Bliss, 208 Broadway, | J. Seymour, Printer.| 1819.| 16mo. pp. [5],-vi, [3],-10-142.

A.B. (1135).

SEARS, REUBEN. A | Poem, | on the | Mineral Waters | of | Ballston and Saratoga, | with | Notes | Illustrating the | History of the Springs | and | Adjacent Country | By Reuben Sears, A.M.| Ballston Spa: | Published by the Author, | J. Comstock, Printer.| 1819.| 16mo. pp. [7],-8-108.

A.B. (1136).

SELDEN, ALMIRA. Effusions | of | The Heart, | contained in a number of | Original Poetical Pieces, | on various subjects.| By Almira Selden.| [7 lines of poetry from Thomson.] | Bennington: | Printed by Darius Clark, | 1820.| 16mo. pp. [3],-iv-152.

A.B. (1137).

SESSIONS, AMASA. Verses, Composed by Amasa Sessons, on the Death of Amasa Robbins, who was killed by the fall of a tree, Holland Purchase, 3d of August, A.D. 1807. [Boston:] Printed by Nathaniel Coverly, [1807] Broadside. 4to. [Two cuts].

(1138).

SEWELL, JONATHAN MITCHELL. Miscellaneous Poems, | with several specimens | from the | Author's Manuscript Version | of the | Poems of Ossian. | by J. M. Sewell, Esq. | Published agreeably to an act of Congress.| Portsmouth: | Printed by William Treadwell, & Co. | For the Author.| 1801.| 12mo. pp. [5],-6-8,-[2],-11-304.

A.B. (1139).

SEWALL, JONATHAN. Rev. Mr. Sewell's | Poem, | on | The Mode of Baptism. | Second edition.| Hallowell: | Printed by S. K. Gilman.| 1820.| 8vo.

(1140).

> Printed on pp. [37]-41 of *Sermon on Infant Baptism,* by Eliphalet Gillet. Hallowell: S. K. Gilman, 1820.   A.
>
> The first edition of the Sermon, with the poem annexed, was printed by Peter Edes, Augusta, 1804. I have not seen a copy of the earlier issue.

SHAW, JOHN. Poems | by the late | Doctor John Shaw, | to which is prefixed | A biographical Sketch of the Author.| Published by Edward Earle, Philadelphia, and | by Edward J. Coale, Baltimore. | Fry and Kammerer, Printers.| 1810.| 12mo. pp. [5],-vi-viii,-[1],-2-252. ˙

A.B. (1141)

SHAW, THOMAS. A Mournful Song. | on *the death of the Wife and Child of Mr. Nathaniel | Knights, of Windham, who fell off the Bridge at the Falls | above Horse Beef Mills, on Presumscutt River, Feb. 22, | 1807, the day after dreaming that she should be drowned, | which she communicated to her husband before the accident.|* Written by Thomas Shaw, of Standwich | Third Edition.] Broadside. B. (1142).

SHAW-STANDISH. Peace. [Verses, n.p. 1815?] Folio broadside. N.Y.P.L. (1143).

SHAW-STANDISH, THOMAS. No. 1. [Cuts of 5 Coffins] | A Mournful Song, | *Occasioned by the Shipwreck of the Schooner Armistice, Captain Douglas, on Cohasset | rocks, August 31, 1815 . . . . bound from Port | land for Baltimore . . . . on which occasion five | persons perished. |* by Thomas Shaw-Standish.| [Cut of a Ship] | [12 lines of Verse.] | 8vo. pp. [1],-2-11. (1144).

On page 7 is *A Solemn Song, on the Volcano of Albay.*

[SHURTLEFF, JAMES.] The | Substance of a Late Remarkable | Dream | In Which Were Presented | The Celestial Worlds | and the | Infernal Regions, | With the | Arch Enemy of Mankind, | with His | Legions Paraded, | Together with his | Instructions to them, | In Which Was Discovered, His Deep Laid Plot | Against the | United States of America | Hallowell (District of Maine) | Printed by Peter Edes | 1800.| 8vo. pp. [3],-4-16. A.B. (1145).

SIGOURNEY, LYDIA HUNTLEY. Moral Pieces, | in | *Prose and Verse.|* By Lydia Huntley.| Hartford: | *Sheldon & Goodwin . . . . . Printers.|* 1815.| 12mo. pp. [5],-vi, [1],-vii-xii, [1],-2-267, [1] and 8 pp. of Subscribers' names.

A.B. (1146).

The author's first book. Some copies were issued anonymously.

[SMITH, EAGLESFIELD.] William and Ellen: a | Poem | in | three Cantos; | with other poetical Works | of | An American.| Published for the Benefit of a helpless Child.| New-York: | Printed by J. Seymour, No. 49, John-Street.| 1811.| 16mo. pp. [5]-vi, [1], viii-xii, [1], 14-158. (1147).

[SMITH, JAMES.] The | Mirror | of Merit and Beauty: | Fifty Female Sketches, | Drawn from Nature.| [3 verses from Pope and 2 from Phaed.] | By a Friend to the Fair. | J.S.M.D.| New-York: | Printed for the Author, | By D. & G. Bruce.| 1808.| 16mo. pp. [5],-6-80. B. (1148).

SNOWDEN, RICHARD. The | Columbiad; | or a | Poem | on the | American War, | in thirteen Cantoes. | [sic] by Richard Snowden.| Baltimore: | Printed by W. Pechin, No. 10, *Second-Street* | [Circa 1805.] 12mo. pp. [3],-4-44.
B. (1149).

SNOWDEN. The | American Revolution.| Written in | Scriptural, | or, | Ancient Historical Style.| "Honi soit sui mal y'Pense" | By Richard Snowden.| Clinton, (Ohio.) | Printed by *Smith & M'Ardle,* at the Office | of "The Ohio Register." | *Year of our Lord,* 1815.| 12mo. pp. [3],-4-170. In same Vol. is the following

The | Columbiad, | or | a Poem | on the | American War, | in Thirteen Cantoes.| By Richard Snowden.| Clinton, (*Ohio.*) | Printed by *Smith & M'Ardle,* | Office of "The Ohio Register."| 12mo. pp. [3],-4-38,-[7]. A. (1150).
Printed rather crudely. The only specimen I have seen from this press, and "the Ohio Register" is not noted by Venable.

[SOMERVILLE, J. S.] Somerville's | Plume of the Classics, | or | Select Classical Pieces, | in | English Verse.| Washington: | Printed for the Author, by Jacob Gideon, Junior | Ninth Street, Near Pennsylvania Avenue | 1820.| 16mo. pp. [3],-4-60. (1151).

SOMERVILLE, WILLIAM C. Lines | on a | Serenade | To the young ladies of Philadelphia, | on the night of the | Illumination for Peace | being Valentines, 14th, Feb. 1815.| By Wm. C. Somerville, of M. | Philadelphia, Feb'y, 1815. | 12mo. pp. [3],-4-14.
(1152).

Southwick, Solomon. Address, | delivered at the opening of | The New Theatre, | in the | City of Albany, | by Mr. Southey, | January 18, 1813.| Written by S. Southwick.| Albany: | Printed by H. C. Southwick, | No. 73, State-Street.| 8vo. pp. [5],-6-14. (1153).

Spence, Lieutenant. Minstrelsey | of | Edmund the Wanderer, | collected by | his early companion, and intimate friend, | Lieutenant Spence | of the United States' Navy.| (Verse quotation, eight lines) | New-York: | Printed by D. & G. Bruce, | Slote Lane.| 1810.| 8vo. pp. [5],-6-83, [2],-86-88, [1],-2-340. [Portraits of "Edmund" and "Licea."]
B. (1154).

Spierin, George Hartwell. Poems, | By | The Late | George Hartwell Spierin, | of | Charleston, South-Carolina, | Student of Law.| [5 verses from Beattie's Minstrel.] | Charleston: | Printed by W. P. Young, Franklin's-Head, | No. 41, Broad-Street.| 1805.| 8vo. pp. [7],-vii-123,-[1]. B. (1155).

Sterry, Abby. H. Effusions, | Religious, Moral, | and | Patri-otic; | in | Prose and Verse | By Abby H. Sterry, New-London: | Printed for the Author: | By Samuel Green | 1818.| 12mo. pp. [5],-6-150. B. (1156).

[Story, Isaac.] A | Parnassian Shop, | Opened | In the Pin-daric Stile; | By Peter Quince, Esq | [4 verses from P. Pin-dar]. | Copy Right Secured | Boston, | Printed by Russell and Cutler, | 1801 | 12mo. pp. [7],-viii, [1], 10-155. A.B.(1157).

> I have seen a copy which had pasted on verso of p. 155 ["Apolo-getical." The author of the preceeding work, &c. [4 lines re-printer's errors] and signed in ink P. Quince. The bracket before "Apolo-getical" is printed before that word and a bracket is after the word "dedicated"] which immediately preceeds the author's signature.

Story, Joseph. The | Power | of | Solitude. | A | Poem | In two Parts | By Joseph Story | [4 verses from Southey] | Boston | Printed By John Russell.| [1802.] 8vo. pp. [7],-8-100. A.B. (1158).

> New and improved edition. Salem, Barnard B. Macanulty, 1804. 12mo, pp. [5],-2-260. [Frontispiece engraved by J. Akin, Newbury-port.]

STRONG, T. The | Tears of Columbia: | A Poem, | to the Memory of | American Heroes and Statesmen. | to which are added | Miscellaneous Odes, &c. | by T. Strong. | [2 lines from Shakespeare.] | Dedham: | Printed by H. Mann—1812.| 8vo. pp. [3],-4-32.   A.B. (1159).

SUTTON, JOHN. Verses on the Untimely Death of Three Brothers that were drowned in Crum Pond, Yorktown, Westchester County on the 3rd day of September, 1809, by John Sutton. Robert Crombie, printer, Peekskill, 1809. Broadside.
                                                                 (1160).

SYMPSON, J. Science Revived | or | the Vision of Alfred. | A poem | in eight Cantos, | with biographical Notes. | by the Rev. J. Sympson, B.D.| Philadelphia, | Printed by John Bouvier, for John Wilson.| 1810.| 16mo. pp. [5],-6, [1],-8-9, [4],-14-207. [Frontispiece.]   A. (1161).

TAPPAN, WILLIAM BINGHAM. New England. | And other | Poems. | By William B. Tappan | Philadelphia: | Printed for the Author, By J. H. Cunningham, | No. 70, South Third-street | 1819.| 18mo. pp. [7],-6-108. [Plate.]   B. (1162).

TAPPAN. Songs of Judah, | and other | Melodies | By | William B. Tappan, | Author of New England and other poems | Phladelphia: | Published By S. Potter & Co. 87 Chestnut Street.| 1820.| 18mo. pp. [7],-vi-xi,-[4],-4-204. B. (1163).

TAYLOR, AMOS. Specimens of Ingenuity in Composition and Poetry. Utica: 1813. pp. 32.   A. (1164).

TERRY, EZEKIEL. A | Divine Poem, | on | Pharaoh to Jacob: | *"How old art thou?"* | By Ezekiel Terry. | Springfield: | Printed by Ashley & Brewer. | [Circa 1801.] 12mo. pp. [2],-3-18.   A. (1164B).

THATCHER, WILLIAM. A | Battle | Between | Truth and Error | Humbly Addressed to the Candid | Lovers of Truth.| By William Thatcher | *Middletown, (Conn)* | Printed by T. & J. B. Dunning | 1808.| 12mo. pp. [3],-iv-vi,-[1],-8-48.
                                                       B. (1165).

THAYER, CAROLINE MATILDA. Religion | Recommended | To Youth, | in | a series of Letters | addressed | to a Young lady. | to which are added, | Poems | on Various Occasions. | by Caroline Matilda Thayer. | Third Edition.| New-York: | Published by J. Soule and T. Mason, for the Methodist | Episcopal Church in the United States.| *A. Paul, Printer.*| 1819.| 16mo. pp. [3],-iv-vi,-[1],-8-220. On p. [159] is title-Poems | on Various Ocasions. | by | Caroline Matilda Thayer.| The poems are on pp. [163]-220.   A. (1166).

THOMAS, DANIEL. A | Poem | Delivered in | Middleborough | September 8th, A.D. 1802 | At the | Anniversary Election | of the | Philandrian Society | By Daniel Thomas | Student of Rhode Island College | Wrentham, (Mass) | Printed by Nathaniel Heaton, Jun.| 1802.| 8vo. pp. [3],-4-12.
                                                        B. (1167).

THOMAS, JOSEPH. A | Poetical Descant | on the | Primeval and Present State of | Mankind; | or, The Pilgrim's Muse.| By Joseph Thomas, | Minister of the Gospel. | [2½ lines from "The Author"]. | Winchester Va. | J. Foster, Printer.| 1816.| 16mo. pp. [3],-iv-219,-[1].   A.B. (1168).

THOMSON, CHARLES WEST. Elliner, | and | Other Poems | By | Charles West Thomson | "Simple flowers, such as the hedge-rows scent."| Philadelphia: | Published by Marot & Walter, | No. 87, Market Street | 1826.| 12mo pp. [5],-6-viii,-[1],-2-98.
                                                        B. (1169.)

TIZZARD, SAMUEL. The | New Athenian Oracle; | or, | Ladies Companion. | In two Books | Book First, | Containing an Extraordinary Variety | of | Questions in Prose, on Moral, | Philo- | sophical and other Subjects, | Together with a Great Number of | Enigmas, Paradoxes, Rebuses, Charades, &c | Also, a Number of Curious | Mathematical Questions.| Book Second | Containing Answers and Solutions | in Prose and Verse.| Designed for the Improvement of the Fair-Sex.| Collected from the most Eminent and Approved Writers.| By Samuel Tizzard *Teacher of the English Language and Mathematicks, in Carlisle.* | [4 lines of Verse] | Carlisle: | From the Press of A. Loudon. (Whitehall.) | 1806.| 8vo. pp. [3],-iv-253-[2]-2-96.   A. (1170).

TONSON, MONS. [3 cuts] Rogers & Victory.| Written by Mons. Tonson, | Late Hair-Dresser to his Imperial and Royal Majesty and Emperor of | the French. Printed and sold by Nath. Coverly, Milk-street, corner Theatre-Alley, Boston. Broad-side. A. (1171).

TOPLIFF, NATHANIEL. Poems, | Moral, Descriptive, | and | Political.| By Nathaniel Topliff, | A Farmer of Dorchester | Boston: | Printed for the Author | *J. Belcher, Printer,* | 1809.| 12mo. pp. [5],-vi-169,-[1]. A.B. (1172).

[TORREY, JESSE.] The | Intellectual Flambeau, | Demonstrating That | *National Happiness, Virtue & Temperance* | Exist in a | Collateral Ratio, | With | The Dissemination | of Phil-osophy, Science, & Intelligence | with an | Appendix | Con-taining several | Splendid Poems on the Advantage | of | *Mental Improvement, and on Charity.*| [7 lines of various quotations] | *By Discipulus Libertatis atque Humanity.*| Washington City | Printed By Daniel Rapine | 1816.| 12mo. pp. [3],-4-143,-[4],-4-35. A.B. (1173).

TOULMIN, J. R. A Little Poem on Peace & War. Second edition Corrected. To which is Added, Two Lesser Poems. [Lex-ington: Office of the Kentucky Gazette? 1803.] (1174).

[TOWSEND, (RICHARD H.)] Original | Poems, | by a Citizen of Baltimore.| Published by Samuel Jefferis, | 212, Baltimore-Street. | Robinson, Printer.| 1809.| 12mo. pp. [5],-vi-x, [1],-2-139, [1] and leaf of Adv. A.B. (1175).

TOWNSEND, WALTER. [Title page gone. First page reads:] [An American eagle bearing a pennant inscribed: "E Pluribus Unum"] Ode | For the Fourth of July, 1803 | By Walter Townsend.| (Set to Music by Dr. Jackson.) [Then the poem begins] 8vo. pp. [1],-2-3,-[1]. B. (1176).

TRUMBULL, JOHN. The | Poetical Works | of | John Trumbull, LL.D. | Containing | M'Fingal, | A Modern Epic Poem, | Revised and Corrected, | With Copious Explanatory Notes; |

The Progress of Dulness: | And a Collection of | Poems | on Various Subjects, | Written Before and During the Revolutionary War | In two Volumes. | Vol. I | Hartford: | Printed for Samuel G. Goodrich, | By Lincoln & Stone | MDCCCXX. 8vo. pp. ([11],-10-235); ([2],-8-177) and slip of "Agents for this work," which is not in all copies. [Portrait and plates engraved by E. Tisdale.]   A.B. (1177).

UMPHRAVILLE, ANGUS.. The | Siege of Baltimore, | and | the Battle of | La Tranche; | with Other | Original Poems | By Angus Umphraville | Aged Nineteen | [4 verses from Virgil] | Baltimore: | Printed by Schaeffer and Maund | 1817.| 12mo. pp. [13],-2-144.   A.B. (1178).

[UPHAM, THOMAS COGSWELL.] The | Home in the West | A Poem | Delivered at Dartmouth College, July 4, 1817.| By a Member of the Junior Class | Hanover: | David Watson, Jun. Printer | 1817.| 16mo. pp. [3],-iv-12. A.B. (1179).

UPHAM. American Sketches.| by Thomas C. Upham.| [3 lines in Latin] | [Cut of an eagle with spreading wings.] | New York: | Published by David Longworth, | at the Shakspeare-Gallery, | *For the Author.*| Feb. 1819.| 16mo. pp. [5],-vi-vii,-[2],-6-120. [Several text illust.]   A. (1180).

[VANVECHTEN, TEUNIS A.] A | Poem, | on | Liberty.| Delivered by one of | the Graduates, at the Annual | Commencement of | Union College, | on the 30*th* July, 1806.| *Published at the earnest request of a number of* | *Gentlemen who heard it.*| Albany: | Printed by Backus & Whiting.| 1806.| 8vo. pp. [3],-4-12.   B. (1181).

[VERPLANCK, GULIAN CROMMELIN.] Dick Shift, | or the | State Triumvirate.| A Political Tale | in | Imitation of Swift | "Till wrapped in terrors of avenging might."| Pursuits of Literature.| New York: | Printed for the Author, | And sold by W. B. Gilley, No. 92 Broadway.| J. Seymour, Printer | 1819.| 12mo. pp. [5],-6-31.   B. (1182).

[VERPLANCK.] The | State Triumvirate, | A Political Tale: | And | The Epistles | of | Brevet Major Pindar Puff.| [6 verses from Dryden] | New-York: | Printed for the Author, | And Sold by W. B. Gilley, No. 92 Broadway, | and other Booksellers | J. Seymour, Printer | 1819.| 12mo. pp. [3],-4-215.   A.B. (1183).

[W., D.] The | Poetical | Nosegay; | or | *The Swindler James Geo. Semple revived* | in the person of | Hugh Workman, | A Native of Ireland.| [5 lines of verse in Latin] | [7 lines] | Copy-Right Secured, | According To Law.| 1800.| 12mo. pp. [11],-2-20.   (1184).

> Copy in N.Y.P.L. imperfect at end. The author's initials "D. W." are on verso of title and at end of dedication.

[W., J.] Farewell to Pittsburgh, and the Mountains, Remarks on the Scenery, A Poem by J. W. Philadelphia: 1818. (1185).

> No Copy located. Title taken from the Sale Catalogue of the library of Rufus W. Griswold, sold in New York, May 1859.

[WADDELL, JOHN H.] A | Fair Epistle | From A Little Poet, | to | A Great Player | [6 verses] | Sold by the Author | New-York, 1818.| 12mo. pp. [5],-6-12.   B. (1186).

[WADDELL.] The Dartmoor Massacre, transposed in verse, from the New York Commercial Advertiser, of the 6th of June last, and the Boston papers of the same month. Being the authentic and particular account of the tragic massacre, at Dartmoor prison, in England, on the 6th April last, in which sixty-seven American sailors, prisoners there, fell the victims to the jailor's revenge, for obtaining their due allowance of bread, which had been withheld from them by the jailor's orders. Boston 1815. 12mo. pp. 8.   A. (1187).

> Another issue N. P. [1815]. pp. 7.   A.

[WADDELL.] Waddell, | to | Coleman.| Facts and Fancy — | As you like it — Go on, or Stop.| [double rule] | New-York: | 1819.| 12mo. pp. [3],-iv, 5-8.   (1188).

> Blue paper cover, with title as given above.
> This curious piece was written by J. H. Waddell and is signed by him at the end of the verses. It is an answer to slurring remarks made by William Coleman, editor of the New York *Evening Post,* regarding Andrew Jackson and the part he took in the Seminole War.

[WALN, ROBERT, JR.] American Bards.| A Satire | [2 verses from Dryden and 3 from Byron] | Philadelphia: | Published for the Author by M. Thomas, | and by Haly and Thomas, New York.| *J. Maxwell, Printer* | 1820.| 8vo. pp. [5],-6-80. A.B. (1189).

[WALN.] Sisyphi Opus: | or, | Touches at the Times.| A Satire.| [4 lines of prose.] | and other Poems.| by the Author of "American Bards."| Philadelphia: | Published by J. Maxwell and Moses Thomas, | and by Haly and Thomas, New York.| 1820.| 8vo. pp. [5],-6-62. [1]. A.B. (1190).

[WARDELL, JOSEPH.] Poems | on | various subjects, | viz. | on the birth of Christ.| His Life, Miracles, Death, Resurrection and Ascention.| His sending the Holy Ghost to carry on | the work of redemption, &c.| The day of Judgment.| On the Joys of Heaven.| Advice to Tale-Bearers, &c., &c.| Printed for the Author.| M, DCCC, IX.| 12mo. pp. [3],-iv,-[2],-7-24. (1191).

WARDWELL. The | Way of the World, | or | A short sketch of the Modern | Customs of Mankind, delineated, | in a variety of methods, both | Metaphorical, Ironical, Miscellaneous, Serous, Humour | ous, entertaining, and | Romantick, | Calculated | to divert, and, at the same time | instruct the Reader | Composed and written in Prose and Verse | By Joseph Wardwell, alias, | Joseph, the Dreamer | [4 verses] | Printed for the Author.| M, DCCC XIII.| 8vo. pp. [2],-iii-24.
A. (1192).

Published in Bristol, R. I.

WARE, HENRY, JR. A | Poem | Pronounced at Cambridge, February 23, 1815, | at the | Celebration of Peace | Between the United States and Great Britain | By Henry Ware, Jun.| Published by Request.| Cambridge: | Printed by Hilliard and Metcalf.| 1815. 8vo. pp. [3],-4-11. A.B. (1193).

WEEKS, JOHN R. In Memory | of | Mrs. Mary Cock, | *Consort of Mr. Thomas Cock, Sen.* | of Mill-Neck, Township of Oyster-Bay; | Who Deceased March 26th, Anno Domini 1806, | Of a Dropsy in the Stomach.| Written in Sincere Regard, | By John R. Weeks.| Broadside of 9 Verses of 4 lines each. Small 4to.   (1194).

WEEKS, JOHN R. *An* Elegy, | On the Death of Mrs. Nancy Underhill, the | beloved consort of *George Underhill,* of Matine- | cock, Long-Island; who deceas'd Sept. 20th, | A.D. 1806, with a Remitting Fever.| *Written as a token of Love and sincere* Regard, | By John R. Weeks.| Narrow 4to. broadside printed on one side only. 10 verses of 4 lines each.
(1195).

WEEKES, REFINE. The | Advantages | and | Disadvantages | of the | Marriage State, | As entered into with | Religious or Irreligious | Persons; | Represented under the Similitude | of a Dream | Versified by Refine Weekes | Stanford: | Printed by Daniel Lawrence | For the Author, 1805.| 16mo. pp. [4],-5-48.   A.B. (1196).

WEEKES. Poems, | on | Religious | and | Historical Subjects | By Refine Weekes | New York: | By James Oran, | No. 5 Burling-Slip | 1820.| 12mo. pp. [7],-4-388.   A.B. (1197).

WEEKES. The | Age of Liberty.| A Poem.| By Refine Weekes.| New-York: | Printed by John C. Totten, | No. 9 Bowery.| 1820.| 12mo. pp. [2],-3-24.   A. (1198).

WELLER, CATHARINE. The | Medley. | by Catherine Weller.| [2 lines from Young] | New-York: | Printed by T. and J. Swords, | No. 160 Pearl Street. | 1810. 12mo. pp. [3],-4-192.
A.B. (1199).

WHARTON, JOHN. The | Virginia Wreath; | or | Original Poems. |by John Wharton, M.D.| Formerly President of the Royal Physical Society at | Edinburg, and Honorary Member of the Medical | and Physical Society of Guy's Hospital, London.| [2 lines from Hor.] | Winchester, Virginia, | Printed for the Author, by J. Foster.| 1814.| 12mo. pp. [3],-4,-[3],-8-105.
B. (1200).

[WHEATLEY, PHILLIS.] A | Beautiful | Poem | on | Providence; | written by a young female slave.| To which is subjoined | A short Account of this extraordinary Writer.| Halifax, | Printed by E. Gay.| 1805.| 12mo. pp. [3],-4-8. (1201).

WHIPPLE, OLIVER. The | Historic Progress | of | Civil and Rational Liberty, | and | Order, triumphant over Faction: | A Poem: | [Quotation from Virgil and translation] | By A Farmer | Portsmouth, | Printed at the *United States' Oracle Press.* | By W. Treadwell & Co. | 1802.| 12mo. pp. [3],-iv-54. B. (1202).

WHITING, HENRY. The Emigrant. A Poem. Detroit: Printed by Sheldon & Reed, 1819. 8vo. pp. 27. (1203).

WHITING, SAMUEL. Elegant Lessons; | or the | Young Lady's Preceptor.| Being a series of | Appropriate Reading Exercises | in | Prose and Verse: | Carefully Selected | From the Most Approved Authors | for Female Schools and Academies | Including Some Remarks upon the Principles of Correct | Reading: With a Brief Dissertation on Poetry, | as a Reading Exercise; and the Dif- | ferent kinds and Constructions | of Poetic Feet | By Samuel Whiting, Esq. | Middletown, Conn., | Printed and Published by Clark & Lyman | 1820.| 12mo. pp. [3],-iv-276. A. (1204).

WHITMAN, BENJAMIN. The | Heroes of the North, | or | The Battles of Lake Erie and Champlain | Two Poems | By Benjamin Whitman, Jr., Esq. | Boston; | Published by Barber Badger | 1816.| 8vo. pp. [11],-12-24. [3 plates.]. A.B. (1205).

WHITWELL, BENJAMIN. Experience, | or, | Folly as it Flies | A Poem, | Delivered at Cambridge, on the Anniversary | of the | Φ B K Society | Aug. 28, 1806. | By Benjamin Whitwell.| [4 verses from Horace.] | Boston: | Printed at the Anthology Office, | By Munroe & Francis | 1806.| 8vo. pp. [5],-6-23. A.B. (1206).

214

[WILLIAMS, JOHN.] The | Hamiltoniad: | or, | an extinguisher for the | Royal Faction of New-England. | wth | Copious Notes, | Illustrative, Biographical, Philosophical, Critical, Admonitory, | and Political; | Being Intended as a | High-Heeled Shoe | For all Limping Republicans.| By Anthony Pasquin, Esq.| [6 verses.] | Copy-right Secured According to Act of Congress.| Sold for the Author, price [   ], at the Independent Chronicle | Office, Court-Street, Boston.| [1804.] 8vo. pp. [3],-4-104. A.B. (1207).
> Piece torn from imprint of copy, which has been examined.

WILLS, ARCHIBALD. A Poem on Door-keeping, addressed to the members of the Honorable the General Assembly. A Dialogue between General Arnold and Lord Cornwallis. A Dialogue between a miser and a spendthrift. An Elegy on the death of Michael Young, and a fable on two Cats and a Monkey in the division of a Cheese. Compiled by Archibald Wills. Raleigh: 1808. 12mo. pp. 12. (1208).

[WILSON, ALEXANDER.] The | Foresters: | A Poem | Descriptive of a | Pedestrian Journey | to the | Falls of Niagara, | In the Autumn of 1804.| By The Author of American Ornithology | Newtown, Penn., | Published by S. Siegfried and J. Wilson | July . . . 1818.| 18mo. pp. [5],-6-106. [Portrait of the author engraved by D. Edwin.] A.B. (1209).

WINCHESTER, ELHANAN. The | Process and Empire | of | Christ; | From His Birth | to the End of | The Mediatorial Kingdom; | A Poem, | in Twelve Books.| By Elhanan Winchester | Brattleboro' | Printed by William Fessenden | 1805.| 12mo. pp. [3],-iv-301,-302,-303-352. A.B. (1210).

WINCHESTER. An | Elegy Upon | *Messrs. John and Charles* Wesley, *George Whitefield,* | *and John de la Fletcher, eminent Ministers of the Gospel,* | Written | By Mr. Elhanan Winchester.| [Two Biblical quotations.] | Weathersfield, Vt.| Printed by Isaac Eddy.| 1815.| 12mo. pp. 11. (1211).

215

WINSOR, WILLIAM. The | Poetic art: | a Poem, | delivered before
the | United Brothers Society, | of | Brown University, | on
their | Anniversary, | September 3, 1811.| By William Win-
sor, A.B.| Providence: | Printed by Jones and Wheeler.|
1812.| 12mo. pp. 12.   A. (1212).

[WOODWORTH, JOHN.] The | Battle of Plattsburgh: | A | Poem,
| In Three Cantos. | By an American Youth.| [2 verses from
Canto 1.] | Montpelier: | Printed by E. P. Walton, | 1819.|
16mo. pp. [3],-iv-46.   B. (1213).

[WOODWORTH.] An | Address to Youth: | by a young man, |
in a | declining state of health.| [2 lines from Christ.] |
Printed at Montpelier, Vermont, | 1819.| 12mo. pp. [3],-4-7,-
[2],-10.   A. (1214).

[WOODWORTH, SAMUEL.] New-Haven, | A Poem, | Satirical
and Sentimental, | with | Critical, Humorous, Descriptive, |
Historical, Biographical, | and | Explanatory Notes.| By
Selim.| [3 lines of verse.] | New-York: | Printed for the
Author. | 1809.| 12mo. pp. [3],-4-34.   B. (1215).

WOODWORTH. Beasts at Law, | or, | Zoologian Jurisprudence; |
A Poem, | Satirical, Allegorical, and Moral. | in Three Cantos.|
Translated from the Arabic of | Sampfilius Philoerin,
Z. Y. X. W., &c., &c. | whose fables have made so much noise
in the East, and whose name has | eclipsed that of Æsop. |
with Notes and Annotations. | by Samuel Woodworth.| [2
lines of verse.] New-York: | Printed and Published by J.
Harmer & Co. | No. 35 Nassau Street. | 1811.| 12mo. pp.
[5],-6-104.   B.A. (1216).

>   The above and *Quarter Day,* were published in a volume containing
>   *Interesting Spanish Tales.* By Rinaldo D'Elville, and *Narrative of
>   the Capture of U. S. Brig Vixen.* With general title-page for all.
>   Each piece is, however, paged sparately, and I believe that the Wood-
>   worth titles were also issued in separate form.

[WOODWORTH.] Quarter-Day, | or | The Horrors | of the | First
of May.| A Poem. | by the author of "Beasts at Law." |
From the Halcyon Press. | New-York: | Printed and pub-
lished by S. Woodworth & Co. | No. 468 Pearl-Street. |
1812.| 12mo. pp. [3],-4-35,-[1].   A.B. (1217).

[Woodworth.] Bubble & Squeak; | or, | A Dish of all Sorts.|
Being a | Collection of American Poems, | Published in New
York; | Comprising | Quarter-Day, or the Horrors | of the
First of May; | Beasts at Law, or Zoologian | Jurisprudence; |
The Fatal Armour; | The Desponding Lovers, | and the |
Capture and Shipwreck of the | U. S. Brig Vixen| New York:
|Printed for the Booksellers. | 1814.| 12mo. pp. [3],-4-35-2,
2-104, [3],-4-22, [5],-4-35, [3],-3-16. (1218).

[Woodworth.] The | Complete Coiffeur; | or | an Essay | on
the | Art of Adorning Natural, | and of | Creating Artificial
Beauty | (*Ornamented with plates*). By J. B. M. D. Lafoy, |
Ladies Hairdresser.| [6 verses.] | New York: | Sterotyped
for the Proprietors, and sold by all | the Principal Booksellers |
1817.| 12mo. pp. [7],-6-98. [Plates.] A.B. (1219).

Woodworth. The | Poems, Odes, Songs, | and Other | Metrical
Effusions, | of | Samuel Woodworth, | Author of "The Cham-
pions of Freedom," &c. | New York: | Published by Abra-
ham Asten and Matthias Lopez. | 1818. | [Portrait of the
author.] 12mo. pp. [3],-iv-288. A.B. (1220).

[Worth, Gorham A.] A | New-Year's-Lay.| Dedicated | to
the Patrons | of | Liberty Hall and Cincinnati Gazette.| Jan-
uary First, | 1817. Address.| [9 lines of Verse, signed "The
News-Boy.] | 12mo. pp. [3],-4-9, and blank wrapper at end.
(1221).

Without doubt by Worth. The poem ends, "and WORTH pre-
sents her Charms."

[Worth.] American Bards: | a | Modern Poem, | in | three
parts.| [2 lines poetry.] | West of the Mountains.| 1819.
[Cincinnati] 12mo. pp. [5],-vi-52. B. (1222).

This is not the work issued in Philadelphia, 1820. See Robert
Waln, Jr.

Wright, Judah. Poems, | On Various Subjects.| By Judah
Wright | Boston: | Printed by Samuel Avery | No. 91 New-
bury Street | 1812.| 12mo. pp. [5],-6-48, and slip of errata
on verso of title. B.A. (1223).

217

WRIGHT, N. HILL. Monody, | on the | Death of Brigadier General | Zebulon Montgomery Pike: | and other poems. | by N. Hill Wright.| [line from Addison.] | Middlebury, Vt.| Printed by Slade & Ferguson. | 1814.| 8vo. pp. [3],-4,-[1],-6-79.   A. (1224).

WRIGHT. The | Fall of Palmyra: | and | Other Poems | By N. H. Wright | Middlebury, Vt. | Published by William Slade, Jun | 1817.| 16mo. pp. [5],-vi-143.   A.B. (1225).

WRIGHT. Boston | or A Touch at the Times | A Poem, | Descriptive, Serious, and Satirical | "Boston folks are full of notions."—Anonymous | By N. H. Wright | Boston: | Printed by Hews & Goss.| 1819. 8vo. pp. [7],-8-24.   B. (1226).

YOUNG, DAVID. The Contrast, a poem in two parts, by David Young. Elizabethtown: Woodruff & Periam, 1804. 12mo. pp. 34.   (1227).

YOUNG. The | Perusal, | or | The Book on Nature Unfolded, | A Poem: | together with a poem entitled | The Contrast.| By David Young. | Newark, N. J. | Printed by John Tuttle & Co. | 1818.| 12mo. pp. 66. Boards, with title repeated on front cover, and advertisement on fourth page of *The Correct and Easy Calculator,"* also by David Young.   A. (1228).

[YOUNG, EDWARD R.] One Year | In Savannah | A Poem, | in Five Parts | [4 verses from Byron.] | Providence: | Printed by Brown & Danforth, | 1820.| 8vo. pp. [3],-4-16.
                                                      B. (1229).

Written to commemorate the Great Fire at Savannah and the Pestilence following.

ANONYMOUS TITLES

ALFRED, an historical poem delivered at the public commencement in Yale College, New Haven, September 11, 1799, written by a Carolinian student in said College. Charleston, J. Cox, 1800. 12mo. pp. 12. (1230).

[CUT OF A SHIP.] America Forever: | or a Defiance to the Bulwark of Religion, | together with | The Yankee Sailor.| ☞ Printed by Nathaniel Coverly, jun. Corner Theatre Alley, Boston. Broadside. A. (1231).

[TWO CUTS.] AMERICAN BRAVERY: or Great Britain, and her copper-colored Allies defeated.| General Tupper, with a detachment of 2000 Volunteers, has completely defeated a corps of Indians and | British Regulars, 1200 strong, and taken the noted Tecumseh Prisoner, who has arrived at Franklinton, Ohio. Broadside. A. (1232).

[THREE CUTS.] THE AMERICAN | Constitution Frigate's | Engagement with British Frigate Guerriere, | Which after an Action of 25 Minutes, Surrendered, and being completely Shattered, was blown up, it being impossible to get her into port. Broadside. A. (1233).

[TWO CUTS.] THE AMERICAN PATRIOT'S, | War Song: | or an Appeal to Freemen. ☞ Printed by Nathaniel Coverly, | jun'r. Corner Theatre Alley, Boston. Broadside.
A. (1234).

AMERICAN PERRY. A Song, Tune—"Abraham Newland." 4to. broadside of ten verses, Published October 6, 1813. (1235).

THE | AMERICAN | POETICAL MISCELLANY.| Original and Selected.| [2 lines of poetry.] Philadelphia: | Published by Robert Johnson, C. & A. Conrad | & Co. and Mathew Carey, | Booksellers and Stationers.| 1809.| 12mo. pp. [3],-4-304.
B.A. (1236).

THE AMERICAN REVOLUTION or National Journal. By Robert Rhymer, Esq. Baltimore: Published by F. Lucas, Jr., No. 138 Market St. Philadelphia; Ash & Mason, 139 Chestnut St Title printed on verso of paper cover; on front of which is Baltimore: sold by J. Murphy, 146 Market St. 12 engraved pages, including title, with illustrations at top of each page.
(1237).

AMERICAN TAXATION: | A Song of Seventy-nine * * * Nathaniel Coverly, Printer, Milk Street. Broadside.   A. (1238).

AMERICAN TAXATION.| This song was written when the trump of war sounded through this happy land, and although | peculiarly applicable to those times, cannot but be received with approbation at the present day. Broadside.   A. (1239).

AN | ATTEMPT | to Vindicate | The American Character, | Being Principally | A Reply | To The Intemperate Animad-versions | of Thomas Moore, Esq. | Philadelphia: | Published by Benjamin Johnson.| T. L. Plowman, Printer. | 1806. 8vo. pp. [3],-iv-43.   B. (1240).

THE | *Anniversary Ode* | of the | Columbian Reading Society.| 1806. 12mo. pp. [1],-2-7.   (1241).
No general title-page.

ANNIVERSARY ODE | of the | Union Book Society. | 1808. 12mo. pp. [1],-2-10,-[3],-2-3.   B. (1242).
No general title-page.

THE ASS ON PARNASSUS; | and | From Scotland, Ge Ho!! | comes | Roderigh Vich Neddy Dhu, Ho- Ieroe!!! | Cantos I. II | of | a poem, entitled | What Are Scot's Collops?| A Prohetic Tale; | written in imitation of | The Lady of the Lake. | by Jeremiah Quiz | Philadelphia: | Published by Mathew Carey | No. 121, Chestnut Street. | 1815. 16mo. pp. [3],-iv-108.   A.B. (1243).

BANKS | IN DANGER, | or | New York in an Uproar | from a | Greenwich | Horse Race.| New-York: | Printed for the author | 1811. 24mo. pp. [3],-4-13,-[2].   B. (1244).

BATTLE OF BUNKER HILL, | This Song was Composed by the British, after the engagement.| Broadside.   A. (1245).
There is another issue with cut at top.   A.

BATTLE OF QUEENSTOWN : | Between the Americans, Commanded by Gen. Van Ransellaer, [sic] and the British by Gen. Brock. [cut]   Canandaigua, October 15, 1812.   ☞   Printed by Nathaniel Coverly, jun.   Corner   Theatre-Alley-Boston. Broadside.   A. (1246).

THE | BIRD OF BIRDS, | or a | Musical Medley; | Being | a Rich and Diversified Collection, | of | *Miscellaneous and Patriotic* | Songs.| Printed and Published | at | New York | 1818. 18mo. pp. [3],-4-141,-[3].   A.B. (1247).

THE | *Blackamore in the Wood;* | or, a | Lamentable Ballad on the Tragical End of a Gallant | Lord and Virtuous Lady; | together | with the untimely death of their two children, | Wickedly Performed by a Heathenish and Blood | thirsty Villian, Their | Servant.| The Like of Which Cruelty was Never | Before Heard of.| New Haven: | Printed for Every Purchaser.| 1802.| 12mo. pp. [3],-4-12.   B. (1248).

THE | BLADENSBURG RACES. | written shortly after the capture of Washington City, | *August* 24, 1814.| [Probably it is not generally known that the | flight of Mahomet, the flight of John | Gilpin, and the flight of Bladens- | Burg, | all occured on the *twenty-fourth of August.*| Printed for the purchaser.| 1816.| 16mo. pp. [2],-3-12.   B. (1249).

[TWO CUTS.]. A BLOODY BATTLE | between the United States Troops under the command of Gov. Harrison, and | several tribes of Indians, near the Prophet's town, Nov. 7th, 1811. Broadside.   A. (1250).

BONAPARTE; | WITH | The Storm at Sea, | Madaline, | and Other Poems.| New-York: | Published by Haly and Thomas, | No. 142 Broadway.| 1820.| 8vo. pp. [3],-iv-92.   B. (1251).

THE BOSTON ASSEMBLAGE, or a peep at Caucus Hall, most respectfully inscribed to the Boston Rebel. By Tristan Trap 'em Esq. Boston: 1812. 8vo. pp. 8.   A. (1252).

221

THE BREECHIAD, | A Poem | By | Theresa | [Quotation from Horace in Latin and its translation] | Boston: | Printed by Belcher and Armstrong.| 1807.| 16mo. pp. [3],-4-22,-[2].
B.A. (1253).

THE BULWARKS OF RELIGION, | Text: Isaiah XXVI. I. ☞ Printed by Nathaniel Coverly, corner Theatre Alley, Milk-Street, Boston. Fifth Edition. Broadside.   A. (1254).

CHESAPEAKE AND SHANNON | A List of the killed and wounded on board the Chesapeake, furnished by | Lieut. Chew, late Purser of the Chesapeake. [Cut] ☞ Printed by Nathaniel Coverly, jun.   Milk-Street; Corner Theatre-Alley, Boston. [1813.]   Broadside.   A. (1255).

THE | CHRISTIAN'S DUTY | Exhibited in a Series of | Hymns, | Collected from Various Authors, | Designed | For the Worship of God, | and for the Edification of Christians | Recommended | To the Serious of all Denominations, | By the Fraternity of Baptists.| [3 verses from the Bible, | Third Edition, Improved | Philadelphia: | Printed for and Published by Peter Leibert | W. W. Woodward—Printer | 1813.| 16mo. pp. [5],-2-331,-[26],-2-28.   A.B. (1256).

COLUMBIA'S | NAVAL TRIUMPHS.| [5 lines from Anll. Mag. Biog. of Decatur.] | New-York: | Published by Inskeep and Bradford, | No. 128 Broadway.| *J. Seymour,* Printer, No. 49 John-Street.| 1813.| 16mo. pp. [7],-8-132.   (1257).

COM. PERRY'S VICTORY on Lake Erie. (Sept. 10, 1813.) Waterford; Printed by Daniel Curtis (1813). 4to. broadside containing eleven stanzas of eight lines each.   (1258).

THE COMBUSTIBLE; | A Heroic Poem.| With notes critical explanatory.| By Johannes Scrawlenburgius.| [2 lines in Latin from Juvenal.] | 8vo. pp. [3],-4-16.   (1259).
Possibly printed in Phila. Circa 1810.

A | CONFERENCE | on | Society and Manners | in Massachusetts.| A Poem.| [3 lines from Bacon] Boston: | Printed by Wells & Lilly.| 1820.| 16mo. pp. [5],-6-70,-[1].   A.B. (1260).

CONSTITUTION AND GUERRIERE. 4to. broadside of eleven verses. N.P.N.D. (1261).

THE | COURT OF NEPTUNE | and | The Curse of Liberty, | with | Other Poems, | on Subjects Connected with the Late War.| [4 verses from Pope] | New York: | Van Winkle, Wiley & Co., Printers | 1817.| 18mo. pp. [5],-vi-106,-[1].
A.B. (1262).

THE CYNICK.| By Growler Gruff, Esquire.| Aided by a Confederacy of | Lettered Dogs.| [2 verses of poetry.] Philadelphia: | 1812.| 16mo. pp. [3],-ii-iv,-[3],-2-210.
B. (1263).

THE DENOUEMENT; | Or *Apollo cured of the Blue Devil.*| Recited on the Anniversary of the Union Book Society, 1807.| 12mo. pp. [1],-2-11. B. (1264).
  The title-page was lacking in copy from which above title was taken. The above is taken from the first page. Probably printed in Washington, D. C.

EARTHQUAKE: | Verses on the Earthquake, in North-America, in the Year 1755, and worthy the | Attention of every Person, particularly as we have | lately had like visitations. [Cut]. ☞ Printed by N. Coverly, junr. Broadside. (1265).
  Printed on the back of "The Reformed Rake."

THE ECHO, | *with other Poems.*| 1807, half title. Eng. title. Noli Me Tangere | [This is issuing from the mouth of a porcupine. The Echo. | Printed at the Porcupine Press | by Pasquin Petronius.| 8vo. pp. xv, [1],-2-331 and 5 leaves of Index. [Engraved title and seven plates.] A.B. (1266).
  By Richard Alsop, Lemuel Hopkins, T. Dwight and others.

[CUT.] EIGHTH NAVAL VICTORY: | Lines, Composed on the capture of his Brittanic Majesty's Squadron, on Lake Erie, by | Commodore Perry.| [1813.] Broadside. A. (1267).

[CUT.] ELEGAIC LINES | on the death of Mr. Joseph Bass, of | Boston, Who set out on a voyage to England for his health, but going | ashore at Bath, (District of Maine) Died Dec. 1802. Broadside. (1268).

ELEGAIC POEM, | on the | Death of Dr. Benj. Rush, | Professor of the institutes and practice of medicine and of clini- | cal practice in the University of Pennsylvania.| Who fell a victim to the prevailing typhus fever, | On the 19th of April, 1813| [line from Ovid.] Philadelphia: | Southeast corner of Chestnut and Fourth Streets | William Fry, Printer | 1813.| 12mo. pp. [5],-6-32. B. (1269).

ELEGIES, | And Other Little | Poems.| By a Student in a College in this State.| [4 lines of poetry] | Baltimore, August 7, 1800.| 12mo. pp. [6]. (1270).

AN ELEGY, Composed on the Death of Vincent Adams and Lucinda Adams; Who were drowned in the River St. Francois, (L.C.) October 22, 1806, the former in the 22nd, the latter in the 19th year of their age. Broadside, folio. (1271).
Printed in Canada.

[CUT.] ELEGY, | in Remembrance of | James Laurence, Esquire: | Late Commander of the United States Frigate Chesapeake. Broadside, printed on silk. (1272).

ELEGY, Occasioned by the Sudden Death of | Hezekiah C. Lee, | of Salisbury, (Connecticut.) | Folio broadside, 2 columns of verse. A. (1273).
Lee was killed in April, 1817.

ELEGY | on | the Death of | Colonel Dan Shaw, | late of Bradford, (Vt.) | Who Departed This Life | November 14, 1814. | also | on the Death of his Sister, | Mrs. Patience Southworth | Late consort of | of | Nathaniel Southworth, Esq. | of Lime, (N. H.) | Who Departed this Life | July 8, 1814.| By a Friend.| Hanover: | Printed by Charles Spear.| October . . . . 1815.| 8vo. pp. [3],-4-8. A. (1274).

ELEGY | On the Death of Commodore | Stephen Decatur, | Who fell in a Duel, by the hand of Commodore Barron, at Bladensburg, | near the City of Washington on the 22d of March, 1820. Printed and Sold by N. Coverly, No. 16 Milk-Street. Broadside. (1275).

AN ELEGY | on the death of Philo S. White, son of Mr. Noah White, of | Sutton, who died August 16, 1819, aged one year.| 4to. broadside of 16 verses in 2 Columns. (1276).

[CUT.] AN ELEGY | on the Death of the late Reverend Charles Warburton, who died | in Boston, July the 1st, 1814. Aged 80. By a Lady of Colour. ☞ Printed by Nathaniel Coverly, jun. | Milk-Street, Boston. Broadside. (1277).

AN ELOGY, | Sacred to the Memory of Miss Polly Holman, who departed this life, May 31, 1814, aged 24 years and 2 months. Broadside. (1278).

EPHEMERA | or | The History | of Cockney Dandies | A Poem, in one Canto | By Blumblery Buzz, Esq.| Professor of Fashions in the Old School. Philadelphia: | Published by Robert Desilver, No. 110 Walnut St. | Thomas Town, Printer, | 1819.| 12mo. pp. [7],-8-22. A.B. (1279).

EPISTLE | TO | Bonaparte. | By a Lady. | Philadelphia, | Published by C. Neal, | No. 201, Chestnut-street.| 1814.| 12mo. pp. [3],-4-11. B. (1280).

EXECUTION OF POWARS, | [Cut of gallows] | for the | Murder of Timothy Kennedy.| [Boston: 1820.] Folio broadside, 32 verses. A. (1281).

EXTRACTS | IN Prose and Verse | By a Lady of Maryland.| Together with a Collection of | Original Poetry, | Never Before Published, | By Citizens of Maryland.| In two volumes.| Volume I | Annapolis: | Printed by Frederick Green | 1808.| 2 volumes. 8vo. pp. [5],-6-364,-[7],-[3],-4-359,-[13]. B. (1282).

THE | FACTOR'S GARLAND, | and, | Verses on the death of | Mrs. Mary Hayward | of Easton.| Wrentham; | Printed for Joseph Ward.| 1812.| 12mo. pp. [3],-4-12. (1283).

FANNY, | continued.| [3 lines from Crabbe's "Tales of the Hall."] | New York: | Printed by William Grattan, | No. 8, *Thames-street*.| 1820.| 8vo. pp. [3],-2-29. B. (1284).

225

FASHION; | Or, the |Art of Making Breeches.| An | *Heroi-Satiri-Didactic* | Poem | By Solomon Irony, Esq.| Life is a pair of Breeches in which mankind are continually fidgeting.| Philadelphia: | Printed By Francis and Robert Bailey.| 1800.| 12mo. pp. [3],-iv-v,-[2],-8-19.   A.B. (1285).

THE FESTIVALIAD. A Singular Poem; written in Commemoration of the Festival of St. John, the first Christian Mason, Celebrated at Dorchester, June 24, 1807. (A.L. 5807.) By Morpheus Stupor. With prefactory remarks, observations, &c., by Hezekiah Hectic. 13th Irish, from Seventh Scotch edition. [Boston]. 1811. 12mo. pp. 42.   A. (1286).

  A Burlesque with Copious Notes, in which well-known Masons of Boston and Watertown are referred to.

FIGHTS OF FAITH, in two parts. Boston, 1820.   (1287).

FRANK; | or, | Who's the Croaker | [4 verses] (1st verse in Latin from Pers. Sat) | New York: | Published by George S. Wharam | 1820.| 12mo. pp. [5],-6-41.   B. (1288).

THE | FRATERNAL TRIBUTE | of | Respect | Paid to The | Masonic Character | of Washington, | in the Union Lodge, | in | Dorchester | January 7th, A.L. 5800. | Charlestown: | Printed by Samuel Etherbridge.| M,DCCC.| 8vo. pp. [7],-8-13,-[2].   B. (1289).

THE | FUDGE FAMILY | in | Washington.| Edited by Harry Nimrod.| [3 lnies from Deodati] | Baltimore: | Published by Joseph Robinson, | *Circulating Library, Corner of Market and Belvidere-Streets.*| 1820. 12mo. pp. [3],-4-109.   (1290).

THE GHOST OF CHRISTOPHER COLUMBUS visiting the United States in the year 1811. A Poem. [Phila.? 1811.] 8vo. pp. 6.   N.Y.P.L. (1291).

  An imperfect copy is in N.Y.P.L.

THE GRUMBLING HIVE; or, Knaves turn'd Honest. Boston: Printed for the People, 1811. 16mo. pp. 18.   A. (1292).

[Two Cuts] Harrison Victorious: | Copy of a letter from General Harrison to the Department of War . . . Head-Quarters, near Moravian Town, on the River | Thames, 80 miles from Detroit, 5th October, 1813. ☞ Printed by Nathaniel Coverly, Jun. Milk-Street, Boston . . . Price 4 cents. [1813] Broadside.   A. (1293).

The Hartford Convention | in an uproar! | and the | Wise Men of the East | Confounded! | together with | a short History of the | *Peter Washingtonians;* | being | the first book of the Chronicles | of the | children of disobedience; | otherwise falsely called | "Washington Benevolents.|| | by Hector Benev-olus, Esq. | [2 lnes of Prose.] | [one line from Bible.] | Windsor, Vt. | Printed for the proprietor of the Copy-Right. . . . 1815.| 12mo. pp. [3],-6-46, and leaf of copy-right.   A.B. (1294).

Hermit, being a Collection in prose and verse.   Park's Press. Montpelier, Vermont. 1808. 16mo. pp. 34.   (1294b).
Signed, *The Wanderer.*

The Hero of the North (Gen. Augustine Taylor) ; or, Knight of the Wooden Sword. A Poem. By the Author. Dedicated to the Officers of the Army. 8vo, sewed, p. 8.   (N. Y., 1813.)
(1295).

The | Heroes of the Lake.| A Poem, | in two books. | written in the Autumn of 1813.| Æmulans Sequor. | New-York: | Printed and published by S. Woodworth & Co. | War Office, 26 Chatham-Street.| 1814.| 16mo. pp. [5],-6-108. [View of Naval battle engraved by Chiquet.]   B. (1296).

Historico Dramatico Ambrosial | Eclogues | By Hengist Hob-nail, | Under graduate of the Agricultural College, and honora-| ry member of the member of the London Horticultural Society | (4 verses from Virgil and 5 from Shakespeare). New York.| Printed for Abram Cox | 1820.| 12mo. pp. [3],-4-16.
B. (1297).

227

HORRID MASSACRE, | at | Dartmoor Prison, England.| [Cut of the Massacre] | Where the unarmed American Prisoners of War were wantonly fired upon by the guard, under the | command of the Prison Turn-Key, the blood thirsty SHORT-LAND; Seven were killed, and about | Fifty wounded, (several mortally,) without any provocation on the part of our unfortunate | American Citizens!—"Blood has a voice to pierce the Skies!"| Folio broadside, poem printed in double column, [Boston! Circa 1815.] (1298).

HOURS OF CHILDHOOD, | and | Other Poems.| [6 verses from Kirke White] | Montreal: | Published by A. Bowman | 1820.| 18mo. pp. [5],-iv-94. A.B. (1299).

AN HYMN | to be sung by the | Episcopal Charity Children, | At St. George's Chapel, | *on* Sunday, *November* 30, 1800—*when a Sermon will be preached, and a Collection made for the | benefit of that benevolent Institution.*| The Music by Mr. Moller.| [at end] Printed by Ming and Young.| Broadside, Small folio. [N. Y. 1800.] (1300).

HYMNS AND ODES, | composed | on the death of | Gen. George Washington: | adapted | to the 22d. day of February, | and dedicated to | those who please to sing them! | (eight lines of prose) | Portsmouth, (N. H.) January, 1800.| Printed at the United States' Oracle Office | by Charles Peirce, sold by him at the | Columbian Bookstore, by groce, | dozen, or single.| 12mo. pp. [4],-5-12. (1301).

[CUT] IN MEMORY of Solomon Snow, a young man of respectability and talents; who was drowned in Crossing | the Kennebec River, from Swan Island to Bowdoinham, August 11, 1811. Broadside. (1302).

INDEPENDENCE | of the | United States.| [4to. broadside. 16 verses in 2 columns. Political poem, dating 1811].
A. (1303).

JAMES BIRD (and other poems.) Philadelphia: [1815.] 12mo. pp. 8. (1304).

> Bird was shot for desertion from the "Niagara," after serving with bravery under Perry.

THE JEFFERSONIAD; | or, | An Echo | to the | Groans *of an* Expiring Faction.| By *Democraticus.* [4 lines of verse] | March 4, 1801 : | *First year of the Triumph of Republican Principle.*| Price—18 Cents.| 12mo. pp. [3],-4-18. N.Y.P.L. (1305).

[CUT] LADY | WASHINGTON'S | Lamentation for the | Death of her Husband.| Printed and sold by Nathaniel Coverly, Jr.| Corner Theatre-Alley, Milk-Street-Boston. [1800] Broadside.
A. (1306).

> There are two issues, in one issue the cut being at the left, the other at the right of title.

[CUT] A LAMENTATION for | Gen. Washington | Esq. Commander in Chief of the Combined Forces of America and | France, during the Revolutionary War, and afterwards President of | the United States of America—who died December 14th, 1799. ☞ N. Coverly, Jr. Printer, Milk-Street, Boston. Broadside. A. (1307).

THE | LAMPLIGHTERS' | Address | to his Patrons | [4to. broadside of 4 verses] January 1, 1819. A.

THE LAMPLIGHTER, | To his enlightened Patrons: | Wishing happiness.| [4to broadside] January 1, 1812. A. January 1, 1816.| The Lampligher | respectfully presents | the | Compliments of the Season.| [4to broadside]. A.

THE | LAMP-LIGHTERS WISH | [4to broadside] January 1st, 1817.
A. (1308).

THE LAST CAMPAIGN of Sir John Falstaff the II. or, the Hero of the Burnt-Corn Battle. St. Stephens: 1815. pp. 26.
A. (1309).

LINES, | Composed on the death of Elias Cummings, son of Rev. Charles Cum- | mings of Sullivan, and Nephew of Enoch Hemmenway, who was | taken and died of the Spotted fever before he returned from | the funeral of his uncle, aged 11 years. [And] Composed | on the Death of | Enoch Hemmenway, | son of Dea. Elias Hemmenway, of Roxbury, N. H. | who died of the spotted fever, Æt. 19 y's. Broadside.
A. (1310).

LINES Composed on the Death of General | Washington.| Broad-
side.   A. (1311).

[CUT] LINES | composed on the Execution of | W. Clement's: |
Who was shot for Desertion, on Fort Independence, Feb. 18 |
having been four times Pardoned, but having last Deserted |
his Post, was condemned to die. ☞ Printed by Nathaniel
Coverly | jun. Corner Theatre Alley. Broadside. A. (1312).

[CUT OF AN EXECUTION] Lines | on the Death of Ebenezer
Ball, | who was executed at *Castine,* October 31, 1811, | For
the Murder of John Tileston Downs.| [Printed, and for sale
by A. H. Holland, *Buckstown.*] Folio broadside printed in
double column. Dated Bluehill, Nov. 1811.
                                          A., N.Y.P.L. (1313).

THE | LOST CHILD: | A poetic tale. | Founded upon a fact. | [3
lines from Anon.] | [2 lines from Anon.] | Philadelphia: |
Published and Sold wholesale by Wm. Charles, | and may be
had of all the booksellers.| 1811.| W. McCulloch, Printer.|
12mo. pp. [5]-vi, [1],-8-60. [6 plates.]   (1314).

[SIX COFFINS] Melancholy Events.| Boston, July 21st, 1813.|
On Monday last, the sloop Liberty, belonging to the garrison
at Fort Independence, . . . was overset. Broadside.
                                                  A. (1315).

METAMORPHOSIS; | or, a | Transformation of pictures, | with |
Poetical explanations, | for the | Amusement of Young Per-
sons, | also | An Alphabet | of | Large and Small Letters |
to | Aid Females in Marking Linen, &c. | Wilmington: |
Printed and sold by Robert Porter, | No. 97 Market Street.|
1814.| 18mo.   A. (1316).

  Consists of 4 folded leaves. Also New York: 1814, with illustrations by Poupard.

MR. PRINTER, The following piece signed "Mechanic," was slily
thrown into my entry late in the evening; to which I have
annexed an answer. And, whereas, the Name of my friend is
unknown, &c. [Signed at end, Pewter Smith.] [Westerly,
May 7, 1802.] [Providence: 1802?] Folio broadside printed
in three columns.   (1317).

[Six Cuts] Most Brilliant | Naval Victory on Lake Erie.|
Glorious News!!! | Enough to stop the boasting and bragging
of our English and Tory Enemies, for a time. Commodore
Perry | has the honor of conquering a whole Squadron of his
Royal Majesty's Subjects and Allies.| The United States'
Flag rides triumphant on Lake Erie. ☞ Printed by Nathaniel
Coverly, jun. Milk-Street, Boston—Price 4 Cents. [1813]
Broadside.   A. (1318).

Musings | at | An Evening Club in Boston.| Somewhat like a
Poem | [9 lines from Montaigne] | Boston: | Printed by True
& Weston | 1819.| 16mo. pp. [3],-4-53.   B. (1319).

A | Narrative | of the Capture of the | United States' Brig
Vixen, | of 14 guns, | By the | British Frigate Southampton; |
And of the Subsequent | Loss of Both Vessels | on a Reef of
Rocks, | off Conception Island.| With some Account of the
Sufferings of the Crew; | Their manner of Deliverance; and |
Final Deposit in the | Prison-Ships at Port Royal, Jamaica.|
The Whole Interpersed with | *Various Remarks relative to
the Treatment shown to, and | Conduct observed by the
Prisoners* | By one of the Vixen's Crew | In a Letter to a
Friend.| New York: | printed and sold at the office of "The
War," | No. 60 Vesey Street.| 1813.| 12mo. pp. [3],-4-34.
                                                              (1320).

A | New History | of a | True Book, | in verse.| [Cut] | For
Sale at A. March's *Bookstore;* price 6 | cents single, and to
those who buy to give away, | 2 dols. pr. hundred.| New-
buryport: 1800?] 12mo. pp. [2],-3-12.   (1321).
    Possibly imperfect as p. 14 is mentioned in Ms. on t.p. of copy in
    N.Y.P.L.

[Cut] A New Song, | On the Death of Robert Howel.| Robert
Howel, an American citizen, pressed into | the British service,
and by Britons most Barbar | ously Murdered on being com-
pelled to fight | on board the Little Belt, against his own
countrymen, | in which unnatural conflict he lost his leg and
thigh, | struck off by a cannon ball, and died in a few hours |
after of the wound.| [Cut and another at end.] Printed and
sold by N. Coverly, Jun., Milk-Street, Boston. Broadside.
                                                              A. (1322).

A New Translation | With Notes, | of | The Third Satire of | Juvenal.| To which are added, | Miscellaneous Poems, | Original and Translated.| New York: | Printed for E. Sargeant, No. 39 Wall Street, opposite the United-States Bank.| 1806.| 12mo. pp. [5],-viii-xxvi, [5],-6-190, [2].   (1323).

Ode in Commemoration of the first settlement of a Congregation of the United Brethren, at Newport, R. I., Nov. 10th., 1758, For the Jubilee in 1808. The Chapel was Dedicated June 26th, 1768. Newport: 1808. 8vo. pp. 10.   (1324).

Ode | Performed at the First Church of Uni- | versalists in Boston, | On the Day devoted to Funeral Testimonies | of Respect, to the Memory of the | Instrumental Saviour of his Country.| George Washington.| [4to broadside of 8 verses] January 12, 1800.   A. (1325).

Olio; | or, | Satirical Poetic-Hodge-Podge, | with | An illustrative or Explanatory | Dialogue, | In Vindication of the Motive | Addressed to *Good Nature, Humor,* and *Fancy.*| [8 verses from Pindar] Philadelphia, printed | 1801 | .[*Copyright secured according to Law.*] | 8vo. pp. [3],-iv,-[1],-4-46.   B. (1326).

On the Death of Mr. John Gale, Com- | posed by his twin-sister. 4to. broadside of 8 verses. [1820].   A. (1327).

On the Death of | Sarah Baker of Pembroke; | who died, May 8th, 1805. Aged 14 years.| Addressed to the School of which She was a Member.| [4to. broadside 16 verses in 2 columns].   A. (1328).

On the | Last Judgment.| [Colopon is] Re-Printed for James Grimes, | Randolph-1801.| 8vo. pp. 23.   A. (1329).
  Advertised as "Just Printed" in Randolph, Vt. in "Weekly Wanderer" of June 27, 1801.

Our Saviour.| A Poem | By a Christian | Illustrated with Engravings | Philadelphia | Published and sold by | Wm. Charles | Price, Plain 12½ cents; Coloured 18¾ cents | 1816.| 16mo. pp. [13].   (1330).
  No title-page. The title is taken from the cover.

The | Pains of Memory; | with some other | Poems.| [Vignette] | New-York: | Printed for the Author.| 1807.| 12mo. pp. [5],-6-76. (1331).

[Cut] A Particular Account of the late Distressing Fire at Portsmouth.| Portsmouth, December 25. Broadside.

A. (1332).

Peace on Honorable terms to America.| [Cut] Folio broadside printed in double column. [N. Coverly, Jun. Boston.] [1815]. N.Y.P.L. (1333).

Peace! Peace! | [2 Cuts] [Printed by Nathaniel Coverly, Jun. Milk-Street, Boston.] [1815] Folio broadside printed in double column. N.Y.P.L. (1334).

The | Pickeroniad | or, Exploits of Faction: | Celebrated in | Mock-Heroic-Al, Serio-Comic-Al | Hudibrastical, and Quiz-zic-Al | Numbers.| Illustrated with explanatory notes. | By Ralpho Risible, Esq.| *Poet-Laureat to their most Dis- honourable Honours, the Grand Knights | of the Most Sublime Order of the Essex Junto,* &c. | [Copy-Right secured according to law.] | Newburyport: | Printed by N. H. Wright.| 1811.| 12mo. pp. [5],-6-36. A. (1335).

A Pinkster Ode, Albany 1803. 12mo. (1335b).

A Poem, on | Jason Fairbanks, | Who inhumanly murdered Miss Elizabeth Fales.| 4to. broadside, 12 verses in 2 Columns, probably printed at Dedham, Mass., 1801. A. (1336).

A | Poem | on | Universal Salvation; | or, | A Gentle Stroke | at | Calvinism. | [3 lines from Wither.] | New York. | Printed for the Author and sold by J. Black, No. 31 Cedar-Street.| 1802.| 12mo. pp. [3],-iv-v, [2],-18-24. (1337).

Poems, | on Different Subjects.| By a Lady | [2 verses] | Boston: | Published by West & Richardson, | No. 75, Cornhill.| E. G. House, Printer.| 1813.| 16mo. pp. [3],-4-117.

B.A. (1338).

A Poet's Progress. | A True Story.| Third impression, | with addition and Improvement.| [3 lines of poetry]. | Sold by the Author. | New-York: | 1818.| 12mo. pp. [3],-4-12.

B. (1339).

A | Poetical Account | of the | American Campaigns | of | 1812 *and* 1813; | with some slight sketches | Relating to the Party Politics | which governed | The United States, | during the war, and at its commencement.| Dedicated to the People of Canada, | By the Publisher.| Halifax: | Printed by John Howe, Jun.| 1815.| 12mo. pp. [5],-6-139.   B. (1340).

The | Political Nursery, | for the Year | Eighteen Hundred Two.| [4 lines of verse from Hartford Guillotina] | Packet-Office, | *Norwich, January 1st.* 1802.| 12mo. pp. [1],-2-16.

N.Y.P.L. (1341).

The Powers of Christianity, or Abdallah and Sabat. A Poem by a Lady. [1 line from Paul.] 16mo. pp. 46 (4), Charleston, 1814.   (1342).

The Prisoner; | or, | A Collection | of | Poetical Pieces, | Written by a Person Confined in the | State prison | *And principally published in the "True American."*] Trenton: | Printed by Wilson & Blackwell, | 1802.| 16mo. pp. [3],-4-24.

B. (1343).

Privateering and Pirateering | Alias, the "Peace Party" at War; | Alias ,the Devil to pay in the | Federal Camp. [Printed by Nathaniel Coverly, jun. Milk-Street, Boston.] [Circa, 1815] Small folio broadside, poem, printed in double column at top, one at each side, cut of sloop and frigate under full sail.   (1344).

The Prize Book, | No. 1. | of the | Publick Latin School | in Boston.| [2 verses in Latin from Horace, | Boston: | Published By Cummings and Hilliard. | Hilliard & Metcalf, Printers.| 1820.| 8vo. pp. [3],-4-63.   A.B. (1345).

The | Progress of Society: | A Poem, | in three parts.| New-York: | Published by D. Longworth, 11 Park. | Clayton & Kingsland, Printers.| 1817.| 16mo. pp. [5],-vi-vii, [6],-14-62, [1].   B. (1346).

234

REFLECTIONS ON LOVE: in a Poetical Epistle. Printed for the author. N. P. 1800. pp. 12. A. (1347).

Signed by the author "D.R.P."

A REMARKABLE | DREAM.| By a young Man in Foxborough.| [Folio broadside, 3 columns of verse.] A. (1348).

Concerning the attempt of the people of Foxborough to settle a new Minister.

THE RETALIATION: | A Poem, | In Sex Cantos with Notes; | being | A counter-part to Fessenden's, | alias | Doctor Caustic's | alias | The Hydraulic Engineer's "Democracy Unveiled."| [Center rule.] | By Cornelius Cantery, Esq.| M.D., L.L.D. Knight of the Rueful Countenance, &c., &c., &c., &c., &c. | [Center rule.] |

> *With true Fessendonian spirit,*
> *I'll* lie *down every whig of merit!*
> *Now Democrats I'll not deceive you,*
> *I'll make you tremble 'fore I leave you:*
> *And if you'll take my best advice, sirs,*
> *You'll all be whist and mute as mice, sirs.|*

[Rule.] | Morris-town: | Printed by Jacob Mann.| 1806.| 8vo. pp. 36. (1349).

A satire on the Federalists, exceedingly coarse, to indecency. A reply to Thomas G. Fessenden's "Terrible Tractoration."

A | RETREAT | From Town | An Epistle in Verse | From the Country.| Boston: | Printed By John Eliot, | No. 5 *Court-Street,* | 1815.| 8vo. pp. [3],-4-24. B. (1350).

RIOT IN BALTIMORE.| Extract of a Letter from Baltimore, dated July 28.| 'The first assault on the Federal Republican office was but a farce compared to the one of last | night . . . . [1812] Broadside. A. (1351).

ROGERS AND BINGHAM.| A Song, written and sung at the celebration in Charleston, S. C.| July 4th, 1811. Songs by the Gross or Single, for sale by Nathaniel Coverly, Jr. Corner of Theatre-alley, Milk-street, Boston, 1811. Broadside.

A. (1352).

THE ROUND TABLE. No. 2. Hartford: 1819. 16mo. (1353).

[CUT] SAW YE my | Hero George: | and the | Rosary.| Lady
Washington left Mount Vernon in June | 1778, in expectation
of meeting her worthy | companion George; on the 28th of
the same | month, found her favourite engaged in the | Battle
of Monmouth: She made the follow- | ing observations.
Broadside.   A. (1354).

THE | SCOURGE | of | Fashion | A. | Poem | By Phylanthus.|
[4 lines from D. of Buck's essay.] | New York: | Printed
by Ming & Young, | No. 33, Liberty-Street | 1800| 12mo.
pp. [5],-6-23.   B. (1355).

[Two CUTS] SHOCKING EARTHQUAKES.| Charleston, (S. C.)
Feb. 7, 1812.| Yesterday morning, about half past 3 o'clock |
the inhabitants of this place were very much | alarmed by an-
other shock . . . ☞ Boston—Printed and sold at the Print |
ing-Office, Corner of Theatre-Alley. [1812] Broadside.
                                                     A. (1356).

A SHORT AND BRIEF ACCOUNT of the Shipwreck of Cap. Joshua
Winslow, | who was overset on Carolina Coast in Lat. 35, 30,
M. N. on the 23d | Day of July, 1788.| 4to. broadside, 3 col-
umns of Verses.   A. (1357).

SIX | POEMS, | on Different Subjects, | relative to | Events of the
late War.| *Composed by a Soldier of the U. S. Army.*|
Printed for the Publisher.| 12mo. pp. [1],-2-24. and blue
paper covers. [Circa, 1815].   (1358).

[CUT] SIXTH NAVAL VICTORY.| The U. S. Brig Enterprise of
14 guns, commanded by Lieut. William | Burrows, took after
an engagement of 45 minutes, the British Brig of | War
Boxer, of 18 guns, Capt. Blyth, who with about 50 of his men
were | killed and wounded. Lieut. Burrows and one man
killed and seven wounded. Broadside.   A. (1359)

[FOUR CUTS] A SONG, | composed on the Evacuation of Boston
by the British Troops, | commanded by General Howe: | who
were panic struck, and thrown into the utmost confusion, at
the appearance of General Washington, | With a Detachment

236

of the American Army, who in one night, (unexpected to the Britons.) | erected strong Breast-Works, with heavy Cannon pointed at the Men of War, | then lying in the Harbour. ☞ Printed by N. Coverly, jun. Corner Theatre | Alley. Broadside.   A. (1360)

SONG, *for* the Anniversary of American Independence, 1819.| E. W. Allen, Printer, Newburyport. 4to. broadside, 4 verses in 2 Columns.   A. (1361).

SPAIN.| An | Account | of the | Public Festival | Given by | The Citizens of Boston, | At the Exchange Coffee House, | January 24, 1809, | In Honor of | Spanish Valour & Patriotism | with the | Regular and Volunteer Toasts, | And all the Original Songs and Odes | Sung on the Occasion.| In which is also Introduced | A Brief Sketch of Spain, | Geographical, Historical and Political.| Spain is not a *dead* but sleeping *Lion.*| Copy Rights of the "Sketch" and "National Ode," having been secured by the author | agreeable to Act of Congress; they are here published by permission of Mr. Paine | Printed | By Russell and Cutler, | And for Sale at their Printing Office in Congress Street. | Boston.| 12mo. pp. [5],-2-36.   A. (1362).

THE SQUARE TABLE. Hartford: 1819. 16mo.   A. (1363).

THE | STARS OF COLUMBIA.| Dedicated | To His Excellency, The | President of the U States, | and the | Officers *and* Gentlemen | of the | Navy, | Likewise | A Comic Patriotic Song, | Called, | Yankee Arguments.| New York: | Published and Sold by Riley & Adams, 23, Chatham-St.| 1813| *Price Six Cents.*| 8vo. pp. [3],-4-8.   B. (1364).

[TWO CUTS] THOU SHALT DO | no Murder.| On Thursday, December 16, Sentence of | Death was passed in a most solemn and | impressive Manner, by the Hon. | Judge Sewall, upon Livermore and Angier, | after a Conviction of the Murder of | Nicholas John Cruay, an Indian, on the | Night of the 23d. November. Broadside.   A. (1365).

[Cut] Thomas Moorehead, | A Ship-wreck'd Mariner, who subsisted fifty-one | days on the bodies of his Comrades.| Taken off the | wreck by the ship Monticello, and arrived at New- | York, the beginning of May, 1809. Broadside.
A. (1366).

No. 1.| The Times; | A Poem, | addressed to the inhabitants of | New-England, | and of the | State of New-York, | Particularly on the subject of the present | Anti-Commercial System | of | The National Administration. | by Miles Standish, jun. | Plymouth: | Printed for the Author.| 1809.| 8vo. pp. [3],-6-27. A.B. (1367).

> I am inclined to believe that this scarce piece was printed in New York, the Plymouth imprint being simply a blind to hide the author's identity and place of residence.

To the Beau Monde.| [Signed John Byrne, advertising in a long poem of 2 columns his merchandize for sale at his store, 5 Hanover Street in Boston. About 1810. Folio broadside]. Another variety, advertising the store at No. 7 Devonshire street, can be dated in 1809. A. (1368).

The | Toddy-Mill, | or the | Humorous Adventures of | Dick Bully. | A caricature: | By Johny Gilpin.| [5 lines quoted.] | Huzza!!! | September 1, 1800.| 8vo. pp. [3],-4-8. B. (1369).

The | Triumph | of | Philanthropy. | Respectfully inscribed | to the | Pennsylvania Institution | for the | Deaf and Dumb.| [2 lines from Cowper.] | Philadelphia: | 1820.| 16mo. pp. [9],-10-34. (1370).

True and Infernal | Friendship, | or the | Wisdom of Eve. | and the | Character of the Serpent, | with the | Situation, Joys, and loss of Paradise.| [2 lines of verse.] | Providence, R. I. | Printed by H. Mann & Co. for the Author.| 1813.| 12mo. pp. [3],-iv-xx, [1],-14-176, [1]. A.B. (1371).

> The running title throughout the work is *True and False Friendship*.

Unparralled Victory.| [3 cuts] | [4 lines] | [7 lines] | [Printed by Nathaniel Coverly, Jun. Milk-Street Boston.| Folio broadside, printed in double column. [1815].
(1372).

THE | UNTAUGHT BARD.| An Original work.| [7 lines of verse] | New-York: | Deare and Andrews, printers.| [dotted line] | 1804.| 12mo. pp. [3],-4-260, [3]. A.B. (1373).

VERSES, | *Composed and Sung at Trenton, on the Delivery of the Funeral Eulogium* | *in Honor of the Memory of* | General George Washington.| 4to. broadside printed in double column, [1800]. N.Y.P.L. (1374).

[TWO CUTS] VERSES | Composed on the Schooner Washington and crew, who was blown off the Coast | on the 24th of November 1811, being bound from New York for Salem: | light, commanded by Nicholas Thomas, after being at Sea 36 days. Broadside. A. (1375).

THE | VICTORS, | An Original Poem.| By a Young Gentleman | of Philadelphia.| [4 lines from Brook's Gustavus Vasa.] | Philadelphia.| Sold by the Principal Booksellers.| 1815.| 16mo. pp. [3],-4-11. (1376).

  Attributed to Charles Brockden Brown, but, he was not the author.

A VIEW of the Democratic Republican Celebration at Westmoreland, N. H. [1813] pp. 12. A. (1377).

THE | WANDERER, | or | Horatio and Laetitia: | A Poem | In Five Epistles| [4 lines from Lake | Utica: | Printed for the Authors | By Seward and Williams.| 1811.| 12mo. pp. [9],-8-138. [2 woodcut illustrations.] A.B. (1378).

  Williams, in *An Oneida County Printer* states that the above was written by the Douglas Brothers, while Bagg *in Pioneers of Utica* gives T. A. Rockwell as the author's name. I am inclined to believe that Williams is correct.

THE | WORK and Contention of Heaven | [at end]. Printed and Sold in New-London. Poem of 24, four line verses in double Column. Broadside [Circa 1800]. (1379).

239

INDEX OF TITLES